Memoirs Of An Unfortunate Young Nobleman Returned From A Thirteen Years Slavery In América

unpublished

№ 2

Charles Richard Fox
I forget when or
where I got this
Production!

MEMOIRS

Of an Unfortunate

YOUNG NOBLEMAN, &c.

MEMOIRS

OF AN

Unfortunate Young Nobleman,

Return'd from a

Thirteen Years Slavery in *America*

Where he had been fent by the Wicked.
Contrivances of his Cruel Uncle.

*A STORY founded on Truth, and addrefs'd
equally to the Head and Heart,*

This is the Heir; come, let us kill him, that the
Inheritance may be ours.

LUKE XX. 14.

————————*Foul Deeds muft rife,*
Tho' all the Earth o'erwhelm 'em, to Mens Eyes.
Spoken by HAMLET of his Uncle.

LONDON,

Printed for J. FREEMAN in *Fleetftreet*; and
fold by the Bookfellers in Town and Country.

M DCC XLIII.

MEMOIRS

Of an Unfortunate

Young Nobleman, &c.

AID me, O Juſtice! be my Guide,
O Truth! while inſpir'd by the
Love of you, moſt amiable Virtues! I attempt to paint the Diſtreſ-
ſes of helpleſs injur'd Innocence :
to trace the myſterious Windings of deep De-
ceit: the cruel Paths of lawleſs Avarice and
wild Ambition : to ſhew how fatal to their Po-
ſterity Variance between the wedded Pair may
ſometimes prove; and how attentive Villany
from thence may form the moſt ſucceſsful Projects. The Story I have to relate is full of Wonders——all the Paſſions are concern'd in it——
I have to treat of ſtrange unnatural Perſecutions
——accumulated Sufferings——numberleſs Dangers——miraculous Eſcapes ——O may my

B   Words

Words have Energy to give each Incident a
true defcriptive Force, to warm the gentle
generous Soul with alternate Pity and Indignation, and make the guilty, tho' ever fo
great in Power, and Wealth, and Titles, ftart
at the Reflection of himfelf.

The Baron *de Altamont* held a very confiderable Rank among the Nobility, but cannot
be faid to have had Sentiments altogether an-
fwerable to the Dignity of his Birth. He
was naturally peevifh: his Ideas were mean,
and confequently his Behaviour unpolite: he
was paffionate, and irrefolute, neither a faft
Friend nor a violent Enemy; and to compleat
his Character, one of thofe who without being *liberal* was *profufe*, and having never
been known to do one great or generous
Action, fquander'd away a very large Fortune
in a fhort Time.

He was married young to a Lady of diftinguifh'd Birth and Beauty, fomewhat rafh
in her Expreffions when provok'd; but otherwife extremely affable and fweet-temper'd:
fhe had alfo a great Share of Wit and an uncommon Vavacity, which enliven'd all the
Converfations fhe came into. In a Word,
fhe had Perfections fufficient to have endear'd
her to any Man who had been fenfible of their
Value; but her Lord, alas! knew not his
own Happinefs: he foon grew fatiated with
the Charms of her *Perfon*, and as to thofe of
her *Mind*, he either wanted Delicacy to re-
lifh them, or was of the Opinion of fome
others, that Wit in a Wife was a Perfection
that might very well be fpar'd. They had not
been

been married many Months before he behav'd
to her with a Coldness, which, conscious of
her Merit, she could ill support: she complain'd of it to her Friends, and that, together with the ill Oeconomy he already difcover'd in the Management of his Affairs,
gave her Father a Pretence to refuse the Payment of some part of the Dowry he had promised in a certain Time after Marriage, and
which being now expir'd, the Baron demanded. Mutual Reproaches occasion'd a mutual
Diffatisfaction between them. However, as
they both were young, the Advice of some
cordial Friends might, perhaps, have convinc'd them how far the Nuptial Vow obliges
those that engage in it to bear with the Fail-
ings of each other; but unhappily for them,
this was so far from being the Case, that on
the Contrary all manner of Stratagems were
put in Practice to widen the Breach between
them, and keep them in a perpetual Difa-
greement.

The Baron's Mother was still living: she
was a Lady of an imperious Nature, lov'd to
be consulted in every thing, and to have her
Opinion taken, whether right or wrong. The
young Baroness had not always paid this
Deference to her, and this created in her
such a Difgust, that it soon after grew into a
Hatred. She detracted from every Virtue—
she magnified every little Inadvertency—she
represented every Failing as a Vice, and was
continually filling her Son's Ears with the ill
Conduct and Indiscretion of his Wife. But
as she had no other View in this than meerly

to gratify her Ill-nature, which probably the
Baron might be acquainted with in other Instances, the Effect would scarce have been
very great had it not been seconded from a
more dangerous Quarter.

The Chevalier *Richard de Altamont*, youn-
ger Brother to the Baron, was a Man of
whom it may be said, without any Danger of
being too severe, that he had all the Vices
center'd in his Compofition: he was proud
and mean at the fame Time——vain-glorious
yet avaritious——ungrateful for good Offices
——revengeful for even imagin'd Injuries——
treacherous when trufted——mifchievoufly inquifitive when not fo—without the leaft Spark
of Honour, Pity, or even common Humanity
——incapable by Nature of doing *any Good*,
and qualified by an *extreme Subtilty* for *all
kinds of Evil*. His Knowledge in all laudable Endowments was fcarce above the Level
of what is ordinarily found amongft the loweft
Rank of Men; but he was a perfect Mafter
in the Arts of Hypocrify and Diffimulation,
and knew fo well when and to whom he fhould
exert thefe Talents, that thofe it moft concern'd to fee into his Soul were leaft acquainted
with it.

This dangerous Perfon being the undoubted
Heir to all his Brother was poffeft of, in cafe
he fhould die without Iffue, had look'd with
an ill Eye on his Marriage; which not being
able to prevent, his working Brain had never
fince been idle to find or make Caufes of
Variance between him and his Lady, in order
to bring about a Separation if poffible. To

this deteftable View the Humours of both the
Perfons he had to practife on, too much contributed. Tho' the Baron, as I have already
taken notice, was far from having any thing
of the truly generous in him, and was not at
all good-natur'd; yet he was eafily led, believed every thing that was faid to him, and
was fure always to be govern'd by the laft
Advice. The Baronefs was gay, a little vain,
loved Company, and her Heart not having
been confulted in the Difpofal of her Hand,
had not a fufficient Stock of Tendernefs for
her Husband, to oblige her to debar herfelf
from any of thofe Pleafures fhe had been
accuftom'd to indulge, tho' never fo much
difrelifh'd by him. The Chevalier, who
knew his Brother perfectly well, and foon
grew no lefs acquainted with the Inclinations
of his Lady, took all Opportunities of con-
firming thofe cenforious Reflexions made by
their Mother: He reprefented her Conduct not
only as too expenfive, but alfo fuch as might
give the World a flight Opinion of her Virtue: Gave broad Hints as if he fear'd that exceffive Love fhe took in Play and Company
had fomewhat in it more criminal than fhe
pretended; and would defire his Brother to
be more watchful over her Behaviour, telling
him, that if fhe was his Wife he could not
approve of the Complaifance fhe fhew'd to
fome of the Gentlemen that vifited her. In
this cruel Manner was the poor Lady tra-
duced; who, entirely unfufpecting any fuch
Treachery, behaved with that Carelefnefs
and Eafe which is infeparable from Inno-

B 3

cence

cence, and which the Guilty but in vain affect.

The Baron, however, prepoffeft by his Mother and Brother, put a falfe Conftruction on all her Words and Actions; and at laft, unable to bear a Behaviour which he imagin'd both impair'd his Fortune and difhonour'd his Family, he told her in plain Terms, that if fhe did not retrench her Expences, and live in a more retir'd manner, he fhould make ufe of the Authority of an Husband to compel her to more Moderation.

How fuch a Speech muft found in the Ears of a Woman of Spirit, who was not confcious of having done any thing to provoke it, let the Ladies judge: Few of them, I dare anfwer, will condemn the Baronefs for refenting it, tho' fome who have greater Experience of the World might perhaps have done it with more Temper; but fhe, fincere by Nature, difdain'd to conceal the Indignation fhe was inflam'd with, and replied to what he faid to her in fuch a manner, as in part juftified his forbidding the Steward to let her have any Money, without an Order from himfelf.

While the cruel Chevalier was thus affifting his Mother in diftracting his Brother's Head with groundlefs Jealoufies, he was no lefs bufy in working up the Baronefs to fuch a Difpofition, as render'd her unable to combat her Husband's ill Humour with any of thofe Arms, which could alone have conquer'd it. Meeknefs, foft Perfuafions, and good Arguments, deliver'd in a tender manner, were what this Difturber of their Peace trem-

trembled at, and therefore took care to deprive her of. Whenever his Brother's Abfence gave him an Opportunity, he made his Court to her with all the Profeffions of a fincere Amity—pretended the greateft Commiferation of her Condition————blamed the Baron for thofe Faults which he had inftigated him to commit, and aggravated thofe he was guilty of by Inclination, which indeed were fuch as a Wife finds it leaft eafy to forgive. 'Tis certain, that to be conftant either in Love or Friendfhip was no part of the Baron's Character; he had many Amours, and as they were generally with Women of mean Beauty as well as Condition, were ftill fo much the greater and more poignant Affront to his Lady, who was always made acquainted with them either by the Chevalier, or fome of the Family whom he had gained over to his Intereft.

How often in their different Clofets did they unbofom themfelves to this perfidious Brother in thefe kinds of Exclamations : *Heaven!* would the Baron fay, *muft my Eftate be ruined—the Honour of my Family difgraced—myfelf abufed by a Woman whofe Duty it is to confult folely my Intereft, Reputation, and Satisfaction!— Does fhe imagine the little Beauty fhe is fo vain of, fhall make me bear her fcandalous Behaviour?*

What unhappy Star, cry'd the Baronefs, *ruled at my Nativity and deftined me to a Man fo every way unworthy of me! plain in his Perfon, weak in his Underftanding, what could my Father find in him to approve?— yet this infignificant Husband, merely becaufe*

he

he is a Husband, must have the Power to pre-scribe Laws to a Woman every way his Equal, in most his Superior. My necessary Expences must *be limited, that he may have the more to lavish on the Wretches he prefers to me!*——Then would she run to her Glass, and having view-ed herself from Head to Foot, *Good God!* said she, *what is there in this Face, this Shape, this Air, to create Disgust!*——no, 'tis the poor Man's want of Taste, *he delights in what is likest to himself——it is* Sympathy—— *and I ought rather to* pity *than* resent *his Folly.*

The most aggravating Circumstance of my Misfortune, cried the Baron when his Jea-lousy was rouz'd by some new Invention, *is, that this Woman is either so very Cunning, or so very Lewd, that she behaves to all the Gen-tlemen that frequent my House with so equal a Complaisance that I know not whom to fix upon as the Author of my Shame——perhaps she sins with every one by Turns, and I am the cursed Dupe of all who call themselves my Friends.*

Thus did they give Vent to their various Agitations when apart, and when together they entertain'd each other either with a gloomy Sullenness or the most piquant Reflections. In fine, every Day furnishing each with some Complaint against the other, the Baron be-came so strongly convinced he was injur'd, and so incensed against his Lady for *imaginary Infidelities*; and she so much to despise him not only for his *real ones,* but for the indifferent Treatment she received from him, that it was

impossible

impoffible for any two People to live together in a more difagreeable Manner.

As they had been married fome Time without the Appearance of any Fruit of the Nuptial Rites, moft People affign'd that Misfortune for the Caufe of the little Harmony which it was vifible there was between them; and poffibly they might not be altogether miftaken in this Point. The Ceremony of Marriage may, I think, juftly enough be compar'd to the well-laying of Bricks for the Foundation of the Manfion-Houfe of eternal Love, but Children are the Cement which muft bind it faft. Few but are delighted to fee in Miniature thofe Images of themfelves, and 'tis fcarce poffible to avoid feeling fome Tendernefs for your Partner in giving them Exiftence. The Baron in particular had been extremely anxious on this Score, and often lamented the little Hope he had of an Heir in all Company he came into. However, what had been his *Wifh* was his Brother's *Fear*; this ambitious Man trembled to think that what in near three Years had not happen'd, a Moment might produce, and that all his Views of Grandeur might ftill be defeated by the Baronefs's becoming pregnant: He therefore aim'd by all the Ways he could to bring about a Separation, not fuch a one as would enable the Baron to take another Wife, but fuch one as fhould put an End to his Apprehenfions of his having any Iffue by this. All his Endeavours to this End had hitherto prov'd unfuccefsful; the Baron, as little as he was now fatisfied with her Society, would not put her

B 5

out of his House, becaufe he then muft hav.
allow'd her a feparate Maintenance; and a
ill as fhe was treated by him, fhe chofe not
to go of her own Accord, becaufe fhe knew
that fhe could not then compel him to it.
This Confideration, and this alone kept them
fo long together, but at laft the Time arrived which gave a fudden Turn to both their
Sentiments.

The greateft Part of the Baron's Eftate lay
not in that Realm where he was born and
ufually had his Refidence, but in one feparated from it by a large Branch of the Sea;
fome very urgent Affairs now demanding his
Prefence there, it was expected the Baronefs
would go with him, nor had fhe herfelf any
other Intention at firft. This very much a-
larm'd the wicked Chevalier, and the more
becaufe he heard the Phyficians fay, that
Change of Air would go a great way in contri-
buting to the Baronefs's becoming pregnant:
To prevent her from taking this Voyage was
therefore all his Subtilty employ'd. *My dear
Sifter,* faid he one Day to her, *How impatient
fhall I be till I hear of your fafe Arrival, and
that you find every thing agreeable to your Merit
and Inclinations!* You are always perfectly good
and obliging, anfwer'd fhe, *but for my Part I
am under no manner of Apprehenfions ; the
Pleafure I take in Travelling more than coun-
terbalances the Danger ; and tho' I never yet
was at Sea, I don't think I fhall be much frighted——then they fay the Country is very fine,
and there is a World of good Company.* There
is the Danger I tremble at for you, Madam,
                                        refum'd

refum'd he, *you know the Unhappineſs of my Brother's Temper——how tenacious of his Honour——and how liable to miſconſtrue every little innocent Freedom in your Sex——And,* added he with a Sigh, *If he ſhould be ſo unjuſt to take any Whim of that Nature into his Head, (as who can anſwer he will not?) how unhappy muſt you be in a Place ſo far removed from any Friend either to adviſe or comfort you!* The Baroneſs teſtified by her Looks that theſe Words made all the Impreſſion on her they were intended for; and having pauſed a little, *Indeed Brother,* replied ſhe, *I am but too ſenſible of the Truth of what you ſay——I foreſee that I muſt live in a perpetual Conſtraint, than which nothing can be more irkſome to a Perſon of my Humour——but I am married, and the Misfortune is irremediable.* With theſe Words ſome Tears fell from her lovely Eyes, which far from melting the inexorable Heart of the Chevalier, made him inwardly rejoice, as convincing him that ſhe was not ſo bent on accompanying her Huſband, but that a ſmall Excuſe would ſerve her to ſtay where ſhe was: It was therefore his Buſineſs to take Care ſhe ſhould not be without one; but thinking he had ſaid enough for the firſt Time, pretended to be angry with himſelf for having mention'd any Thing to anticipate her Diſquiet, and concluded with telling her he hoped there would be no Occaſion for thoſe Fears his Friendſhip for her had made him entertain.

From her Chamber he went to that of the Baron, and finding him alone, *Well,* ſaid he,

B 6 *I juſt*

I just come from visiting my Sister——She is extremely gay, and pleases herself much with the Amusements she expects to find at the Castle de Altamont——You will certainly have a good Companion of her during your Voyage. You tell me News, reply'd the Baron; for I imagin'd she was as little satisfied with going, as I must own to you, I am with taking her.——— But, pray, what Amusements are they which she expects, and are so delightful to her in Idea?———O! it is easy for your Lordship to guess, reply'd the Chevalier, knowing her Disposition so well as you do,——Invitations,——Balls, ——Entertainments.———I assure you she expects to attract an universal Admiration, and that the fine Baroness de Altamont will be the Toast of the whole Kingdom. And pray what Figure does she think I am to make all the Time? cry'd the Baron sullenly. That of a Husband, answer'd the Chevalier with a Sneer. By Heaven! she shall find herself deceived in her Imaginations, resumed the other; I am a Husband 'tis true, but will prove myself a Husband that knows his Power, and is resolv'd to exert it——Alas! my Lord, said the Chevalier, you know her Pride and the Violence of her Spirit, and this Striving for the Mastery would but serve to make you the Talk of the whole Country.——In my Opinion it would be better you should, before you set out together, let her know how improper it will be that she should give Encouragement to any Addresses or Gallantries that may be offered her; and oblige her to give her Word and Honour to live in a manner agreeable to your Inclinations.——If you can bring her to

this.

this Promise,—continued the cruel Incendiary, even tho' she should break it, as I much fear she will, and force you to make Use of the Proofs you have over her, she would then have no Pretence to complain. My dear Brother, cry'd the Baron, it is excellently well thought on,—how happy am I to have the Advice of such a faithful Friend!

The two Brothers were continuing their Conversation, when the old Baroness came into the Room, with a Countenance which shew'd something had extremely ruffled her. They both rose to pay her the Respect due to a Lady of her Quality and their Mother, which she seeming to take little Notice of, threw herself into an easy Chair, and after a Moment's Silence, I know not, said she, addressing to the Baron, how you will relish what I am going to say; but I cannot help telling you, that if you take your Wife to Altamont, you will be made the Jest of the whole Country round: I only just now offer'd to give her some Advice concerning the Regulation of her Conduct; and she has treated me in such a manner as I would not have taken from any other Person in the World.——In fine, her Head is so intoxicated with Pride and Vanity, that she is above all good Counsel,——quite abandon'd,——has no Regard for her own Character, nor that of those who belong to her, and will bring us all into Disgrace, if some Method is not taken to oblige her to be more discreet at least, if not more virtuous.

The Baron then made her acquainted with what he intended by the Advice of his Brother
ther

ther to propofe to her, and as the Time prefix'd for their Departure was near at Hand, it
was agreed that he ought not to defer what he
had to fay to her, and fhould therefore mention
it the fame Day at Dinner, and alfo that the
old Baronefs and the Chevalier fhould be witnefs of what pafs'd on that Occafion.

While this Contrivance was forming in the
Baron's Chamber, his Lady was venting in
Tears the Vexation fhe labour'd under. The
old Dowager Baronefs had been reproving
her paft Conduct, and giving Leffons for
her future Behaviour, in a manner fo arbitrary
and infulting, that it forced from her fome
Expreffions, which, had fhe been more Miftrefs of her Paffion, fhe would not have made
ufe of to the Mother of her Husband. Hearing afterward that fhe ftay'd Dinner, and
not doubting but the fame Difcourfe would
be revived, fhe fent her Woman to excufe
her coming to Table, under Pretence of being indifpofed.

The Baron, who was determin'd now to
fpeak the whole of his Sentiments, and chofe
to do it in the Prefence of his Mother, flew
into a Rage at receiving this Meffage, and
bad the Perfon who brought it tell her Lady,
that he had more than ordinary Reafons to
defire her Company at that Time.——that he
commanded her to come, and was refolv'd to
be obey'd.

Whatever Right the Name of Husband gives,
the young Baronefs could not fubmit to a
Mandate deliver'd in that arbitrary manner,
and return'd for Anfwer, that not being well

in

in Health, she could not imagine a Husband that *loved her* would wish she should hazard being worse, by complying with his Desires; and one that had not that Consideration for her, was not worthy of being obey'd.

You see, Son, said the old Baroness, *the Violence of her Spirit, and what kind of Treatment you are to expect if you offer to controul any Thing she thinks fit to do, tho' never so shameful for herself, and injurious to you. I could wish, indeed,* said the subtle Chevalier, *that my Sister would avoid being seen so frequently in Publick Places, or, when there, be a little more serious : She is now going to a Country where the Ladies are very censorious, and the Men very presuming : Her excessive Gaiety, I am afraid, will draw Scandal from the one, and give too much Encouragement to the other, and both join to disturb my Brother's Peace of Mind.*

Many other things of this Kind were added, till the Baron became so exasperated, that he swore not to take her with him, but upon Condition she would make great Submissions to him, and give him the strongest Assurances in her Power, of behaving in a manner quite the Reverse of what she had hitherto observed. In the Height of his Passion he was for running to her Chamber, and telling her how ill he was satisfied with her ; but his Mother opposed it; and after many Debates what was best to be done, they at last concluded, that after Dinner the Chevalier *Richard* should represent to her the Disposition of the People she should live among in case she went with the

Baron,

Baron, and endeavour to convince her, that an Alteration in her Conduct was absolutely necessary: After this, he was to let her know, that the Baron expected she should make him a solemn Promise never to play, or be seen in any Company he should not approve of her being with.

Nothing could be more agreeable to the Chevalier than being employ'd in this Negotiation, yet did he seem to undertake it with the greatest Reluctance, feigning to be prevailed upon only by the Consideration, that since it was necessary to know her Sentiments, he was the fittest Person to sound them, as the Dowager Baroness had so lately been disconcerted by her, and the Baron was too much incensed at that Time, to argue with that Moderation the Occasion required.

But before he went, he reminded his Brother, that it was very probable she might seemingly consent to every thing he desir'd, as her Heart was so much bent on going, and might afterwards deny that she made any such Promise. *It would therefore be better, in my Opinion, said he, that your Lordship should put down in Paper what you expect from her, and oblige her to sign her Name to the Conditions; and then, in case of Non-performance, you may put what Restriction you shall find necessary upon her: She will not presume to complain when you have her own Hand to produce against her.*

This Advice was received with a loud Approbation both by the Baron and the old Lady, and

and the former called for a Sheet of Papers and immediately wrote as follows:

I Acknowledge myfelf to have been infinitely to blame in not having confulted, as I ought to have done, the Honour and Satisfaction of my Husband and Family, and do hereby promife to be more regular in my Conduct for the future: Particularly, I engage myfelf to renounce all kind of Gaming, to keep no Company of either Sex but fuch as fhall be approved of by him, and in every thing to conform myfelf to his Pleafure, as becomes a loving, virtuous, and obedient Wife: Defiring that whenever I fwerve from this Promife, or difcover an Inclination to relapfe into my former Follies, this Teftimony, which I fign with my own Hand, may rife up in Judgment againft me.

The Dowager Baronefs was in Raptures at this Revenge on her Daughter-in-law, for the late Rebuff fhe had given her; and the Chevalier, for ftronger Reafons, hugg'd himfelf in the Affurance of his wicked Aim's Succefs. He affum'd, however, the moft troubled Countenance, when he came into the Baronefs's Chamber, and after a long Prelude, teftifying the great Regret he had in being obliged to execute a Commiffion which was fo fhocking to himfelf, and would be fo ungrateful to her, he at laft prefented the Paper to her, telling her at the fame time, that fhe muft either fign it, or give over all thoughts of going to *Altament* Caftle.

Pre-

Prepar'd as she was, by what he had said, for something more than ordinarily alarming, she no sooner cast her Eye on the first Line of this imperious Scroll, than the Disdain it fill'd her with shew'd itself in every Feature: The farther she read, the more inflam'd she grew; but the Conclusion put her beyond all Patience— she tore the Paper in a thousand Pieces, and made the bitterest Exclamations on the Severity of her Fate. The Chevalier, under the Mask of endeavouring to appease her Rage, took care to blend such things with his Persuasions, as but provok'd her more; and when he begg'd to know what Answer he should give the Baron, *Tell him,* said she, *what you have seen me do; and if that is not sufficient to convince him what I think both of him and his impudent Proposals, tell him, I despise and hate the one, and will sooner go alive into my Grave, than even pretend to allow the Justice of the other.* It is not to be suppofed the Chevalier made any real Attempts to alter this Resolution in her; but, glad he had brought things to this Height between them, return'd to the Baron with an Account, in which he omitted nothing that might prevent any relenting Thoughts from rising in his Breast.

A Man of much less Artifice than the Chevalier *Richard* might indeed have succeeded in this Point; for where there is no Love, there must be a greater Fund of Good-nature than the Baron was poffeft of, to have made any Husband recede from what he had once determin'd, without some small Submission on the Part of the Wife.

An

An immediate Stop was now put to all the Preparations that had been making for the Baroness's Departure; but she saw it without Regret, and, far from abating any thing of that Resolution she had testify'd to the Chevalier *Richard*, she sent her Woman to tell the Baron, that she should sleep in her own Chamber, and suppofed he would not be difpleafed at the Abfence of a Perfon he had thought fit to treat in the manner he had done her. *She is much in the right,* cry'd he, when this Meffage was deliver'd to him, *she cannot oblige me more than by keeping out of my Sight,—not only now, but for ever.*

Thus did the Diffatisfaction they long had more fecretly harbour'd for each other, break into an open Quarrel; and there being no more than two Days between that in which it happen'd, and that prefix'd for the Baron's Departure, he went without taking any Leave of her, or even feeing her, tho' fhe was in the fame Houfe.

Before he went, however, fhe fent to know what Appointments were allotted for her Maintenance in his Abfence, and to whom fhe was to have Recourfe for the Payment: To which he return'd for Anfwer, That fhe had already coft him more than he had received with her; and that Part of her Fortune being ftill in the Duke her Father's Hands, fhe muft apply to him; to whom, perhaps, fhe had been a better Daughter, than to him fhe had been a Wife.

This was a mortal Stab to the poor Baronefs: She knew the Duke was ftern, haughty,

and

and made small Allowances for the Frailties
of Women, and thofe fhe had been guilty of
having been reprefented by the Baron's Friends
in their worft Colours, fhe fcarce doubted but
fhe fhould meet with a greater Share of Reproaches than Relief.——She foon found fhe
had not been deceived in her Conjecture ;
Whatever the Duke's private Opinion was,
he feem'd to think her Conduct moft to be
condemn'd, and told her, that fhe muft not
expect he would give any Countenance to a
Woman, who, by her own ill Management,
liv'd in a State of Separation from her Hufband.

To add to her Misfortune, and give her
Father yet a greater Pretence for refufing his
Protection, the old Baronefs, pretending fhe
had Proofs that fhe had wrong'd her Husband's
Bed, exhibited a Libel againft her for Adultery, in order to obtain a Divorce, that her
Son might be enabled to marry again, fhe having a young Lady of a confiderable Fortune in
her Eye for him, when that fhould be brought
about.

This terribly alarm'd the Chevalier *Richard*.
He had compafs'd what he aim'd at in occa-
fioning a Separation, and if his Brother fhould
marry again, all he had done was of no Effect ; fo that as Poifons of a different Nature
deftroy each other's Force, when applied at
the fame time, fo did the Malice of thefe
two, working for contrary Ends ; and the Efforts privately made by the Chevalier fruftrated all his Mother's Endeavours : Heaven or-
daining, that the worft Enemy the Baronefs
had

had now did all the Offices of the moſt cordial
Friend.—In fine, the Proſecution was dropp'd;
but it made ſo great a Noiſe, that thoſe Perſons who before had ſupply'd her with Money,
now refuſed to give her Credit, and ſhe was
driven to the extremeſt Straits that perhaps
any Woman of her Birth and Quality ever labour'd under. She had Recourſe again to the
Duke her Father.—She wrote, ſhe implor'd;
but for a long Time in vain.—At laſt he conſented to pay what Debts ſhe had contracted, and
give her a Sum of Money ſufficient to enable her
to appear in a manner ſuitable to her Dignity,
on Condition ſhe would go to her Husband,
and attempt a Reconciliation with him by
ſuch Ways as he ſhould approve. It was to no
Purpoſe ſhe pleaded the ill Uſage he had given
her, and that as it was the Effect of his Choice
that ſhe remain'd behind him, there was little
Probability he would receive her if ſhe went;
the Duke was obſtinate, and told her that till
he was convinced ſhe ſeriouſly endeavour'd it,
he would neither give her the leaſt Aſſiſtance,
or ever ſee her Face again.

What could ſhe now do? How avoid the
cruel Extremity? There was no Refuge for
her, ſhe muſt either ſtarve, or do what was
little leſs irkſome to her; and after having
endured the moſt cruel Conflicts within herſelf which Party to take, ſhe at length yielded
to her Father's Will, and he performing the
Promiſe he had made, even more liberally than
ſhe had expected, ſhe ſet out with a gay Equipage, but ſad Heart, for the Kingdom where
the Baron now was.

Her

Her Voyage was prosperous; the Winds and Waves, more favourable than her obdurate Husband, brought her safely to the Port, which being a considerable Distance from *Altamont* Castle, she began to reflect, that as she was compell'd to come by her Father, it would be Prudence in her to do something on her own Part to oblige her Husband to receive her in such a Fashion as should not occasion any Discourse of their Disunion in a Place where she was so much a Stranger. To this End she struggled with her Resentment, and by Degrees got so much the Mastery of it, as to submit to write to him in these Terms:

To the Baron DE ALTAMONT.

My LORD,

AS there is nothing more common than for People to change their Ways of thinking, you will not be surprized that mine has not been unalterable, or if you are, I flatter my-self it will give you no Displeasure. By the Date of this you will find I am in ****. I thought proper to acquaint you with my Ar-rival, and that to morrow I set out for *Alta-mont*. As my following you, without being either *follicited* to it by your *Affection*, or *com-pell'd* to it by your *Power*, is an undeniable Token I am sincere in my Desires of a Recon-ciliation, and determin'd to do every thing I can to preserve a future Harmony between I hope you will have so much Regard to the
Honour

Honour and Satisfaction of us both, as to receive me in a manner becoming the Husband of an

Affectionate and Virtuous Wife,

M. DE ALTAMONT.

This Letter she sent by the Post, and it probably might have had the Effect it was intended for, had it been the first Harbinger of her Approach; but tho' she had communicated her Intentions of going to the Baron to very few, yet was not the Secret so closely kept, but that it came to the Knowledge of the Chevalier *Richard*, who, alarm'd at it, immediately sent an Account to his Brother, as follows.

To the Baron DE ALTAMONT.

My LORD,

TO prevent an Astonishment which might, perhaps, render you unable of reflecting what would best become you to do, I thought it my Duty to acquaint your Lordship, that the Baroness is now on her Journey towards *Altamont*,——You have been inform'd from time to time, in what Manner she has behaved since your Departure, and though I cannot approve the Measures our Mother took, because, as it was impossible to procure a Divorce, the Disgrace in part retorted upon you, yet I cannot see how you can receive so offending a Wife, without being look'd upon as the tamest of Husbands.——I have always
wish'd

with'd a Reconciliation between you, but fear
it will not now be for your Honour to agree
to it: I leave it, however, to your Lordſhip's
ſuperior Judgment, and have the Honour to
be, with the greateſt Sincerity,

Your Lordſhip's moſt devoted Servant,

and affectionate Brother,

RICHARD DE ALTAMONT.

This was alſo accompany'd by one from
the Dowager Baroneſs, full of the moſt undif-
guiſed Invectives againſt her Daughter-in-law,
ſo that, with this ſtrong Prepoſſeſſion, there
was little Likelihood a Letter from a Wife unloved, and much ſuſpected, could have any
very great Influence. Had he known ſhe intended to come while ſhe was on the other
Side the Water, 'tis probable he would have
ſent to have prevented her Embarkation; but
as ſhe had made the Voyage, and was already
in the Kingdom, he knew not how to put a
Stop to her Journey, and leſs in what Faſhion
he ſhould behave on her Arrival at the Caſtle.
He imparted the News of her Approach to
none of his Acquaintance: He neither went
himſelf to meet her on the Road, nor ſent any
of his Retinue to conduct her. The Baroneſs, who imagined that he would at leaſt
have paid her this laſt Compliment, after the
Letter ſhe had ſent him, which ſhe imagined
a ſufficient Submiſſion for much greater Errors
than hers had been, was ſtung to the very
Heart

Heart when she found herself within twenty Miles of the Castle, and no Appearance of any Person sent by the Baron : Glad would she have been to have had it in her Power to have turned back, but the Circumstances she stood in with her Father would not permit her to testify, by such a Step, the Disdain she had of the Slight now put upon her. As she drew nearer to her Journey's End, the more her Perplexity increased, when, on a sudden, she recollected that a young Lady she had been extremely intimate with, in her Virgin-State, had married into that Country, and lived somewhere in these Parts. —— A Thought came presently into her Head, which giving her some Satisfaction to pursue, she ordered a Servant to enquire after this Friend, and being informed that her House was not above a League distant from where they now were, and within a small Mile of *Altamont*, she directed her Coach to stop there, under the Pretence that being a little indisposed with the Fatigue of travelling, she would refresh herself before she went any farther.

The Lady received her with all imaginable Demonstrations of Joy, and they immediately renewed that Friendship for each other, which Absence had only interrupted. They gave each other a brief Account of their Adventures since their parting, and the Baroness, in the Conclusion of hers, told her that if she might flatter herself with a few Days Welcome at her House, she would feign herself indisposed, and send to let the Baron know she was there. Her fair Friend approved of her

C   Pro-

Project, and the rather because her Husband, being very well acquainted with the Baron, she thought he might be able to mediate Matters so as to bring about a perfect Reconciliation. As she was a Woman of great Prudence, she failed not to represent, in such touching Terms, to the Baroness, how much it concerned her Interest and Reputation to be well with her Husband, that she began seriously to resolve to bear with more Moderation than she had hitherto done, whatever was disagreeable in the Temper of a Man to whom she was bound for Life; and, that if he would do his Part, to contribute all in hers to live peaceably together. In order to this it was agreed, that she should write a second Letter, the Contents whereof were these:

To the Baron DE ALTAMONT.

My LORD.

CHange of Air, or the Fatigue I have endured, rendered me unable to reach the Castle, tho' so near, and I was obliged to stop at the House of one of my Friends, whom I hear with Pleasure is also yours: I need not mention the Chevalier *du Pont*, because he is so good as to be the Bearer of this; and has promised, since my Illness will not yet permit me to remove from hence, to conduct you to her who much desires to see you, after so long a Separation, and to exchange Forgiveness

ned with you for the Caufes that occafioned
it.

Your moft affectionate Wife,

M. DE ALTAMONT.

These were Submiffions, which, in fpite of
all Remonftrances, nothing but the Neceffity
of the Baronefs's Affairs could have extorted
from her Pride on this Occafion, her natural
Sincerity was put to a no lefs fevere Tafk,
and fhe found it the greateft Difficulty in the
World to affume a Countenance and Behaviour to the Baron fo as not to contradict her
Letters when he fhould arrive.

The Chevalier *du Pont* found him in an
extreme ill Humour ; he told him he was unacquainted with the Baronefs's Behaviour towards him, or he would not have undertook
the Office he now did — fwore he would never fee her Face more, — accufed her of a
thoufand Irregularities, if not Vices, and concluded with faying, *It was impoffible fhe
could ever alter her Temper and Conduct.* To
all this the other faid little till he had railed
himfelf quite out of Breath, and exhaufted all
the Venom his Mother and Brother's Letters
had infufed into him, but then exerted all the
good Underftanding he was Mafter of, than
which few Men had a greater Share, to bring
this incenfed Hufband to put a lefs fevere
Conftruction on his Lady's paft Actions, and
a better Opinion of her prefent Intentions.
The Baron's natural Docility contributed very

much

much to enforce the Arguments of his Friend, and in a few Hours he was as willing to believe every thing in her Favour, as before he had been to her Prejudice. *Come,* faid he to the Chevalier, *let us go and fee this poor Penitent : Whatever fhe has been guilty of, I dare fwear her Punifhment, fince I left her, has been equal.*

The meeting of thefe two was odd enough, the Baron put on a haughty Gravity, which was wholly unnatural to him, and only affumed, becaufe he thought it would become him at this Juncture, and excite Refpect in his Lady. The Baronefs affected an Humility, which fhe was far from feeling, but had its Effect on her Hufband; while the Airs he gave himfelf only ferved to make him appear more contemptible in her Eyes.

But this mutual Conftraint lafted not long; whether it were that Abfence had given the Baronefs all the Charms of a new Beauty, or that he was really ftruck with fome Remorfe for the unkind Treatment he had given her; to which foever of thefe Motives it was, none but himfelf could determine; but he had not been half an Hour at the Chevalier *du Pont's* before he became exceeding good-humour'd, and even fond of his Lady. The Returns fhe made were highly obliging to him, and finding him fo much more complaifant than fhe expected, wrought fo far on the natural Sweetnefs of her Difpofition, that all her late counterfeited Softnefs was converted into a real one ; and whoever had now feen them together, would have believed them an extreme

happy

happy Pair, and that they were incapable of having ever difagreed.

The Baron would not quit the Chevàlier *du Pont*'s that Night, but early the next Morning went home to order Things for the Reception of his Lady. In the Afternoon he return'd with two Coaches-and-fix and all his Equipage, and towards Evening the reconciled Couple, accompanied by the Chevàlier *du Pont* and his Lady, went together to the Caftle of *Altamont*, where for fome Days there was nothing but Feafting, Mufick, and Balls, to entertain the Nobility and Gentry of thofe Parts, who hearing the Baronefs was arrived, came to pay their Compliments to her. Every Body was charm'd with the Perfon and Converfation of this Lady, and the Baron having now none to miflead him, was mightily pleas'd at the Congratulations made him on his Choice, and the Praifes which all Degrees of People gave her.

To add to his Contentment, or rather to give him an Extafy he had never known before, the Baronefs became pregnant: His Fondnefs of her increafed from the Moment of this happy Difcovery; fhe was highly fatisfy'd herfelf, and began now to find a real Tendernefs for her Hufband.

While this Harmony fubfifted, the Baronefs brought into the World a Son; that Son, whofe Adventures have fince made fo great a Noife in the World. — O! who that then beheld the fmiling Babe, Heir of three Baronies, and a much fuperior Title in Reverfion, Idol of his Parents, and Objcft of the Con-

gratulations

Gratulations and Rejoicings of a whole Province, could have imagin'd he was born to suffer Woes sufficient to make him regret he ever had Existence, and almost accuse Heaven of Partiality! Little, alas, does the fond Mother, when pressing her darling Infant in her Arms, think of the Miseries that may be destin'd for its Portion: But to return —

Our young Chevalier was baptized by the Name of *James*, in Compliment to a noble Lord a near Relation of the Baron's, and at whose Death he expected a considerable Addition to his Estate, and soon after committed to the Care of a young Woman in the Neighbourhood, called *Juggan*, who, tho' a plain Country Creature, had the good Fortune to have her Milk approved by the Physicians above that of others, who came to offer themselves, of a superior Class. She performed indeed all the Duties of a Nurse with so much Exactness, that the Baroness was very well satisfied with her.

The Baron had now no Reason for Complaint against his Wife, yet in time he grew peevish with her, would have Starts of Passion tho' no Cause to alledge for them; but she knew it was natural to him, and had learned Philosophy enough to bear it with Patience; as also his refusing to let her accompany him to the Capital, whither he often went himself, and would sometimes stay a Month or six Weeks together. 'Tis certain he had his Reasons for depriving her of the Pleasures that great City affords, but they were chiefly on his own Account; he less

feared

feared she should indulge herself too much in them, than that her Presence would be a Bar to his Enjoyment of them; for tho' no Man was more frugal and parsimonious when at home, he regarded no Expences for the Gratification of his Appetites when abroad; and as his darling Pleasures were Wine and Women, he seldom lay one Night alone, or went sober to Bed during his Continuance in Town. But the Baroness was altogether ignorant of this, as also that by being the Dupe of several of his dissolute Companions, he had been obliged to mortgage great Part of his Estate, and had beside contracted many other large Debts. Happy had it been for her, if she had never been acquainted with what was entirely out of her Power to remedy, or when she was so, could have concealed her Knowledge.

The Chevalier *James* was about four or five Months old, when one Day his Nurse having brought him into her Chamber, she was praising his Growth to a young Lady who happened to be with her when *Juggan* came in : *Yes,* cried the silly Tatler, *his Nurse has a double Reason to take Care of him. A double Reason,* said the Baroness, *I don't know what you mean, but I should be glad she had a Thousand, so he throve the better for them.* In speaking this she happened to cast her Eyes on *Juggan,* and saw her Face was covered with a scarlet Blush, which a little surprizing her, made her ask the Lady, what double Reason it was she supposed her to have? To which the other would have avoided giving any direct Answer, saying they were Words

C 4   with-

without Defign, and had no Purport. This
yet more exciting the Baronefs's Curiofity,
fhe told her it was to no Purpofe to deny
that fhe had that Moment fomething in her
Thoughts, and fhe would never forgive her if
fhe made a Secret of it. *Then if you muft know*,
faid the Lady, *it was a foolifh Fancy juft then
come into my Head, that there is a great
Refemblance between the Features of the Chevalier* James, *and Nurfe* Juggan's *own Child.
That's an odd Whim indeed*, cry'd the Baronefs coldly, *there is feldom any remarkable
Likenefs where there is not fome Mixture of
the fame Blood.* She faid no more, nor did
the other continue the Difcourfe, but *Juggan's* Colour remain'd all the Time fhe ftaid
in the Room, and had all the Tokens of a
violent Confufion upon her. The Baronefs
was little lefs diforder'd, tho' fhe conceal'd it,
and affoon as the Perfon, whofe filly Inadvertency had given her this Alarm, had taken her
Leave, fhe began to reflect very deeply on
what fhe had faid. -- *A double Reafon*, and *the
Likenefs between the Children*, fhe thought
were odd Expreffions, and muft have fome
Signification. — She had feen *Juggan's* Child,
and had thought him a fine Boy — and
fhe had been told fo, began to think he
indeed fome little Refemblance of the Che-
lier *James*.-- She remember'd too that fhe
often afk'd *Juggan* where her Hufband
and why he did not live with her, and that
the Woman had only faid, he was gone beyond Sea, but never cared to mention him,
to be afk'd any Queftions concerning him.
the

this put together, infused a Kind of Jealousy
in her Heart. — She thought it was not impossible but the Child who was thought like
the Chevalier, might be got by the same Father. — The Blushes and Confusion the
Nurse was in at the Mention of a Resem-
blance between them, help'd to strengthen
this Suggestion in her, and she became so uneasy, that resolving to be assured what Grounds
there were for it, she rung her Bell for her
Woman, to whom she repeated all that had
past, and charg'd her, by all the Duty and
Affection she had for her, to found the Bottom of this Matter; which she told her she
might easily do, by enquiring among the Servants what Kind of Man *Juggan*'s Husband
was, what his Profession, how long he had
been absent, and whither he was gone, and
such like Questions. By the Answers made
to her she doubted not but she should be able
either to confirm the Truth of her Suspicions,
or wholly banish them. *Charlotte*, for that
was her Name, seem'd very unwilling to be
employ'd in this Affair, and would fain have
persuaded her Lady to entertain no such Con-
jectures, but the Baroness was obstinate to be
obey'd, and the other was obliged to promise
she would do all in her Power to give her the
Satisfaction she required.

Difficult it was for her to resolve in what
manner she should behave in this Business:
That *Juggan* never had been married to any
Man, and was made a Mother by the Baron,
was scarce a Secret to any in the whole Province but the Baroness, and that she had not

heard.

heard of it was owing wholly to the Prudence
and Good-nature of her Acquaintance, as well
as of those about her.　Loth she was to be the
Person that should inform her Lady of a
Thing which she knew would give her so
much Uneasiness, and as she seem'd so bent
on the Discovery of the Truth, was fearful of
incurring her Displeasure by concealing it, if
ever it should come to her Ears by any other
Means.　She evaded it however for some Days
by one Pretence or other, till the Baroness beginning to accuse her of trifling with her, she
found a Necessity of confessing that there was
some Discourse concerning a Kindness the Baron had testify'd to *Juggan*, but that no-body
could be sure of any such thing ; and if it were
so, it was before her Ladyship's Arrival, and
therefore she had the less Cause to resent it.

　　She was going on to excuse the Baron as
well as she could for this Accident in case it
had really happened, which yet she would
not seem to be assured of, but the Baroness
stopt her Mouth.　*As for the Certainty of it,*
said she, *I am well convinced, but if I pardon that Effect of a loose and wandering Inclination in him at a time that I was absent
and at Variance with him, I know not how I
ought to resent his permitting a Strumpet to
give Suck to my Son and his own lawful Heir.*
Charlotte would now again have interposed,
but the Baroness bid her leave the Room.

　　Here ceased that Tranquility of Mind she
had enjoy'd since her being at the Castle of
Altamont ; for tho', as she told her Woman,
there might be some Allowances made for his

Amour

Amour before her Arrival, yet the entertaining the Woman he had been thus guilty with
in Quality of a Nurfe to his Legitimate Son,
was a Proof he ftill had a Regard for her;
and from this Moment the Baron never mentioned her, or look'd upon her, but the Jealoufy of this unhappy Lady made her imagine it was with Tendernefs. She had ftill,
however, the Prudence not to let him perceive
fhe knew any thing of the Difcourfe concerning this Affair, nor, for the Sake of her Son,
who not being yet wean'd, might fuffer by
the Change of Milk, did make any Propofal
to remove him from her Breaft. — She labour'd, however, under a fecret Difcontent,
which, by the Conftraint fhe put on herfelf
in concealing, wrought a vifible Change both
in her Perfon and Behaviour. The Baron obferv'd it, and perhaps guefs'd at the Occafion,
but took no Notice to her either of the one or
the other; he grew every Day more cool, fhe
lefs tender, and a kind of forced Civility was
all that now remain'd between them: As
there was no Quarrel, and each kept their
Thoughts in their own Breaft, there was no
room for any Friend to attempt the Redrefs of
what they could not but obferve.

How long they might have continued in
this inactive Infenfibility Heaven only knows.
Chance rouzed the Seeds of Paffion in the
Souls of both. The Baronefs, one Evening
pretty late, indulging her Difcontent in a
Grove adjacent to the Caftle, her Meditations
were interrupted by the Sound of Voices behind fome Trees; fhe thought the one was

no

no Stranger to her Ears, and the other the Baron's: She rose from the Bank she had been sitting on, and drawing softly to the Place whence the Sound proceeded, was convinced of what she before believed, and saw by the Light of the Moon, which then shone very plain, her Lord and one of her Maids in such an Attitude, as could leave no room to doubt the shameful Business they met there upon. Tho' she had moved with as much Circumspection as possible, the rustling of her Garments making them turn their Eyes that way, they immediately saw and knew by whom they were thus surprized. — Could the Baroness have retreated without being known to have been a Witness of their Guilt, the same Prudence which had made her silent in the Affair of *Juggan*, might perhaps have made her seem ignorant of this; but as this could not be done, she could not, without the utmost Meanness, stifle her Resentments. The Maid had no sooner beheld her Face than she fled the Place with all the Speed she could; but the Baron remain'd, as neither dreading any Reproaches, nor asham'd of deserving them. *Is it thus, my Lord,* said she, *that you requite my Study to oblige you? Is this my Recompence for secluding myself from all the World, renouncing every Pleasure that my Rank and Youth might claim, and fixing my whole Satisfaction in your Content? To wrong me with one of my own Servants, nay, one of the meanest of them too, is too cruel an Indignity.* Here her Tears stopt the Progress of her Words.

You make a mighty Merit, answered he, *of*

living

living decently when you had neither *Means* nor *Opportunities* of carrying on your *Gallantries* any longer; but if you had half the *Wit* you would be thought *Miſtreſs* of, you would not bring to my *Memory* what I have been willing to forget, nor by giving a *Looſe* to your impertinent *Curioſity* force me to tell you to your *Face*, that whatever I may do is, beſide the *Privilege* of my *Sex*, fully juſtified by your own *Example*.

These laſt Words deſtroy'd all the Patience ſhe would fain have preſerved in ſo ſhocking an Adventure.—*By my Example*, cried ſhe! *then I ſhould proſtitute myſelf to one of your Grooms or Footmen;*—but know, injurious *Man*, I have a Soul that ſcorns ſuch Meanneſs. The Baron then told her that *Virtue* ſupported only by *Pride* was little to be valued, and treated all ſhe ſaid to him with ſuch an Air of Contempt, that not being able to find Words to vent the Rage ſhe was poſſeſt of, it ſeized upon her Spirits, and ſhe fell into a Swoon. He left her in that Condition, but aſſoon as he got into the Caſtle acquainted her Woman with the Condition ſhe was in, on which ſhe ran immediately to the Place he had directed, and with the Aſſiſtance of ſome other Servants brought her to herſelf. She was led between them to her Chamber, where by that time the Baron was undreſs'd and gone to Bed. As ſtrong as her Reſentments were, ſhe recollected the ill Conſequences that had attended her beginning a Separation of this Sort, and reſolving to give him no Pretence for acting as he before had done, made her Women put her into Bed, where they ſlept

or

or rather quarell'd together the beft Part of
the Night. Each faying what they could to
mortify the other, *Juggan* was not forgot;
but he feem'd not to regard even her Knowledge of that Amour, and anfwer'd her Up-
braidings either with retorting her Accufa-
tions on herfelf, or with fuch a ftabbing Indifference and ill-natur'd Calmnefs, that never
Woman fuffered a greater Humiliation.

Company happening to come the next Day
to dine with them, they were both wife eno'
to conceal what had paft by behaving to each
other as ufual; but as foon as they were alone
their Ill-humour return'd, and fo continued,
that from that time forward no more Endearments paft between them. The Baron went
foon after to the Capital, where he ftay'd feveral Months, return'd to the Caftle meerly
for Form's fake, then to the Capital again,
which he now made much more his home
than his own Province. The Baronefs, who
by his laft ill Treatment had recover'd all
her former Contempt of him, received him
with Conftraint, and parted with him without
Regret; it was juft the fame with him; and
thus did they drag on a mutual Difcontent upwards of three Years, during which time the
Chevalier *Richard* arrived at the Caftle,
who was far from defiring to fee more
Unity between them; for tho' the Birth of
the Chevalier *James* had defeated all his
former Projects, yet had he ftill others no lefs
pernicious than the former. Perceiving that
his Brother, in fpite of his Indifference for the
Mother, exceedingly carefs'd the Son, he fpar'd
no Pains to alienate his Affections, and at
                                          laft

laſt prevail'd ſo far on his Credulity as to make him ſometimes ſuſpect he was not of his own Begetting; but theſe Imaginations came but by Starts,——Self-love prevailed,——He found a Pleaſure in thinking he was the Father of a Legitimate Offspring, and therefore would indulge it; which the Chevalier perceiving contented himſelf with infuſing that cruel Opinion into others, and forbore mentioning it any 'more to his Brother, endeavouring only to keep him as much as poſſible at a Diſtance, to the end he might become more indifferent to him. Not that he could imagine this would forward his own ambitious Views; for as the Chevalier *James* was born in Wedlock, whether he really was of the Baron's begetting, or whether he believed him ſo or not, was of no Conſequence; for being born of the Baroneſs entitled him to the Succeſſion of all the Baron either had, or might be poſſeſt of; but the wicked Chevalier *Richard*, incapable of being moved by the growing Beauties of his Infant Nephew as by all the Impulſe of Blood and Nature, look'd on the ſweet Innocence with an implacable Hatred, as being born in his Deſpite, and the ſure Bar to all his Hopes of Greatneſs. He never heard that he was taken with any of thoſe little Ailments to which Children are incident, but he wiſh'd they might be fatal to him; and indeed, conſidering the Cruelties he ſince has practiſed on him, nothing is more ſtrange, than that he did not contrive ſome Means to make them ſo; but if any ſuch abhorr'd Deſign ever came into his Head, the Execution of it was fruſtrated by Providence,

and

and as there is no Proof there ought to be no Accusation.

The young Chevalier, unhurt by his cruel Uncle's ill Wishes, liv'd and grew the only Solace of his Mother's melancholly Hours: The Care and Tenderness his Nurse had for him, endear'd her also by Degrees to the Baroness; and the more so, as she lost that Boy who was said to be of the Baron's begetting, and doubtless was so, since she who best could tell, at length acknowledged it.

The continual Riots the Baron liv'd in at the Capital obliging him to repeated Mortgages, he bethought him of breaking up House-keeping, disposing of the Castle of *Altamont*, and the Lands adjoining to it for his own Life: He had no sooner taken this into his Head than he put it into Execution, and the unhappy Baroness was told at once that she must remove. *Whither?* demanded she. *Even where you please, Madam,* reply'd the Baron; *my Misfortunes have reduced me to sell all I was possest of for the Payment of my Debts; I have no longer wherewith to support you, and as you have no Friends in this Kingdom, your only Resource in my Opinion is the Duke your Father.* She was sometime before she could give Credit to a Misfortune so unlook'd for; and which she could not imagine by what Chance had been brought upon her; but on enquiring further she soon learned the cruel Certainty and the Causes of it. Finding no Remedy she prepared for her Departure with that scanty Pittance the Baron thought fit to bestow on her, but which he pretended was all

he

he could fave out of his Bankrupt Fortune: She defired to take her Son with her, not doubting but her Father would have Compaffion on the Heir of *Altamont* ; but this the Baron would by no means permit, and all her Tears and Prayers were vain : He told her that if fhe defired he fhould continue his Affection for him, or believe he had that Share in him fhe pretended, fhe would not make any Efforts to feparate him from a Father who had hitherto ufed him as his Son. This filenc'd her Intreaties, and having taken a mournful Farewell of that dear Babe, and thofe who had fhewn a Friendfhip for her, particularly the Chevalier *Du Pont* and his Lady, fhe quitted the Caftle of *Altamont*, and foon after the Kingdom, with no other Comfort, Company, Equipage or Retinue than *Charlotte* her Woman.

The Baron now eafed of his Wife, and the Burden of a Family, and Mafter of a good Sum of ready Money, returned with his Brother to the Capital, where amongft low Company and in the meaneft Manner of Living more was prefently confumed, than with good Oeconomy might have fupported him according to his Rank a confiderable Time.

In fine, having fold his whole Eftate for Life, and fquander'd all the Purchafe, he became fo extremely deftitute, that he wanted even the common Neceffaries of Life : In this Diftrefs he was advifed by fome of his Companions to raife Money by giving Leafes in Reverfion of a very great Eftate, which muft infallibly devolve on him at the Deceafe of the
present

prefent Poffeffor, who was extremely ancient.
He fell immediately into this Scheme, but the
Chevalier *James*, as he was yet an Infant,
and confequently could not be confulted, was
an Impediment to the Execution of it: No
body being willing to purchafe Leafes which
they knew would not ſtand good without
Confent of the Heir. To remedy this, it
was agreed that the Chevalier ſhould be removed from a great School where he then
was, and put to a private Place, and a Report fpread that he was dead: —— Letters
were forged to corroborate this as a Truth,
and the Chevalier *Richard*, now fuppos'd
Heir to his Brother, join'd in the Leafes, by
which they jointly received large Sums.

Soon after this, the Baron feem'd to grow
tired with the Variety of Women he had enjoyed, and to fettle his whole Heart on an
agreeable young Lady, call'd *Helena*: Whether a Man of his Temper could be capable
of a true Affection I will not fay; but he
was fo intent on poffeffing her, that finding
fhe was not to be gain'd but on honourable
Terms, he gave out the Baronefs was de
and married her publickly.

His Fondnefs for her continu'd, to the W
der of all that knew him, after Enjoym
and tho' having no Children by her, he
defirous of calling home the Chevalien
yet had fhe that Afcendant over hi
prevent it, and by continual Infinuation
his firft Wife was of fo loofe a Cha
that it was fcarce probable the Child was
wrought fo far upon him as to make him

tally neglect the young Chevalier, who being in an obscure Place and among poor People, became very ill used by them on his Father's ceasing to pay for his Board and Learning as he had been accustom'd.—And tho' the Misfortunes of this young Nobleman were almost of equal Date with his Birth, yet it was but now he began to feel them in the Want of those Things his young Apprehension made him know he stood in Need of ——— his Clothes were tatter'd and too little for him —— his Fare was hard, and allow'd him but in scanty Portions——all that could cherish or delight him was denied——no Tenderness, no soft Indulgence shewn to him——no Recreations permitted him——not look'd on but with Frowns—— not spoke to but with Reproaches ——continually reprimanded and often beat in the most cruel Manner, either for doing somewhat he ought not, or for not doing what none took the Pains to instruct him in—while others of his Age were at their Exercises of Learning, he was either employ'd in drawing Water, cleaning Knives, and such like servile Offices—a Sweeper of that School he should have studied in, and the Drudge of those he ought to have commanded did he continue for more than two whole Years, when growing more sensible of his ill Usage he began to murmur at it, on which they told him that they had kept him only out of Charity all that time, and if he did not like his Way of Life he might go and seek a better. The poor Innocent thinking nothing could be worse than the present Calamity,

mity, took them at their Words, and without either Clothes, Money, or the least Instruction where he might find his Father, turn'd his Back upon that Scene of Misery to enter upon one which presented him with greater still.

Not knowing where to go, he wander'd along the Road till he came to a small Village, where his little Limbs, for he was yet but a little more than ten Years old, became so weary that he sat down on the Threshold of a Door, and wept bitterly for want of Food : Several look'd on him as they pass'd ; but he knew not how to ask Relief : At length, a good old Woman brought him a Piece of Bread, which his eager putting to his Mouth making her see he was very hungry, she added to it some cold Meat and a Draught of Butter-milk and Water. With this Refreshment he was enabled to prosecute his Journey, but whither he knew not, being wholly ignorant where the Baron lived, or any other Person to whom he might apply.—His Fate, however, led him to the Capital, and having never before been in any great City, he was amazed to see such a Concourse of People, all with busy Faces, hurrying about the Streets.—The fine Shops and gilded Signs were also Objects of Admiration to him, and for a Time made him forget even Hunger; but the Calls of Nature will not long be hush'd by external Objects———he felt the Pinch of an empty Stomach, and fell again into Tears.———No Body here offering him any thing, he at last forced himself to ask Compassion———the Manner in which he implor'd—the reluctant

Bash-

Bafhfulnefs that fhew'd itfelf in his Voice and Eyes, join'd with a certain Something in his Countenance, which in fpite of his Diftrefs fpoke him above what he appear'd, excited a Pity in every one that faw him, and made him rarely fue in vain. When Night came on he took Shelter in a Church Porch—hard Lodging for the Heir of a Family, which for Antiquity and Noblenefs is inferior to few, except of Royal Defcent, in _Europe_—yet fo it happen'd, and the Diftreffes which this young Nobleman endur'd in common with thofe born of the moft abject Parents, may ferve as a Leffon to thofe who too much glory in their Birth, to abate their Arrogance on that Score, by fhewing that a Lord when he wants Bread, feels the fame Hunger as a common Man.

Early the next Morning he quitted his uneafy Bed, and now remembering that he had heard his cruel Schoolmafter talk of writing to the Baron at this City, he went up and down feveral Streets enquiring for the Baron _de Altamont,_ but was a long time before he met with any one that knew him : at laft he was inform'd that fuch a Nobleman had liv'd there, but that he had left the City fome time, and few People knew whither he had retired. This Intelligence was perfectly true, for the Baron had contracted frefh Debts, and to avoid the Importunity of thofe who had given him Credit, was gone to live with his Lady, now call'd Baronefs _de Altamont,_ in a fmall Village fome three Leagues diftant from the Capital.

Our

Our illuftrious Fugitive was now without
any Hope, any Shadow of Relief. —— His
young Appetite was keen—— Hunger prefs'd,
—— He faw feveral Boys about thofe popu-
lous Streets earning Bread by going on little
Errands, and as he had none to give it him,
and by fome churlifh People (Church-wardens
or Overfeers 'tis poffible) threaten'd to be fent
to the Houfe of Correction for afking it, he
enter'd himfelf among that wretched Frater-
nity, and by doing as they did, procured for
himfelf the fame miferable Subfiftence.

O! had the Baronefs now feen her Son,
that Son fhe fo fondly loved, wandering from
Door to Door, —— his tender and fine form'd
Limbs expofed half naked to the inclement
Air, —— no Lodging but the open Street, —
his Food cold Scraps ; and what wou'd more
have pierced her Soul, a Companion for Va-
gabonds, ——unknowing, uninftructed in every
Thing that raifes the human Species above
Brutes.— Had fhe but even in Dreams beheld
him thus, no Defperation would have equal'd
hers, the dreadful Idea would have turn'd her
Brain: and the moft raging Madnefs have en-
fued ; but fhe was not fo unhappy as to fufpect
it. At her Departure from the Caftle fhe had
conjured *Juggan* to write often to her, and
give her a faithful Account of the young Chevalier's Condition.——The poor Creature was
punctual in obeying this Injunction, and acquainted her when he was taken from her on
he Score of Education, and alfo when he was
moved from that School to another, as fhe
fuppofed for more Improvement. —— She
wrote

wrote according to the Information she received, and doubted not the Truth of herself. To believe he was well, and in Favour with his Father, was all the Confolation the Baroness had in a Condition melancholy enough: Her Father, prepossess'd with false Idea's of her, refused to see her after her Arrival, allow'd her only a small Pension the common Necessaries of Life. — All her Kindred shun'd her, ——— her Acquaintance slighted her, and every one censured her as having done something, tho' none could say of what Nature, that merited the Misfortunes she sustain'd. She heard some talk of the Baron being married, but she gave herself no Trouble to enquire into the Truth of it. ——— Love and Jealousy are strong Passions, and her Spirits were now too much depress'd to be capable of feeling them.

Her Son was not yet of an Age to be sensible of the Misery of his Condition in such a Manner as to have any Effect on his Mind, — he was never sad but when cold or hungry, — had a great deal of Alertness in his Nature, and inherited all the Passion of his Family, which frequently occasioned him many Blows from those of his Companions, who had the Advantage of him in Strength.

It happened one Day that some Boys, superior to himself in all Appearance, fell upon him, and beat him for something they imagin'd he had offended them in, calling him at the same time Dog, Scoundrel, Blackguard, and such like foul Names, which, less able to endure than the Blows, he told them they ly'd,

——— that

—— that he was better than any of them, for his Father was a Lord, and he fhould be a Lord too when he came to be a Man. ——
Several idle People being gathered together to fee this Battle, hearing him fay this fet up a loud Laugh, and from that time he was call'd in Derifion nothing but *My Lord.*

Sometime after this, a good fober Perfon, who was ftanding at her Door, and heard this Denomination given to him, call'd him to her, and feeing he was far from being of that deform'd Make which is a Reafon among the Vulgar for conferring the Title of *My Lord*; *Tell me,* faid fhe, *why they call you* My Lord; —— *that is not your Name, fure?* No, Madam, anfwer'd he brifkly, *my Name is* de Altamont; *but I fhall be a Lord when my Father dies.* Ay! faid fhe, very much furprifed, *who is your Father? The Baron* de Altamont, reply'd he, *and my Mother is the Baronefs* de Altamont, *but fhe is gone out of the Kingdom, and they fay I fhall never fee her again. Who tells you all this?* again demanded fhe. *O! I know it very well,* cry'd he, *I lived in a great Houfe once and had a Footman, and then I was carried to a fine School, and was reckon'd the head Boy of them all, and had the fineft Clothes.* —— *and after that I was carried to another School, and there they abufed me fadly, and turn'd me away, becaufe they faid my Father would not pay them any Money for me.* The Woman liftened with the utmoft Attention to what he faid, till perceiving he had done, afk'd him why he did not go to his Father; *I don't know where to find him,* anfwer'd the

poor

poor Innocent, and fell a crying. *Do you think you should know him if you saw him?* said she. *Yes, very well,* replied he, *tho' it is a great while since I saw him ; but I remember he used to come in a Coach and six Horses to see me, when I lived at the great School.*

Nothing could exceed the Amazement which the Account he gave of himself excited in the Person who heard it ; but willing to try him farther, *I know the Baron* de Alta-mont *very well,* said she, *he never had but one Son, and he is dead. Indeed, Madam, I tell the Truth,* cry'd he, *and if any Body told you I was dead they ly'd.——I never was sick but once, and that was when I fell down and cut my Forehead with a great Stone ; here is the Mark of it,* added he, putting back his Hair ; and shewing her a large Scar above his Eye-brow. *My Father knows it well enough,* said he, *for he came when my Head was bound up, and was very angry that they had taken no more Care of me.*

The Person who was thus inquisitive, kept a great Eating-house, and the Chevalier *Richard* came frequently there : And whenever the Baron came to Town, as he sometimes did tho' very privately, this was always the Place where he appointed to meet those with whom he had any Business. She had heard there was an Heir in the Family, and that he was dead ; and to be told he was alive, and reduced to the miserable Condition this Boy was in, seem'd a Thing incredible ; but then again the Particulars he repeated, the Confidence with which he spoke, and the innocent Grief he

express'd

expreſs'd at not being able to find his Father,
would not ſuffer her to believe him an Impoſtor. She ruminated a good while, and reflecting on the Affair of the Leaſes which ſhe
was perfectly acquainted with, and the Baron's,
ſecond Marriage, ſhe grew aſſured in her
Mind, that for the ſake of raiſing Money, and
getting a Wife, he had renounc'd his Child.
The Thought of ſuch a Barbarity ſtruck her
with Horror.———She ſhudder'd at the unnatural Deed, and making the Child come
in, ſhe order'd her Servants to clean him, and
ſent one out to buy ſome Neceſſaries for cloth-
ing him, while another ſpread a Table for
him with ſuch Food as for a long Time he had
not taſted. He was almoſt beſide himſelf at
the Kindneſs he received———he wept for Joy
as he had lately done with Grief, and was ready
to fall down and worſhip his Benefactreſs.

Had ſhe purſued her firſt Intention, which
was to write to the Baron, the young Chevalier
might perhaps have had a laſting Cauſe to
bleſs her ; but on recollecting that the Chevalier *Richard* came often to her Houſe, ſhe
thought it better to relate the whole Affair to
him ; in the mean Time ſhe kept the young
Penſioner in her Houſe, tho' without acquainting any of her Family with his Name or Quality. She examined him concerning his Education, and receiving from him an Account
how he had been treated at the laſt School, was
ſhocked beyond Meaſure to find a Genius, in
which Nature had not been failing in her Part,
ſo cruelly denied all the Means of Improvement.

It

It was not many Days before the Chevalier *Richard* came, as she expected. She immediately took him into a private Room, and acquainted him who she had in the House, and the Means by which he came there; News little pleasing to the Hearer.———At first he said she was imposed upon———that his Nephew was dead———*At least*, said he, recollecting himself, *the Boy we call'd so; but his Mother was the most vicious Woman in the World, and he was no more my Brother's Son than he was mine. I can say nothing as to that*, replied this good Woman, *I had not the Honour of being acquainted with his Mother, nor even ever saw her; but whatever she was, as there was no Divorce between my Lord and her, and a Child was born, he must inherit, therefore ought to have been educated in a Manner befitting the Honours he must one Day receive.* The Chevalier *Richard* said little to this, but order'd her to let the Boy be call'd; on which he was so, and immediately came in.

He was all new cloth'd, genteely tho' not rich, and a certain Nobleness in his Air, the fine Proportion of his Limbs, with the loveliest Hair in the World, gave no small Addition to his Dress. He entered the Room with such a sweet Humility in his Countenance, as considering he was before two Persons, to one of whom he had such great Obligations, and the other who appear'd to be a Man of Quality by his Garb, for he knew him not, and paid his Respects in so graceful and engaging a manner, that sure no Heart but that of his obdurate Uncle, could have been unmelted

at

at feeing him thus relieved by a Stranger from the forlorn Condition he was lately in.

But this cruel Man look'd on him with a revengeful Ire, which at that Time he wanted Artifice to conceal, and was visible to the charitable Benefactress of the young Chevalier. His large and fiery Eyes sparkled with a kind of greedy Malice to destroy the helpless Innocent : Had they been alone together, 'tis possible something might have happened that would have prevented these *Memoirs*, and a Son of the Baron *de Altamont* been no more remember'd. *What Name is this you take upon you?* cry'd the unnatural Uncle, with a Fierceness that made the young Chevalier tremble, yet did not fright him from avowing the Truth. *I take none upon me, Sir, but that which I brought into the World with me, and was always call'd by*, answered he; *no-body will say but I am the Son of the Baron* de Altamont. *By whom?* demanded the Chevalier *Richard*. *By his Wife, the Baroness* de Altamont, return'd the other, with more Resolution than could have been expected from his Years, and the arbitrary Manner in which he was interrogated. *Then you are a Bastard*, cry'd the Chevalier *Richard, for your Mother was a Whore. I cannot help it, if she were*, reply'd the Baron's Son, *but I never heard any body else call her so ; and if I were a Man, you should not call her Whore nor me a Bastard, whoever you are*. His little Heart, ready to burst at these opprobrious Names, sent the Tears into his Eyes as he spoke this, which moving the Woman of the House,

House, *Fy, Sir,* said she, *'tis cruel to insult the poor Child——be cannot help his Mother's Faults if it were so.* That's true, reply'd the Chevalier *Richard; but when I think how my Brother has been used by that vile Woman, it puts me past all Patience.*

As he was speaking this, the Chevalier *James* look'd earnestly on him, and presently cry'd out, *O, Sir, you are my Uncle Richard, I remember now very well, you came once to our School with my Father.* I knew nothing of it, said the unrelenting Man, and turn'd out of the Room. The Woman of the House follow'd, and having argued a good while in favour of the Child, he at last promised to speak to his Brother, and that he should be taken better Care of for the future; but desired she would keep him close, and not mention any thing of the Affair, because it would give an Uneasiness to the Baroness, meaning his Brother's present Lady, if she should hear any thing of it.

Glad she had obtain'd this Promise, she return'd to the young Chevalier, who she found crying bitterly at the Unkindness of his Uncle. She bid him be of good Heart, for he was in a better Humour now, and would let the Baron know he was with her, and that he should go to School again, and have the same Education other young Gentlemen had. This a little reviv'd him; for never any one of his Age more passionately long'd to be Master of those Accomplishments he had seen in others.

But while he was delighting himself with

the

the Imagination of being made what he ought to be, his wicked Uncle was contriving the Means to make him what none who are happy enough to be baptiz'd into the Christian Faith, either ought or legally can be : In fine, of sending him into *America*, to be disposed of as a Slave, whence there was little Probability he would ever return, to become a Claimant for that Dignity and Estate his Ambition and Avarice made him covet for himself.

He kept his Word indeed, and inform'd the Baron of the deplorable Condition his Nephew had been in, and the way he came to be relieved ; and remonstrated to him, that the Child ought to be sent somewhere for Education. This he thought proper to do, because he doubted not but he would be made acquainted with the whole by the Person herself, when next he came to Town. The Baron could not but feel some Remorse at having abandon'd a Child, who had not attain'd yet to Years capable of offending him ; 'tis possible too had some Desire of seeing him ; but the artful Chevalier took care to prevent that, by reminding him, that as it would be of ill Consequence the young Chevalier should be known to be living, till after his Decease, on account of the Leases ; it would be better he should be sent immediately to *St. Omer's*, *Bruffels*, or some other Place, where he might at a cheap Rate receive an Education suitable to his Birth. This Advice had all the Appearance in the World of good Reason, and the Baron readily pursued it, giving his Brother at the same time Money to reimburse the Person who had taken

fo much Pity on him, and to provide every
thing requifite for him. The Chevalier took
upon himfelf the Care of finding a proper
Place to fend him to, and the whole Management of the Affair; and the two Brothers
were extremely fatisfy'd in their Minds, the
one for having now the Opportunity of doing
what he was fenfible he had too long neglected;
and the other in having it in his Power to remove, as he flatter'd himfelf, for ever, the Bar
of his ambitious Views.

The firft Step this inhumane Uncle took,
was to agree with the Mafter of a Ship bound
for *Penfylvania*, for a certain Sum of Money,
to tranfport the Chevalier *James* thither, and
then he was to make what Advantage he could
of him, by difpofing him in the Plantations to
who bid moft. The Story he invented to
bring the Mafter of the Veffel into this Project was, That the Boy being the natural Son
of a Perfon of Condition, and not meriting
the Protection of his Father, on account of a
Propenfity to vile Actions, it was thought proper to fend him where he might have lefs Opportunity of following his Inclinations. Whether this gain'd any real Credit with the Perfon
to whom 'twas told, cannot be faid, but it
ferved him as an Excufe for entering into a Bargain he was fure to be a Gainer by.

The Veffel not yet having taken in her Lading, the Chevalier *Richard* thought it improper his Nephew fhould continue any longer
where he was, fo removed him to a Houfe, the
Mafter of which being entirely at his Devo-
tion, he was kept there conceal'd till every

thing

thing was ready for his going on board; but told the Woman, when he took him away, that he was to embark that Moment for *St. Omer's.*

Not many Days after this, the Baron *de Altamont* was taken ill, and died: He was too suddenly snatch'd away to settle his Affairs, or make any Declaration concerning his Son, as it is probable he would, had he thought himself so near his End. As he had lived for a great while extremely private, his Death made no Noise, and would scarce have been mention'd, but for the Debts he left unpaid. The Chevalier *Richard* immediately took upon him the Title of Baron *de Altamont*, and with it the Estate appertaining, the late Possessor being able to dispose of it only for his own Life.

The young Chevalier, now real Baron, was kept too close a Prisoner to hear any thing of this Change in his Family; and the Ship being ready to sail in a short time, he was convey'd privately on board, knowing no other than that he was going somewhere for Education; and as he had been told, that nothing should be wanting to repair the Time he had already lost, he run over in his Mind all the Sciences he remember'd to have heard the Names of, and computed how long the Study of each would take him up. In this manner did he amuse himself till they got out to Sea; but then a sudden Storm arising, less agreeable Ideas took the Place of those I have been mentioning. Whenever he cast his Eyes on the tumultuous Waves, which beat on every Side the Vessel, and sometimes rose above it, the Sight struck Terror to his little Heart. The Dread of Death

seems

feems implanted in the Nature of Human Kind as a peculiar Curfe, fince no other Species of created Beings are capable of it; but with us, the Young, the Old, the Innocent, the Guilty, the Monarch on his Throne, the Wretch that groans in Chains, all equally languifh in one common Apprehenfion of that tremendous Change! Happinefs fhudders at it, nor can Mifery give it Welcome. Our young Traveller, tho' yet unknowing he had been betray'd, and wholly ignorant of the Miferies he was deftined to, fuffered fo much from his Fears of drowning, as made him wifh himfelf again on Shore, even in the Condition from which the good Woman's Pity had relieved him. To thofe who experience Variety of Ills the prefent ftill feems worft.——Alas! he little thought that when the Danger he now dreaded was over, he fhould receive a Shock to which all he had hitherto met with would be trivial.

The Hurricane, which had continued near three Hours, being ceafed, and the Waves refuming a more fmiling Face, a Cloth was fpread in the Captain's Cabbin for him to take fome Refrefhment after the late Fatigue, which he had no lefs Share in than the inferior Sailors. The Chevalier *James*, who had been there during the Storm, was going to fit down at the Table, *Hold, Youngfter*, cried one of the rough Tarpaulins, pulling him away, *Do you think you are to be a Mefs-mate with the Captain?* Two Cabbin-boys that were waiting, fet up a loud Halloo at the fame Time, which fo much furprized the beguiled Innocent, that he had not Power to make any Reply. *The Boy would not choofe the worft Company, I find*, faid the

Cap-

Captain, *if he were left to himself; but he will know his Distance better hereafter.*

The Chevalier *James* reflected as much as his young Comprehension would permit on this Treatment; and as they had told him that his Passage was paid for, and he was going to an Academy for Education, he could not imagine the Reasons for their not paying him the Respect due to his Birth: He spoke not a Word however, till the Captain having dined upon such Fare as is usually eat at good Tables on Shore, he had his Allowance given him of Salt Beef and Peas, and that in such a Manner, as but in the short Time he was a Vagrant in the Streets, he had never even seen. He now began to mutter, and say, that as soon as he got out of the Ship, he would send his Father an Account how they used him. None but the Captain himself knowing upon what Terms he had been entered, or the Motives of his Transportation, his Discourse was as strange to those he directed it, as theirs had been to him: On his mentioning however that he was going to *St. Omers* in order to study, and that his Father was a Lord, they easily found he was ignorant of his Condition, and some there were, who, having Hearts less rugged than their Appearance denoted, very much compassionated him. What he said coming to the Captain's Ear, he was obliged to relate the Story to the Ship's Crew, as he had heard it from the Chevalier *Richard*, and by this Means the unhappy Youth became acquainted with the Treachery of his inhuman Uncle, and that instead of being made an accomplished Nobleman, he was going into the worst kind of Servitude.

Com-

Complaints he uttered, the piteous Cries and Exclamations he sent forth on the Discovery of this unparallel'd Cruelty, were so violent, that the Captain fearing, in his Desperation, he might throw himself overboard, and by that Means deprive him of the Advantage he might make of him, was obliged to order he should be put into the Hold, and a Watch set over him, till he became more reconciled with his Destiny. In this Calamity did he make manifest a Greatness of Spirit wonderful at his Years——He refused all Sustenance, nor Hunger, nor Drowth, nor Faintness, could prevail with him to take the least Refreshment; and when by the Captain's Command they forced any thing into his Mouth, he would not suffer it to go down his Throat, but spit it back again before the Faces of those that attempted to make him swallow it, tho' they enforced their Arguments by some Blows, and Menaces of more and much severer. He thought not now of dying, or the Fears of it were lost in the present Agonies of Despair and Rage ; and having persisted in this Resolution without the least Appearance that any thing could terrify him out of it, the Captain thought proper to try what soft Usage and Persuasions would avail. To this End, he bad those he had intrusted to look after him, to bring him into his Cabbin, where the Light, after having been kept so long in Darkness, and his Weakness, thro' Fasting, made him fall into a Swoon the Moment he entered ; proper Care being taken, he soon recovered, and the Captain began to sooth him with the kindest Words he could make use of, told him that

it

it was without his Knowledge that his Men had dealt so urgently with him, and that he should have every thing he liked that the Ship afforded during the Voyage, and that when they came on Shore he would do his utmost to place him where he should be well used. *But I shall have no Learning, and shall be a Slave,* said the Chevalier. *Yes, yes,* replied the dissembling Captain, *you will have Opportunities enough to learn any Thing——nor is there any Thing so terrible in the Name of Slave as you imagine—'tis only another Name for an Apprentice—you will only be bound for a certain Time, as many Noblemens Sons in* England *and* Ireland *are; and when your Time is expired you will be your own Master.*

All this was insufficient to restore any Kind of Contentment to the Chevalier; he sighed grievously, and said, *God would revenge his Cause upon his wicked Uncle, who had told all those Lies on him, and he was sure sent him unknown to his Father, because he would not let him see him.* That is no Fault of mine if it be so, answered the Captain ; *but if you will promise me to eat and drink, and be chearful, I'll endeavour to speak to your Father myself at my Return, and persuade him to send for you again.* But can I come away if I am bound? demanded he. Yes, if your Father send, replied the other. These Words easily deceived a Heart that knew no Guile, and dissipated some Part of the Gloom that had hung on the again-betray'd Chevalier: A little Persuasion now sufficed to make him eat and drink what was set before him in the Captain's Cabbin, where from that Time forward
he

he always din'd and sup'd, and was used with
so much Tenderness, that not knowing the Interest the Captain had in his Life, and the
Recovery of his good Looks, he thought him
the best Friend he had in the World, and flatter'd himself that he would not only take care
to put him to a good Master, but also procure
his Liberty in a short Time.

These delusive Hopes, added to good Eating
and Drinking, and civil Behaviour, recover'd
the Rose in our young Voyager's Complexion,
and on their landing he seem'd to have lost
nothing by the Fatigues he had endured ; so
easy is it to repair the Decays of Youth, while
Age in vain endeavours to retrieve the Plump-
ness in the once-fallen Cheek.—It was now the
Captain's Business to dispose of his Property
to the best Advantage he could for himself;
which he did without any Regard to the Promises he had made when he was under Apprehensions of losing him. The Person he
sold him to was a rich Planter in *Newcastle*
County, who after paying the Money agreed
on between them, took home the young Chevalier, and immediately enter'd him among
the Number of his Slaves.

On parting from the Captain, he had begg'd
him not to forget letting his Father know his
Condition, which the other to please him as-
suring him of, he followed his Master with
less Reluctance than was expected from him,
considering the Spirit he had shewn on board.

A new World now opened itself to View of
the Chevalier *James*, in which every thing he
saw was strange to him : The Habits and odd
Manners

Manners of the *Indian* Men and Women, the various Birds, and four-footed Animals, so different from those of *Europe*, would have afforded an agreeable Amusement to his attentive Mind for a considerable Time, had he been permitted to indulge it; but *Drumon*, so his Master was called, soon found him other Employment.——He had slept but one Night in the House of Bondage, when he was called up at Day-break, and sent to work in the Field with his Fellow-slaves.

The Labour that fell to his Share, and several others that Day, was cutting of Timber to make Pipe-staves, which Commodity is a considerable Branch of the Traffick of that County: This was a Work our noble Slave was so little skill'd in, and was indeed so much beyond his Strength, that he had many Stripes for his Aukwardness before he had any Meat. This first Day gave him a Sample of what he was to expect, but as he hoped from the deceitful Promises the Captain had made him, that it would not be of any long Continuance, he set himself with all his Might to do the best he could to gain the Favour of a Person in whose Power he soon found he was as absolutely as an Ox or an Ass, or any other Property he had made Purchase of; but there are a Sort of People in the World that are not to be obliged, and the greater your Endeavours for that End, the less will be your Effect. *Drumon* was one of these, and among the Number of Wretches under his Command, there was not one who could do any thing to please him. ——He seemed to take a savage Pleasure in adding to the Misery of their Condition by continual ill Usage, and to do every thing in his Power to degenerate them from the Human Species, and render them on a Level with the mute Creation.

Nothing is indeed more strange than that any who have ever known a better State, can support with Life the Hardships of an *American* Slavery, which is infinitely more terrible than a *Turkish* one, frightful as it is represented; for besides the inceffant Toil they undergo, the Nature of their Labour is such, that they are obliged to be continually exposed to the Air, which is unwholesome enough, the Heats and Colds which the different Seasons of the Year bring on these Parts, being far greater than any we know in *Europe*. Then, after being allow'd no Shelter from either of these Extremes, all the Refreshment afforded them is *Pone*, or a Sort of Bread made with *India* Corn, heavy on the Stomach, and insipid to the Palate, with a Draught of Water, or at best mingled with a little Ginger and Molosses; they feast when a Dish of *Homine* or *Mush*, both which are made of the same kind of Corn, is set before them, moistened with the Fat of Bacon or Hog's Lard. This is the manner in which the Slaves or Servants to the *West India* Planters in general live; but some Masters there are that appear more human than *Drumon*, and soften in some measure the Severity of those poor Creatures Fate by gentle Words; whereas that cruel Monster, as I said before, took a Delight in heightning their Calamities. Nor Age, nor Sex, nor the Accidents which occasioned their being in his Power,

could

could move him to the leaft Compaffion, but
on the contrary, thofe received the worft Treatment from him that were intitled to the beft.
The Chevalier *James* was not the only one
who experienc'd this cruel Partiality, there
was among the Companions of his Servitude
a female Slave of near fixty Years of Age, but
who had fomething in her Air and Afpect, that
in Spite of her mean Habit, denoted her to
have been a Perfon little accuftomed to the
fervile Offices fhe was now employed in. This
Woman had been the Wife of a Perfon of fome
Confideration in *England*, but her Bloom being paft, and a new Beauty having attracted
the Inclinations of her unfaithful Husband, he
contrived to get rid of her, by trapanning her
on board a Veffel bound for *Penfilvania*, and
having made a League with the Captain in
the fame Manner the Chevalier *Richard* had
done concerning his Nephew, got him to
tranfport her, where fhe fell to the Lot of the
pitilefs *Drumon*. At firft he put her to wait
on his Wife, believing, as fhe had been well
educated, fhe might be of Service to work Plain-
work for the Family, but finding her Eyes were
too much impair'd by the Tears fhe fhed
at the unnatural Barbarity fhe had met with,
he fent her to the Kitchen, and made her prepare that wretched Suftenance allowed for the
Slaves, and when it was ready, carry it to them
in the Field. As there was a great Number
of them, and fhe had frequently fome Miles
to go where many of them happened to work,
this was a Toil the Delicacy of her Conftitution could ill fuftain: Several times in a Day
would fhe fall down through Faintnefs, but
unavail-

Unavailing were Complaints; the Anfwers fhe received were Curfes, and the moft fcurrilous Taunts. Once fhe attempted to fend a Letter to fome Friends in *England*, in hope of being redeem'd, by the Money being return'd to *Drumon* that he paid for her; but fhe was betray'd in this Defign, and as he chofe to part with none of his Slaves, he made her be chaftifed with the moft cruel Stripes, by way of Example to the others.

I know not but it is a fort of barbarous Po-licy in thefe Planters to ufe their Slaves ill, efpecially when the Time for which they are bound is near expir'd; becaufe, by the Laws of that Country, when any of them run away, if they are retaken, as they commonly are, they are mulcted for that Difobedience, and oblig'd to pay, by a longer Servitude, all the Expences and Damages the Mafter pretends he has fuftain'd by their Elopement; fo that by this means fome of them ferve double the Years they are contracted for: Thofe therefore who are fo unhappy, either by their own Inad-vertency or the Cruelty of others, to be fent thither, have no real Remedy but Patience, fince, in feeking any other, they but prolong their Mifery, and give a Shew of Juftice to the Perfecutions inflicted on them.

This Leffon the afflicted Woman, I have juft been fpeaking of, was continually preach-ing to our young Chevalier.—She had often obferv'd the Tears trickling down his Cheeks when fhe brought him his Food, had heard him utter the moft piercing Lamentations, when he imagin'd himfelf alone, and believing

ing by every thing she saw both in his Perfon
and Behaviour, that he was of no mean Ex-
traction, she took a very great Fancy to him,
and extremely pitied him ; but much more
fo when afterwards she heard from him the
foul Play that had been offer'd him : In fpite of
her own Woes she had fome Tears to fpare
for his ; and perceiving that he lamented
more the being deprived of an Education fuit-
able to his Birth, than all the Hardships he endured, she thought she could never enough
admire fo juft a way of thinking in one fo
young. She had been a very great Reader,
was well acquainted with Hiftory and the
World, and, tho' a Stranger to the dead Lan-
guages, knew very well the Subjects on which
the antient Hiftorians, Poets, and Philofophers
had wrote, by having been converfant with
the beft Tranflations of them. She now call'd
every thing she could to her Remembrance
for the Advantage of this noble Slave ; and
whenever she had an Opportunity, wrote it
down on Paper, and gave it to him when she
brought his Food. By this means he became
acquainted with feveral remarkable Occurrences
of the *Greek* and *Roman* Empires, as well as
the Revolutions of a later Date, and nearer
home. She gave him alfo an Account of all
the great Families in *Europe*, particularly thofe
of his own Country ; and when, among that
illuftrious Catalogue, he found an Action great
or noble done by fome of his own Anceftors,
his young Heart was ready to burft, between a generous Ambition and the Impoffi-
bility there was that he fhould ever be able
to

to imitate them. So great was his Defire of Knowledge, that whenever he was a Moment out of Sight, he would pull out thefe little Pieces of Paper, and read them till he got them by Heart: In this Employment being often catch'd, he endur'd many Stripes for neglecting his Work, yet did not the Smart deter him; and never any Boy fuffer'd more Correction for his little Propenfity to Learning, than our young Chevalier did for difcovering a greater than perhaps was ever known at his Years.—How much the Pity! how irreparable the Lofs to the Publick, fo rifing a Genius fhould be cruſh'd by fuch a Series of Cruelties and Misfortunes! Who can fufficiently deteft the bafe Ufurper of his Right, who not content to deprive him of his Title and Eftate, deprived him alfo of all the Improvements of the Mind?—The Place he fent him to, the Station he ordain'd him to, were fuch as, according to all human Probability, muſt have corrupted both his Soul and Body; yet fo wonderfully did Providence interpofe in favour of this young Innocent, that his pure and florid Blood flow'd thro' his Veins untainted, either with the inclement Air, coarfe Food, or hard Labour he fuftain'd; and his Mind, at the fame time, retain'd its fweet Simplicity, imbibing nothing of the Principles of thofe he was among, nor the leaft Tincture of their Manners.

His Sentiments and Behaviour render'd him fo dear to the old Slave, that he fcarce could have been more had he been her own Son. He had no lefs Regard for his kind Inftructrefs: When-

Whenever he had any Ceſſation from Labour, inſtead of diverting himſelf as the other Servants did, he paſt thoſe Moments with her, asking her Queſtions concerning the Motives of ſuch Tranſactions, as ſhe had ſet down in the Papers ſhe gave him; and made ſuch judicious Remarks ſometimes upon them himſelf, as perfectly aſtoniſh'd her. He had an excellent Memory, which made every thing his own that he once heard or read; and as his Capacity enlarg'd with the Increaſe of his Years, his Idea of Men and Things ſtill grew more clear and diſtinct. On reflecting on the Vices of Mankind, he look'd on Avarice and Ingratitude as the moſt contemptible, and at the ſame time moſt dangerous to Society; and concluded, that a Man poſſeſt of their oppoſite Virtues could not but be good in all Circumſtances of Life:——What could be more juſt than this Obſervation? what better could all the Learning of the Schools have enabled any one to make? Since, if we look into the Seeds of Ill, we ſhall find that all the Miſchiefs, Murders, Frauds, and Oppreſſions that happen in the World, owe their Riſe to one or both of theſe pernicious Qualities.

It was in Contemplations of this Nature that our illuſtrious Slave beguil'd four Years of the ſeven he was bound to ſerve; at the End of which Time the good Woman to whom he was ſo much indebted for the forming his Mind to Virtue, died; and as her Society had been his only Comfort, ſo was her Loſs an inconſolable Affliction to him.——He now felt all his Woes with double Weight, having ne none to advife him how to bear them. His Slavery became fo infupportable to him, that now for the firft Time he began to entertain Thoughts of making his Efcape: They reach'd no farther, however, than to form a continual Defire of doing it, no Opportunity for a great while offering that could give him any Hope of fucceeding in fuch an Enter-prize.

He lay down in his little Hamock one Night fo full of difturb'd Meditations, that all the Wearinefs he felt after a Day of very great Toil, could not for fome Time make him fall into a Sleep; and when he did, his active Fancy, or rather fome fupernatural Caufe (as the future Accidents of his Life would make one think) prefented him with Images which his waking Thoughts never could have produced.

He imagin'd that, inftead of the wretched Furniture his Bed was compofed of, he was lying on a beautiful green Bank on the Side of a Meadow, the Verdure of which was ena-mell'd with a great Variety of the fineft Flowers both for Colour and Fragancy he had ever feen;—the Sun feem'd as near fet-ting, and gilding the Tops of diftant Hills, added to the Agreeablenefs of the Profpect; when all at once the Rays withdrew,——a heavy Cloud overfpread the Hemifphere,———— all appear'd brown and difmal, but chiefly that Part where the Dreamer lay: He turn-ed his Eyes upwards, and beheld a little above his Head a Balance of enormous Size, felf-poiz'd, and hanging in the Air, each Scale

by

by turns feeming more ponderous than the
other, and threatning to defcend and cruſh
him with its Weight.————Frighted, yet unable to detach his Sight, or rife from the
Place he was in, he continued gaizing till the
Phænomenon, as if pluck'd by a Hand unſeen,
inſtantly flew up, and was loſt in Air. This
no ſooner difappear'd, than others, and yet
more dreadful Objeſts ſtruck his wandering
Eyes: Before him, but very high in the
Cloud, he faw a great many Globes cut croſs
with numberleſs Lines which ran diametri-
cally athwart each other, and from each
Globe or Sphere a fiery Arrow feem'd to
dart directly on him; at a greater Diſtance,
and as far as he could difcern, a Sword of a
moſt tremendous Length, that pointed towards him, brought up the horrid Rear; the
Blade looked blue with Keenneſs, the Hilt
was envellop'd with clotted Gore, and Spots
of the fame Colour tinged in various Places
that thick Cloud in which theſe Wonders were
exhibited.

The Chevalier remembered in his Dream,
that he had heard the Sailors, when he was
on Board, talk much of the *Zodiack*, and of
ſtrange Figures that poſſeſſed the ſeveral
Houſes, and the confus'd Idea he had of what
they called the *Signs*, made him at firſt i-
gine they were what he faw; but then, tho'
afleep, recollecting that he had never heard a-
mention of a Sword, he grew terrified, an
confidered the whole Apparition as a Men-
from Heaven; this beat ſo ſtrongly on
Apprehenſion, that it broke the Bands of Sl-

and he awoke cover'd all over with a cold Sweat.

The Objects of his Dream had been so perfect and distinct, that he could scarce believe he had been asleep, but had verily and indeed seen them with his waking Eyes : 'Tis certain they made such an Impression on him as was never to be erased ; and whenever afterwards he was in any real Danger, or under the Apprehensions of falling into any Misfortune, the fiery Arrows and that dreadful Sword were always present to his Mind.

The particular Relation I have made of this Dream, will doubtless be look'd upon as a piece of Impertinence and Folly by those who pretend to be too wife to pay any Regard to what they call only the Effect of a disturb'd Imagination; but whoever shall have Patience to go through these Memoirs, and compare the Accidents which afterward befell the Dreamer with the Particulars of his Dream, they will be apt to confess with me, that it must be somewhat more than the vague and inconnected Ideas, which rise either from the Fumes of a distemper'd Body or disturb'd Mind. I grant indeed, that for the most part what we call Dreams proceed from one of those two Causes ; but to maintain there never was or can be any other assign'd for them, and that they always are without any Signification, is running counter both to Sacred and Prophane History, and must be allow'd to be as great a Proof of an *arrogant Obstinacy,* as giving Credit to *all,* without Distinction, is of *Weakness* and *Superstition.* Whence or

by

by what Means thefe internal Warnings are
communicated to the Soul while the Body fleeps,
I fhall not take upon me to difcufs; and only
add, that the Opinion I have that fuch Things
do fometimes happen, is founded not only on
the Accounts given me by Perfons whofe good
Underftanding as well as Veracity I have no
Reafon to doubt, but alfo on my own Obfervation and Experience.

As the Chevalier *James* increas'd in Years,
fo did his Difdain of Slavery increafe with
them : The nearer he approach'd to Manhood,
the more impatient he grew to attain the Qua-
lifications requifite for that State, efpecially
in Perfons of his Rank ; and when he reflected
on the Time he had loft, and in which others
make fo great a Progrefs in Education, he became almoft defperate, and tho' naturally of
the fweeteft Difpofition, could not forbear in-
veighing againft the Barbarity of his Uncle
Richard in Terms no lefs fevere than juft ; but
the wild Woods and Fields wherein he work'd
were the only Witneffes of his Complaints ;
he had none near him that deferved his
Confidence, and tho' compelled to be an Affociate in their Labours, he never partook in
any of their Pleafures, if the rude Riots which
on fome particular Days were permitted them,
can be call'd fo.

But tho' he maintained this becoming
ferve towards them, they did not obferve
fame with him ; one in particular had
exclaim'd againft the Miferies of their Slav
and the Cruelty of *Drumon*, and declared
him that as foon as any Opportunity offer

would run away. The Chevalier liſtened to what he ſaid, but without giving any other Anſwer than that he was afraid ſuch a thing was impracticable, till one Day as they were at Work together at ſome Diſtance from the reſt, he told him that he had heard of a Ship that had juſt taken in her Lading, and was ready to ſail from *Dover*, a great Sea-Port Town in the next County, and was bound for *England*; therefore, ſaid he, if you will bear me Company, we'll e'en make the beſt of our Way toward it this Night. The Chevalier's Heart beat high at the very mention of quitting the ſhocking Life he had ſo long endured, and knowing in other Inſtances that the Fellow who made this Propoſal was of a reſolute and daring Spirit, did not ſcruple to believe he was determined to do as he ſaid, and having aſked ſome farther Queſtions, to all which the other anſwered as if the Thing was eaſy to be accompliſhed: It was agreed between them that in the Dead of the Night, when the whole Family were aſleep, they ſhould ſteal out, and ſet forward on their Journey. The Chevalier had ſome Difficulty in the Fears that the Captain would not admit them as Paſſengers, as they had no Money; but the other told him, that he had heard who the Captain was, and knew he was very intimate with ſome Friends he had in *England*, and on that Account would ſtay for the Payment of their Paſſage-money till they came on Shore, and that then they might ſend to their Relations. This ſatisfied our noble Slave, who having nothing in View but the

E   regain-

regaining his Liberty and returning to *Europe*, did his Bufinefs that Day with a more than ordinary Alacrity, and at Night about the ufual Hour went to his Hammock, as did the other Slave, to give no Sufpicion to the Family. An Enterprize of fuch Moment to the Perfons who undertook it, might be fuppofed to fill their Heads fufficiently to keep them waking; and the Chevalier *James* being otherwife far from a heavy and fluggifh Conftitution, it was little to be imagin'd he fhould now neglect the Hour in which he had promifed to meet the intended Companion of his Flight; yet fo it happened: He no fooner laid himfelf down than he fell into the moft profound Sleep he had ever known, and opened not his Eyes till he was called to his daily Labour. Amazed he ftarted up, and looking round him, found the Sun was high advanc'd, —the Rage he was in with himfelf for having, as he thought, by a fatal Sloth, loft the Opportunity of recovering his Liberty, is not to be expreffed. He was in this Agony of Defpair and Self-condemnation, when all on a fudden he heard a great Confufion in the Houfe: He ran to know the Occafion, and heard his Mafter had been robb'd: That a Bag of Money had been taken out of his Buroe, and feveral fmall Pieces of Plate which ftood in a Corner-cupboard in the Parlour.— All the Slaves and Servants were immediately call'd together, and *Jacob*, for fo the Fugitive was called, being miffing, they no longer had any Difficulty in gueffing who had been the Thief. On this, Perfons were immediately difpatch'd in fearch of him all round the County,

County, and fuch proper Meafures taken in the Purfuit, that the Chevalier doubted not but he would be foon brought back. How did he now blefs the happy Sluggifhnefs he fo lately curft! How admire the Goodnefs of all difpofing Providence, that would not fuffer him to be thought the Partaker of this Wretch's Guilt, as he muft have been had he been the Companion of his Flight. As he was extremely Juft in his Nature, and difdain'd a bafe Action even more than a mean Servitude, he would fooner have chofe to have languifhed out his whole Life in the one, than have committed the other to gain not only his Liberty, but all other things the World call good. He now even became fo fcrupulous, that he knew not, if an Opportunity of efcaping without Danger fhould offer itfelf, whether he ought to accept it; becaufe, as he was the Property of *Drumon,* and his Service purchafed by him, for a certain Time, it feem'd not ftrictly juft he fhould deprive him of himfelf without any Affurance of having it in his Power to return him as mu Money as the Refidue of his Time with him might be worth. How truly worthy of a Nobleman were Sentiments fuch as thefe! How few are capable of entertaining them, efpecially at his Years, and in fuch Circumftances, I might fay of his Humour too; for tho' he was good-natur'd almoft to an Excefs, yet he was liable to Paffion, Rafh, and Impetuous, when urged; this indeed may be faid to be the only Shadow to his Virtues, and it cannot be too much lamented that he was not in his early Years under that proper Re-

E z gulation,

gulation, which might have fhewn him the
Error, and inftructed him how to correct it
in its firft Approaches. But this was a Difpofition he had yet little Opportunities of
indulging, and as the Sparks of it could not
fhoot out till afterwards, perhaps that very
Reftraint it was that made them blaze with
greater Fury when let loofe.

The unfortunate *Jacob* was the next Day
brought back, bound Hand and Foot, to receive the Punifhment due to his double Crime:
He had not gone more than twenty-feven
Miles when he was taken, and the Money and
Plate was found upon him unimbezzled, and
juft as he had purloin'd them. As foon as
they carried him before *Drumon*, he ordered
him to be ftrip'd down to the Wafte and tied
to a Poft before the Door, and then to receive
twenty Lafhes from each of his Fellow-flaves.
After this he was put down into a Dungeon,
and kept there for four Days, at the Expiration
of which he was re-fold to a Planter in *Phi-
ladelphia*, and never appeared again at *Newcaftle*.

It muft be confeffed that this Fellow de-
ferv'd even more Correction than he met with,
and by the Laws of that Country ought to
have been branded on the Forehead ; nor was
it out of Pity to him that *Drumon* remitted
that Part of his Punifhment, but that knowing
him to be a daring defperate Fellow, he had a
mind to part with him, which he could
have done on fuch good Terms had he given
him that Mark of Guilt,—Thus can the m

cruel Tempers shew Mercy when they find it is their Interest to do so.

He made use however of a very wrong Policy, in my Mind; for instead of using his Slaves with more Gentleness, in order to prevent their following the Example of *Jacob*, his Barbarity after this increas'd; and on the least Murmur from any of them, he would cry, *What, you want to do as the Rogue* Jacob *did; but you see what he got by it, and you, perhaps, may not come off so easily.* 'Tis certain that nothing is more difficult than for a Slave or Servant in *America* to make his Escape without being re-taken, because the Master spares no Expence for that Purpose as it all falls upon the Slaves, and they are compell'd by the Laws to serve so much longer. But yet would they be prevail'd upon to try the Sweetness of that Service which proceeds from *Love* rather than *Fear*, I fancy they would find their Account in it; and by endeavouring to engage the *one*, find they would have no Occasion for inspiring the *other*. It is infinitely more difficult to command with Discretion than it is to obey: Few know how to make a right Use of Power: They shew too great a Consciousness of it, and imagine they cannot be *Rulers* without being *Tyrants*, and this it is that gives Asperity to Subserviency; and it is this mistaken Exertion of Authority that occasions Rebellions in States, and Elopements in private Families.

The Chevalier *James* had now attain'd to seventeen Years, more than five of which he had languished in this miserable Bondage, but

he

he was so far from being more easy by being
so long inur'd, that his Impatience to be eased
of it grew stronger every Day. His Labour
was toilsome and incessant, his Fare was hard
and insufficient for the Calls of Nature ; the
Blows he frequently received were painful ;
yet were all these the least galling Portions of
his Slavery : The Reflection how and by whom
he had been trapan'd into it, was infinitely
severer than all his Body could endure.———
Resentment against that Author of his Woes,
his inhumane Uncle, was a continual Vulture
preying on his Peace, and he would have done
every thing, hazarded every thing, and suffered every thing, to obtain the Satisfaction of
upbraiding and exposing him for the unwarrantable and unnatural Act.

It was in one of these Fits of Rage and Desperation, that, unmindful of the Difficulties
he was to encounter, and the Prolongation of
his Slavery if he succeeded not in his Enterprize, that he quitted the House of *Drumon*,
determined rather to suffer himself to be cut
to pieces than brought back. To this end he
took a Hedging-bill with him, that in case he
should be overtaken by any that might be sent
in Pursuit of him, they should not find him so
easy to be taken as *Jacob* had been. As he
was well-limb'd, and extremely nimble, he
had gain'd many Miles before he was miss'd
but as soon as he was so, Men and Hor
were sent after him. They posted directly
ward *Delawar* River, that being the R
the run-away Slaves usually take, in hope
finding some Ship where they might e
th

themselves. This was the Chevalier's Design, but through Eagerness to be too quick for his Pursuers, he mistook his way at first setting out, and without suspecting he had done so, kept running on till, instead of *Delawar* he came to *Sarsquahanna*, a large River, that parts the Province of *Pensilvania* from the five Nations of the *Iroquois.*

Tho' he had never seen *Delawar* River since his landing, the little he remember'd of it, serv'd to assure him this was not the same: He was not dismay'd at it, however, for as he saw some Shipping, tho' at a great Distance, he hop'd he should be able to find some means of getting nearer them, either by Boat or travelling on by the Coast. He perceived also, that he was not far from a Town, but he chose not to venture to it, but to take Shelter in the Covert of a Wood for that Night. Early the next Morning he renewed his Journey, but whither he directed his Course he was wholly ignorant, for though he met several People he durst not fall into Discourse with them, or ask them any Questions, for fear of being suspected. In fine, he wander'd thus for three Days, without any other Sustenance than what the Woods afforded, and growing too faint to travel farther, as well as desperate of ever getting out of that Country, he laid himself down at the Foot of a Tree, thinking to rise no more, when a strange Chance brought him at once Relief and fresh Calamities. It was near the close of Day when he took up this melancholy Lodging, and Night had not yet drawn her

Curtain

Curtain over that Hemisphere, when he was
surprized with the trampling of Horses coming
towards him in as full a Gallop as the Thicknefs of the Wood would permit : On lifting
up his Eyes he faw two Men well mounted,
one of whom had a Woman behind him, and
the other a large Portmantle and feveral Bun-
dles. As thefe did not feem to be Purfuers,
and were Faces he had never feen, he took
Courage, but much more fo, when after they
had ftop'd, he heard him who had the Woman with him fay, *Come, my Dear, 'tis time
now for you to take fome Refrefhment, and I
think we cannot find a more convenient Place.*
With that he alighted, and having with the
utmoft Tendernefs helped her to do the fame,
the other jump'd from his Horfe, and taking
hold of the Bridle, as alfo of that which he
who feem'd to be the Mafter had newly quitted, faften'd both to a Tree very near that
where the Chevalier was. He then unty'd
one of the Bags, and taking out a Napkin,
fpread it upon the Grafs, and fet before them
fome choice Food and a Bottle of rich Wine.
The Gentleman and Lady fat down and began to eat very heartily, at the Sight of which
our almoft famifh'd Wanderer figh'd inwardly, but could not refolve with himfelf to venture forth and intreat to be a Gueft. On raifing his Head to look on them, however, he
made fome ruftling among the Leaves of fome
Shrubs which grew about the Tree, and he
concealed him from the Eyes of thefe New
comers ; that little Noife he made alarm'd
the vigilant Waiter, and turning to fee when

it proceeded, he plainly faw the difconfolate
Youth. *A Man!* cry'd he, *we are betray'd*;
and at the fame time ftruck at him with the
Cutlafs fuch a Blow, as, had it not mifs'd him,
would have cleft him in two. The Lady
fhriek'd, and the Gentleman (for fo he appeared) drew his Sword, and was coming to fecond
his Man in the Deftruction of a Perfon they
fuppofed to be a Spy; but the Chevalier perceiving their Miftake, and the imminent Danger he was in, ftarted up, and falling on his
Knees, *Spare, I befeech you, Sir,* faid he, *an
innocent Youth, who was brought hither by
his own Misfortunes, and had no Defign to difturb, or be a Spy upon your Actions.* Thefe
Words, and the Sight of him, which excited
rather Pity than Indignation, made the Stranger put up his Sword; but the Lady, not yet
quite affured her Apprehenfions had been
vain, asked him who he was, and what had
occafioned his being in a Place fo unfrequented? On which he found himfelf obliged to
make a brief Recital of the Caufe, as the only
Means of avoiding that Death their Sufpicions
threaten'd, and another alfo, which he faw it
was in their Power to preferve. He had
no fooner ended his little Narrative, than
Chearfulnefs return'd to all their Faces, and
finding by the Conclufion of his Hiftory the
Want he was in of their Affiftance, they made
him fit down, and partake with them of what
they were eating. In the Circumftances he
then was, fuch an Invitation was not to be re-
fufed; he accepted it thankfully, and being
feated as they were while the Repaft lafted,

E 5 the

the Stranger told him, that as he exprefs'd an
Impatience of returning to *Europe*, if he could
keep Pace with their Horfes, he might go with
them to *Apoquinemink*, where a Veffel waited
for them to carry them to *Holland*, in which
they would take care he fhould have a Paffage.
This was joyful News indeed to the Chevalier,
and he told them he did not doubt but the
Defire he had of getting out of that Country,
would give him Strength and Nimblenefs
enough not to quit their Company, in fpite of
the Fatigues he had fo lately endured.   Scarce
ever in his Life had he felt that Satisfaction he
now did: He look'd on thefe People as his
guardian Angels, and fent from Heaven for his
Deliverance.   *But,* faid the Lady, *we are in
Danger of being purfued as well as you, and
therefore muft travel all Night.*   This was ftill
more pleafing to the Chevalier; for *Apoquinemink* being in the Neighbourhood of *Newcaftle,*
he might have been in Danger of being difcovered by fome one who poffibly had feen him at
Drumon's.

   After they had refted themfelves a fhort
Space, they remounted and purfued their
Journey through the Foreft, the Chevalier following as faft as he could, imploring Heaven
to give him Strength to keep up with them.
whether his Ability would have conformed to
his Inclination is uncertain, but they had not
left the Foreft above three Furlongs, before
they heard a great Number of Horfes following in full Speed, and prefently faw Light
behind them —— Nothing could equal the
Alarm this gave both the Gentleman and his
fair Companion, efpecially as they drew more
near,

near, when looking back, she screamed out, *'Tis he, 'tis he himself, we are lost for ever!*——— There was no time for further Speech, those they dreaded in an Instant were upon them.—— The Lady flung herself off the Horse, and ran as if to seek some Covert,——The Gentleman drew his Sword and the Servant his Cutlass, and faced about on those that came to attack them: The Chevalier too, thinking he ought in Honour to do his best in the Defence of the Company he was with, began to lay about him with his Hedging-bill; but the Combat was too unequal, and tho' they fought like Men who knew inevitable Death attended them if taken, they were presently surrounded, and all of them made Prisoners: The Lady was taken up in a Swoon and laid before one of the Vanquishers, her Companion and his Servant were bound on their own Horses, and the unfortunate Chevalier had both his hands ty'd and fasten'd to the Tail of one of their Horses, and in this wretched Plight were they conducted to a little Village, where they remained till Morning, but in different Rooms; and as soon as Day-break, bound as before, and made to travel in the same Manner, stopping no more till they arived at *Chester* Town, where they were all immediately carried to the common Jail, and lodged apart as they had been at the Village.

Here, as 'tis common in such Places, when any new Prisoners are brought in, to canvass their Characters and Crimes, was the Chevalier made sensible who the Persons were he had been with, and also those who had deprived them

them, of the Means of purfuing their Intentions.

He heard that the Lady was the Daughter of
a rich Trader at *Chefter* Town, and that being
difcovered to have an Inclination for a young
Man very much beneath her, fhe had been compell'd by her Father to marry one he made
choice of for her, but for whom fhe had an
extreme Averfion: That fhe afterwards kept
Company privately with her firft Lover, who
was the Perfon taken with her, and they agreed
that fhe fhould rob her Husband of every thing
of Value that fhe could conveniently take, and
go with him to live in fome foreign Country;
but that their Defign being overheard, it was
difcovered to her Husband, who prefently got
a Warrant and proper Officers to apprehend
them; that he had joined himfelf, and all his
Friends in the Purfuit; and that, as he had
been fo fortunate to overtake them, it was not
to be doubted but he would profecute them,
and all concerned in their Enterprize, with the
utmoft Rigour of the Law.

The Chevalier *James* fhudder'd at this Difcourfe, he was troubled for the Delinquents,
and was under fome Apprehenfions for himfelf,
notwithftanding the little Share he had either in
their Crimes or Adventures. He now perceiv'd
how dangerous a thing it is to affociate one's
felf with Perfons one has no Knowledge of; but
in the Condition he was at that Time, who
could have blam'd him for acting in the manner
he did?

In the Morning they were all brought forth
and carrried into the Court of Judicature, where
the

the Trial lasted not long; all the Husband accused them of was proved upon them, and those unhappy Lovers, with the Man who attended them, were all three condemn'd to die. Concerning the Chevalier *James* there was a Demur: His being found in their Company, and joining with them in opposing those who came to apprehend them, seem'd to render him a Partner in their Crime; but then his Youth, and the full Account he was now obliged to give of himself, and the Accident by which he came to be with them, pleaded strongly in his Favour. But the Point was a long time in debate, and the Judges not being able to decide it, he was remanded back to Prison, with Orders given to the Jailor, that he should be brought every Day to the Market-place, and exposed to publick View, in order that if any one that saw him should prove he had ever been at *Chester* Town before his being brought thither as a Prisoner, he should be look'd upon as accessary to the Robbery, and suffer the same Fate with the others.

For five Weeks did he continue in this dreadful Suspence: innocent as he knew himself not only of the Crime, but also of having before that fatal time been ever near that part of the Country, there must be something terrible in a Situation such as his, where his Life depended on Chance.—How often has it happen'd that one Man has been mistaken for another? and he could not be certain that this would not be the Case with him. The Accidents of his Life had hitherto been so unfortunate, that he might with Reason fear the worst; but he was at last eased of these Apprehensions, prehenfions, tho' by a way little lefs dreadful than the Certainty of thofe Apprehenfions would have been.

Some Affairs of Traffick brought *Drumon* to *Chefter*, he faw his Slave, and having enquired into the Motives of his being thus expofed, was prefently made acquainted with the whole Hiftory of his being apprehended, and the Caufe of it; on which he went immediately to the Juftices and claimed him as his Property: The Time of his running away, as fworn to by *Drumon*, agreeing exactly with the Account the Chevalier had given of himfelf, this unhappy Nobleman, who feem'd born to be deliver'd only from one Mifery to fall into another, was acquitted of any Partnerfhip in the Crimes of the condemned Perfons, and *Drumon* rejoicing he had fo unexpectedly recovered his Fugitive, took him home as foon as the Bufinefs which had occafioned his coming to *Chefter* was compleated.

Before their Departure they had the dreadful Spectacle of the two unhappy Lovers Execution, than which nothing was ever more pity-moving. He feem'd all Defpair and Grief, but it was that his lucklefs Paffion had brought fo amiable a Creature to Deftruction—She fwoon'd, and half anticipated the Work of the Executioner, to fee the only Man fhe had ever loved about to fuffer for her Sake. They embraced, and when feparated, broke from the Arms that held them and embraced again, and when by greater Force reftrain'd from any further Adieus of that kind, the Soul of each feem'd to iffue in a mutual Shriek.

All who were capable of Tears wept at their Fate, and the general Voice condemned the Father of this beautiful Criminal, who by compelling her Inclinations gave Source to this Scene of Woe. The Chevalier above all was particularly touch'd; the Kindness they had shewn in the few Minutes (for it reach'd not to an Hour) he was with them had so won upon his grateful Heart, that it was ready to burst with Grief, and render'd him in a manner forgetful of his own Concerns. During their Stay at *Chester*, the cunning *Drumon* contented himself with only reproaching him for quitting him without having done any thing, as he said, to give him a Pretence for it, reserving the Chastisement he intended for him till he had him again safe at *Newcastle*; but on their Arrival there he let all his Fury loose, and represented the Loss his Flight had been to him, and the Expences he had been at in endeavouring to retake him with such Exaggerations, that the Justices mulcted him for two Years, so that he had now four Years to remain a Slave. Not content with this, the revengeful *Drumon* set him Tasks utterly impossible to be perform'd, gave him Stripes without Mercy for his enforced Disobedience, and Food in such scanty Portions, that it might be said was only sufficient to keep him from perishing.

In short his Usage, always bad, was now become intolerable, and such as would doubtless have tempted the Chevalier to have ventured a second Flight, had he not been too closely watch'd to obtain any Opportunity. As the only Redress left for him, and that a

poor

poor one, he went to the Justices and made
his Complaint; on the hearing of which *Drumon* was ordered to dispose of him to some
other Master: Which was soon after done to
one of the same County; but the still-unhap-
py Slave found no Change in his Condition
by this Change of Hands; the Person whose
Property he was now become, being of as cruel
and inexorable a Disposition as *Drumon* himself. There was indeed so little Difference
between their Usage of him, that to give a
Description of it would be only repeating
what has been already said. He bore it however for three Years, having still in mind the
Danger he had been in when taken by the
People of *Chester*; and had perhaps continu'd
a Twelve-month more, which would have
compleated his whole Time, had he not fallen
in Company with some Sailors, who persuaded him to enter himself on board the Ship
to which they belong'd, promising to conceal
him till they sail'd, which they said would be
in a few Days. The Discourse he had with
them of *Europe*, particularly of his native
Country, renewing his Impatience to return,
he resolved to venture once more, and accordingly accompanied them to the Vessel. But
before they could get on board, the Master,
by some of his Spies, being informed of this
Design, sent after, and had him taken. For
this Offence he was mulcted no less than four
Years, a most unreasonable Time; but several of the Slaves having been lately discover'd
in an Attempt to make their Escape, this Severity was inflicted on him as an Examp
a

and Terror to the reſt ; and in this Inſtance, as well as in many others, he ſuffered for the Faults of others more than for his own.

This laſt Misfortune ſo ſunk the Spirits of our illuſtrious Slave, that in a ſhort time he was ſcarce to be known : Inſtead of his once freſh and roſy Colour, a livid Paleneſs over-ſpread his Cheeks——his Eyes loſt great Part of their former Luſtre, and were continually caſt down——his Sprightlineſs was converted into a kind of dead Sloth——a Melancholy which is not to be expreſs'd hung upon his Heart, and ſhew'd itſelf in all his Looks and Actions. The great Change that appear'd in him giving his Maſter ſome Apprehenſions of loſing him, he began to treat him with ſome-what leſs Auſterity, and gave his Wife, who of herſelf was a very good Woman, Permiſſion to take him into the Houſe, at ſuch times as he was abroad, and give him part of ſuch Food as they eat at their own Table, as if un-known to him. Ill-judging Man! he imagin-ed that to ſhew the leaſt Kindneſs to a Slave himſelf, would be derogating from his Au-thority ; but ſuch is the Temper of moſt, who from a low Fortune riſe to Riches and Power, without having been bleſt with an Education to inſpire better Notions; or elſe having them from Nature, which is very extraordinary, but when found in any one, as greatly to be ap-plauded.

The Chevalier received the Favours ſhewn him by his Miſtreſs with a becoming Gra-titude, but though ſhe even exceeded her Com-miſſion, and he wanted for nothing as to Eat-ing

ing and Drinking, yet this Kindness contributed little to the Dissipation of his Sadness
——a deep Sense of his Misfortunes had now
took hold of him——the ardent Desire he had
from Nature to attain those Accomplishments
he had an Idea of, made him look back with
Horror upon the precious Years, which should
have been employed in learning them, irreco-
verably lost in an ignominious Slavery——He
knew what he *ought to be*, and to think he never *cou'd be* what he ought and wished to be,
was a Dagger to his Soul, which gave Wounds
too severe for any thing in the Power of those
he was among to heal.

He was one Day sighing over some Meat
that was given him by his Mistress, when she
being called out of the Room on some Occasion, she ordered her Daughter, a very amiable young Creature of about fourteen or fifteen
Years of Age, to give him a little Can of Wine.
——The Girl readily obeyed, but presented it
to him with a trembling Hand, and so visible
a Confusion, that the Chevalier, sunk as he
was in Sorrow, could not help taking Notice
of it, and asked if she were not well? *Not
very well,* answered she, *I have an ugly Pain
at my Heart. I am sorry for it,* said he, *but
you will soon be well again*——*Distempers of
the Body are easily removed; but those of the
Mind are terrible indeed.* In speaking these
Words he gave a Sign, which shew'd he felt the
extremest Anguish of the Ailment he had mentioned. *I know,* resumed she, *there is nothing
so much to be pitied as a troubled Mind: But
do you think you are the only Person that is*
unhappy ?

unhappy ? I'll warrant there are many People in the World that have greater Cause for Sadness than you. That cannot be, cry'd the Chevalier, *but if it were so, the Knowledge of others Woes would be far from lessening mine. That's true indeed*, said she, *but I would put you in mind of something that would make you bear your Misfortunes with more Patience —— Consider*, James, *that all this Affliction will rather add to them than any way diminish them——pray therefore be more chearful—— indeed I would do any thing I could to make you so ; for I pity you from my Heart* — She was going to add something more, possibly what would have let him into the secret Source of that Pain at her Heart she had complain'd of, but her Mother's Return prevented her, and she drew back to a Window, where she stood looking out without taking any farther Notice of the Chevalier at that time.

Having finished his little Repast, he went to Work without thinking any thing farther of his young Mistress's Behaviour, than that it proceeded from Good nature ; but he was soon convinced that the Miseries he had undergone thro' the Severity of the Father, were fully revenged on the Daughter ; this young Girl being possest of a Passion for him more violent than is ordinarily found in Persons of her tender Age. The Accident which discovered it to him was this :

A young *Indian* Maid, whose Parents liv'd in the Neighbourhood, and who on that Account had frequent Occasions of passing thro' those Woods and Fields in which the Chevalier

lier, was ufually employ'd, had diftinguifh'd
him in a particular manner from his fellow
Slaves; and as the Women of that Country have
either lefs Modefty or more Simplicity than
thofe born and bred up in *Europe*, fhe made
no Efforts to conceal the Tendernefs he had
infpired her with, but on the contrary took all
Opportunities to be in his Company; fhe
would fit whole Hours by him while he was
felling Timber, help him to gather up the
Branches, and do every thing her Strength
would permit to affift him in his Labours. ——
She told him fhe could never love any but
him, and that if he would marry her when
he had ferved out his Time, fhe would work fo
hard that fhe would fave him the Expence of
two Slaves. The Chevalier, whofe Trouble
was too great to admit Room for any Sentiments of that kind, much more for one of her
Condition and Country, plainly told her, that
he would not have her think of any fuch thing;
for as foon as his Time was expired he was
refolved to return to *Europe*. ——On this fhe
fell a weeping; *But*, faid fhe, *cannot you take
me with you?*——*I will go with you all over
the World if you will but love me.* Alas!
replied he, *I would not be fo cruel to take you
from your-Parents and your Country*——*befides,
one of your Nation would not be fo well received in mine; and there are a great many
other Reafons*, added he, *why I cannot marry
you.* Thefe Words were no fooner utter'd,
than fhe fcreamed out fomething in her own
Language which he did not underftand, and
immediately fell into a Fit. Neither Gratitude

tude nor Compaffion would admit he fhould
neglect any thing in his Power to bring her
to herfelf; and having nothing elfe at hand, he
catched up a Piece of Wood that had a Hollow
in it, and ran to a Brook and filled it with
Water, which he threw on her Face, and took
her in his Arms to lift her from the Ground;
juft he was feating her on a large Arm of a
Tree which he lately had fell'd, *Maria*, fo his
Mafter's Daughter was call'd, under Pretence
of taking the Air, came into the Field, and
faw the Action in which he was employ'd. ——
She was now feiz'd with another and more
tormenting Paffion than Love, and is the greateft Curfe of it; I need not fay I mean Jealoufy, few that have known the one in any very
great Degree but have experienced the other;
Poor *Maria* now felt the force of both, and
was very near being in the fame Condition
with the *Indian*; but her Pride rendring her
difdainful of fuch a Rival, was in this Juncture
of fome Service, and enabled her to draw towards them with a Defign of reproaching
him for the Choice he had made of a Miftrefs,
in an Air which he might take only for Ral-
lery. As fhe came more near, fhe heard him
fay, *Turquois*, my dear *Turquois*, moderate
your Paffion; and then faw the new-recover'd
Maid throw her Arms about his Neck, and
print feveral Kiffes on his Cheeks: Such a
Sight put her paft the Power of executing her
Defign, and inftead of laughing at him as fhe
intended, fhe flew to the *Indian*, and having
pufh'd her roughly away, turned to the Chevalier, and gave him a Box on the Ear, calling
him, at the fame time, ungrateful and bafe.

Poor

Poor *Torquois* ran away frighted at her Rage, and the Chevalier himself was so much astonished at it that he had not Power to speak——At last, after she had over and over repeated the Word *ungrateful*, he broke Silence. *I cannot imagine*, said he, *what you mean by accusing me in this manner——it is not in my Nature to be ungrateful, and I am sure I must have been so if I had let this young Maid have died for want of any Assistance I could give her.* What then, cry'd she, *is it by Kisses and Embraces she was to be kept alive?* Go, continu'd she, *I hate you, now I have seen you in her Arms.* It was not my Inclination to be there, answer'd the Chevalier, *but if it had, I see no great Cause for Astonishment in a Man of my Age, and even much less that it should be an Offence to you;* —— however, added he, *I have that Respect for you as to be sorry to do any thing you should think is such.*

In the time he was speaking, she reflected a little on her Behaviour, and perceiving the Imprudence she had been guilty of, was ready to die with Shame —— She put her Handkerchief before her Face to conceal the Blushes she could not restrain, and by that Action added to the Chevalier's Surprise: *What is the Meaning, Madam, of all this?* said he; *if to speak to* Torquois *be imputed to me as a Fault, I will avoid her as much as I am able;* ——*I assure you I never encouraged the frequent Visits she has made me in this Forest, and am truly sorry for her Sake that she ever came here.* For her sake! cry'd she, *I fu*—

*pofe fhe came here to pleafe herfelf; but if fhe has
got any hurt by it, fhe will do well to keep away
for the future.* I hope fhe will, faid the Chevalier. *That depends very much upon yourfelf,*
refum'd *Maria* haftily, *and if you think it
worth your while to oblige me, you'll never fpeak
to her again*——*but do as you think fit,* added
fhe, preventing him from replying—*I lay no
Injunctions upon you* ——*if you value her more
than me, you may continue your Acquaintance*—
*I fhan't give myfelf any Trouble about it, nor
will ever fpeak to you again.* With thefe
Words fhe turned from him, and went away,
as not defiring any Anfwer. He attempted
not to follow her, or dive into the Myftery of
her Behaviour. Unpractifed as he was in
Love, Nature was too good an Inftructrefs not
to make him know her Refentment proceeded
only from the Excefs of her Affection; and
tho' fhe told him not in plain Words, as the
fimple *Indian* had done, that fhe lov'd him,
the manner in which fhe acted at feeing them
together as plainly difcovered it.

He found himfelf now with two Miftreffes
of different Complexions and Manners; the
one was born and bred in *Paganifm,* tho'
with her Family lately turned to the Worfhip
of the true God, more out of Form than Faith.
She was not above thirteen Years of Age, but
tall, and had an admirable Shape; her Features were regular to a Nicety; her Eyes full
of Sweetnefs and Luftre, and her Skin fo
much whiter than what is ordinarily found
among the Natives of that Country, that fhe
might very well have paffed for an *European,*
and if here would have been called a brown

Beau-

Beauty: She was innocent, good-natur'd, and knew not the Art of disguising her Thoughts; but as the *Iroquois* in general are impatient in Misfortunes, and restrained by no Considerations whatever from gratifying their Inclinations, she shewed that she degenerated not from her Race, but had in her Composition all the Violence, all the Resolution, tho' not all the Thirst of Revenge some of them have manifested.

Maria was a very lovely Creature too, but just the opposite of all this; she was extremely fair, had yellow Hair, fine blue Eyes, which spoke the Tenderness of her Heart, but was a little vain and inclin'd to Coquetry. She was much admired and complimented by the young Men; but tho' she was pleased with their Addresses, none of them made any Impression on her Heart; the agreeable Slave, without attempting or even once thinking of such a thing, reigned sole Master there—From the first Moment she saw him, she lov'd, and though she had good Understanding enough to know, that in spite of all the Discourse there was of his being a Man of Quality, there was little Probability that her Father, who was very wealthy, and had no Child but herself, would ever consent to dispose of her to one who was in the Condition of a Slave; yet was her Passion too strong for all Impediments, and she thought, if she could but but once engage his Affections, to run all Hazards with him. To this End she had made him all the Advances Modesty would permit, and the Insensibility he shewed either of *them*, or of that

Beauty

Beauty which the Praises daily given it had made her think confiderable, gave both her Love and Pride the feverest Mortification; but as both thefe Paffions are apt to flatter with delufive Hopes, fhe confoled herfelf with a Belief that there ftill would come a *Time* when he fhou'd grow lefs indifferent. The furprizing him with *Torquois* in the manner already mentioned, deftroying at once this pleafing Expectation, and adding Jealoufy to her former Anxieties, made her now feel all the Tortures of defpairing Love and humbled Vanity.

Few Men but would have taken fome Pleafure in being beloved by two fuch fine young Creatures as *Maria* and *Torquois,* nor was our Chevalier of fo cold a Conftitution as to render him incapable of being moved by Beauty, had not the whole Affections of his Soul been fo taken up with the Defires of quitting that Part of the World, that every thing in it was diftafteful to him. He pitied both thefe Girls, but had not the leaft Spark of Inclination for either; and the Apprehenfions that the Violence of their Paffion might produce fome ill Confequence, though of what kind he could not forfee, gave no fmall Addition to his former Difcontents.

In order to prevent any Increafe of this unhappy Paffion, and fhew how little he was defirous of encouraging it in either, he took pains to fhun the Society of both as much as poffible. To avoid feeing or fpeaking to *Maria,* he came very little to her Mother, choofing rather to relinquifh that Refrefhment fhe had of late afforded him, than give any Opportunity to her Daughter of entring into any Converfation

F   with

with him——and to be out of the way of *Tor-quois*, he put his Master in mind of some Fences that were broke down, in a Piece of Ground at a good Distance from that in which he used to see the *Indian* Maid, and obtained leave to go with another Slave, and repair the Damages.

As neither of them wanted Sense, both easily saw into the Meaning of this Behaviour, and each imagining herself slighted for the Sake of the other, conceiv'd the most inveterate Hatred for her supposed more happy Rival.

In vain for several Days did both endeavour to find an Opportunity of reproaching him; he kept so far out of the Walks of the one, and so artfully avoided being alone with the other, that neither had the Advantage each so ardent-ly desired. At last *Maria*, impatient to vent the various Agitations she was full of, knowing where he worked, resolved to make a Pretence for going thither; *Torquois* having also disco-vered where it was, had the same Intention, and happened to make choice of the very Day and Hour *Maria* did. In a little Meadow which bordered on a River, unhappily these rival Beauties met:——They saw, and each guessed the other's Business, and, fired alike with jealous Rage, mutually meditated how to disappoint it. *Maria* imagined she might awe the *Indian* by some Looks and Words she was preparing to accost her with; but *Torquois*, more violent, gave her not the leisure: She no sooner had her in her Reach, than like an in-censed Lioness, she threw herself upon her, and seizing her by the Throat, griped her Neck so fast between her Hands, that she was

very

very near being ſtrangled. *Maria* was naturally timid, and leſs ſtrong than her Rival, but
the Pain and Fear of Death ſhe was in, redoubled her Vigour, and enabled her to make ſuch
a Struggle, that ſhe at length unlooſed herſelf,
and flew with the utmoſt Speed towards the
Place ſhe intended to go—*Torquois,* finding her
Prey eſcaped, and doubting not but ſhe was
gone to make her Complaint to the dear Object of her Wiſhes——Mad with Deſpair and
fruſtrated Revenge, ſhe ran directly to the River, and plunged headlong in, putting an End
at once to her unhappy Love and Life.

Maria being at a good Diſtance, turning
back her Eyes to ſee if ſhe was purſued, ſaw this
dreadful Cataſtrophe of her Rival's Fate, which
frighting her little leſs than the Danger ſhe had
been in herſelf from her Fury, ſhe began a
Scream, which continued till ſhe came within
hearing of the Chevalier and his Companion.
They turned about amazed whence the Sound
proceeded, but much more at the Sight of their
young Miſtreſs, pale, breathleſs with Flight
and Fear, and all the Signs of Horror in her
Countenance.

Both aſked the Cauſe at once, but neither
could be reſolved—She had Power to ſay no
more than —————— *Torquois! O Torquois!* and
fell into a Swoon ; they did what they could
to recover her, but in vain, and they were obliged to take her up and carry her home between
them, in all appearance dead. Her Mother, at
ſeeing her thus brought, was reduced almoſt to
the ſame Condition—her Father was alarm'd
——all the Family was in the utmoſt Confuſion

F 2 ————the

——the Slaves were queftioned concerning the
Occafion; but they were as ignorant of it as
thofe that asked——*Maria* herfelf could only
unravel the dreadful Myftery, and fhe yet gave
no Signs of ever being capable. The Terror
fhe had been in thro' the rough Ufage *Turquois* had given her——the extreme Hurry of
Spirits——the unufual Emotion of her Body,
and the Horror the latter Part of that Adventure had occafioned, fo feized upon her Vitals,
that none was ever more near Death without
dying. Her Youth however, and the Goodnefs of her Conftitution at length furmounted
the rude Shock fhe had fuftained: She opened
her Eyes, but could fay nothing for a long
time but *Turquois*. It was to no Purpofe, that
her Father, Mother, all prefent endeavour'd
to get an Explanation; the young *Indian's*
Name again repeated was all fhe had the Power to fpeak. A Phyfician was immediately
fent for, who gave it as his Opinion, that her
Diforder was merely on her Spirits, and therefore fhe muft have had fome very great Fright.
This the two Slaves confirmed the Truth of,
by relating in what manner fhe came to them.
Silence and Repofe being judged moft proper to
recover her, every body but her Mother, who
would needs watch by her, quitted the Chamber, and her Father with fome others of the
Family went into the Court-yard talking of
this ill Accident, and expreffing their Impatience to know the Truth of it.

As they were in this Difcourfe, they faw a
great Crowd of People coming that way——
who as they drew more near, perceived they
had

had a dead Body laid on fome Planks———on
looking farther they found it was poor *Turquois*
———That unhappy Maid having been feen by
fome People on the other Side of the River commit this Act of Defperation on herfelf, feveral
had Compaffion enough to jump in with a
View of preferving her; but their Care in that
Point being vain, they had however taken her
up, and were now carrying her to her Parents
Houfe. The Father of *Maria* expreffing fome
Wonder, and Defire of knowing what Motive
could have induced her to fuch a Deed, one of
thofe Men who helped to carry her, faid, *Nay,
we know nothing of that, but it may be your
Daughter* Maria *may be able to inform you
fomething of the Matter; we faw them together
juft before, and they feemed as if they were ftruggling with one another, whether in Jeft or Earneft
I cannot pretend to fay.*

My Daughter! cry'd he, *you muft be miftaken, I don't know that fhe was acquainted
with her.* *He tells you Truth,* faid another of
the Fellows, *we all faw her———fhe was dreft
in Blue, and after they parted fhe ran up towards the Field Dike.* That was the Grounds
where the Chevalier and the other Slave had
been at Work.

The Father of *Maria* was very much furprized at this Account, which agreeing fo well
with the Colour of his Daughter's Clothes that
Day, and the Place from which fhe had been
brought by his Servants, affured him there muft
be fomething in it; but tho' he was not able
to form any Guefs what fhould have brought
them together, much lefs the Occafion of their

F 3 ftrug-

ftruggling, he judged there muft have happened,
fomething very extraordinary, and which he was
uneafy till he was acquainted with.

The Chevalier *James*, who ftood by and
heard all this, was much lefs in the Dark.——
He doubted not but they had quarrell'd, and
fear'd the unhappy Motive had been himfelf.
This threw him into frefh Perplexities, and
tho' in examining into all the Particulars of his
Behaviour to them both, he could find nothing
to condemn, yet could he not reflect on fo fad
an Accident, of which he had been the innocent Occafion, without the moft poinant Grief
and Bitternefs of Heart.

The Mother of *Maria*, when inform'd by her
Hufband of the dreadful End of *Turquois*, and
what was faid concerning her Daughter, was
all impatient to know the Certainty from her
own Mouth; but as fhe was then afleep, the
Tendernefs fhe had for her, made her willing
to poftpone the Gratification of her Curiofity.

Maria foon awoke, but in a high Fever, and
too delirious to give any Anfwers that might
be depended on to the Queftions put to her;
what fhe faid ferving only to make them know
there was fomething in her late Adventure
which they could not comprehend. She often
in her Ravings called out for *James*, asked
where he was, and two or three times faid fhe
fuppofed he was gone to *Turquois*. This was
indeed a fufficient Reafon to make them think
that Slave was fome Way or other concern'd
in the Myftery; but which Way to make him
unravel it they were at a Lofs: To menace
him, in order to oblige him to fpeak, they
doubted

doubted would be in vain, and might only put him on disguising the Truth; after many Expedients which all seem'd impracticable or uncertain, they at last hit on one which proved effectual.

As *Maria* was continually repeating his Name, it seemed highly probable she had something to say to him of Moment: He was therefore, without her being ever mentioned to him, ordered to carry some Billets into her Chamber, and place them in a particular Part where she could not avoid seeing him as she lay in Bed; the Curtains on that Side being left open on Purpose. The Father and Mother, when they heard him coming, concealed themselves in a Closet, where they could easily hear every Thing that passed, and had contrived before to send all the Servants out of the Way, that what Conversation should happen between their Daughter and the Slave might not be interrupted.

This Stratagem succeeded to their Wish: He had no less Impatience to speak to *Maria* than she had discover'd to have some Discourse with him; and seeing there was no body in the Room, ventured to draw near to the Bed-side, and in a low Voice, *Madam*, said he, *for Heaven's sake inform me the Occasion of your late Fright, and what happened between you and the unfortunate* Turquois. *All your Care is still for her*, cry'd she fiercely, *no Matter what becomes of the undone* Maria. *Ah, Madam, say not so*, replied he, *I call Heaven to Witness I have all the Respect for you which I ought to have, and 'tis that Respect as much*

F 4   *as*

as the Pity *I have for her unhappy Fate, that makes me impatient to know the Source of so fatal an Accident.* O *the ungrateful Creature,* cry'd she with Vehemence, *can you deny that you yourself is the Source? was it not her Love and Jealousy of you that made her attempt my Life, which failing in, Rage and Despair made her destroy her own?* As the Chevalier was wholly ignorant of what had paſt between them, he expreſt the utmoſt Surprize at hearing she had been in any Danger from the Fury of the young *Indian*; on which *Moria* gave him the full Account of every Particular, concluding with many Reproaches for his Falſhood. *Falſhood!* said he, *to whom, or in what? I call God to* Witneſs *I neither had nor pretended any Affection for that unfortunate Maid; but on the Contrary did every thing in my Power to diſcourage that Inclination she seemed to have for me.* ——*No, Madam,* continued he very gravely, *I never yet knew what it was to love any Woman; nor is there any Probability that while I remain in the Condition of a Slave, I should have Leiſure to entertain any such gay Fancies.* Maria ſigh'd, and made no Reply to theſe Words; and he went on, *My Thoughts,* added he, *are all taken up with doing my Duty as far as I am able to thoſe to whom I belong; and when the Time shall happily arrive to reſtore me to Liberty, I shall have Avocations of a different Nature than Love to engroſs my Attention.* You ſpeak, said she, *as if Love was a voluntary Paſſion; but it may be you'll be convinced to the Contrary some Time or other. When I am it will be*

Time enough to think of it, anfwer'd he. With thefe Words he turned away, and began to place the Billets as he had been order'd; but fhe called him haftily two or three times, which obliging him to go towards the Bed again. *Ungrateful, ftupid, infenfible Man!* cry'd fhe, *will you not tell me?—What?* Madam, demanded he. *Nay,—nothing,—'tis no Matter,* replied fhe, with a Voice that fhewed fhe was in an extreme Agitation. *Yet you might fay, methinks,* continued fhe, after a Paufe which fome Sighs had occafioned, *You might fay you did not hate me, or that you were forry for me, even though it were not true. I have no need of Diffimulation,* anfwered he, *in this Cafe; for nothing can be more real than my Concern for your Diforder; and I am fo far from hating you, that I would do any Thing in my Power to prove the Refpeƈt and Value I have for your good Qualities;—As for any Thing farther, you already know my Sentiments, and I need not repeat them.* He faid no more, but turned away a fecond Time, nor would her Pride permit her now to call him back: How long fhe would have remained in that Mind is uncertain; for her Parents having now difcover'd the whole of every Thing they had defired to know, thought the Converfation had lafted long enough, and came by another Way from their Concealment into the Chamber. The Chevalier was glad of their Prefence to put an End to any farther Talk between him and their Daughter, and after he had done the Bufinefs he came there upon, went out of the Room, little fufpeƈting they were fo well acquainted with his and her Sentiments. Neither did they

F 5

take

take the leaft Notice to *Maria* of what, they had heard, fearing it would increafe her Malady.

They were, however, extremely troubled at finding her Heart had thus engag'd itfelf, but had nothing for which they could blame the Slave: It was eafy for them to perceive he had done nothing to contribute towards the Inclination fhe had for him, and could not help confefling that they were under an Obligation to him for not making all the Advantages he might have done of it. Had fhe been in Love with an ordinary Slave, or one whofe Soul had been as abject as his Circumftances, would he not have privately married a young Girl, who was the Heirefs of Wealth fufficient to have tempted a Man far above the Condition of a Slave? or had not the Object of her Affections had a Share of Difcretion, and Senfe of Honour rarely to be found at his Years, would not the Virtue of fo amiable a Maid been in very great Danger? The Mother of *Maria* trembling at the Efcape fhe had had, expatiated largely on it to her Husband, and gave the higheft Encomiums on the Prudence and Temperance of the Chevalier *James*; her Husband, in Spite of his natural Roughnefs, was fenfible of the Truth of what fhe faid, and join'd with her in his Commendations. They then began to confider by what Means they fhould put a Stop to this unlucky Paffion, and both agreeing that in order to reftore the Tranquility of their Daughter, it was neceffary this dangerous Slave fhould be removed; the good Woman propofed giving him his Freedom, and permitting him to
                                                            return

return to his native Country, which would not only effectually eafe them of all Apprehenfions on his Score, but alfo be a juft Recompence to him for the Honour and Integrity of his Behaviour in an Occafion which appeared to them fo full of Temptation. The Husband feem'd to approve of what fhe faid, and promifed to fend him away by the firft Ship that failed for *Europe.*

The Chevalier in the mean Time was ruminating on the Capricioufnefs of his Deftiny, which ordered it fo that whether he was lov'd or hated, each alike contributed to render him unhappy.——Not all the Severity he had endured, either from the Cruelty of *Drumon,* or his prefent Mafter, had given him more real Pain than the defperate Paffion of *Turquois,* and the Apprehenfions he had for the Fondnefs of *Maria.* The Extravagance of thefe young Womens Behaviour, made him reflect more deeply than he had ever done before on that Paffion which had influenced it ; and the dreadful End of the Lady and her Lover, which he had been Witnefs of at *Chefter,* now coming frefh into his Mind, he concluded that there was nothing a Heart ought fo much to guard itfelf againft, as Sentiments which were liable to produce fuch pernicious Confequences.

He had not that Day been fent into the Field as ufual, under the Pretence of their having fomething to employ him in at home, becaufe of having an Opportunity to fend him into *Maria's* Chamber for the Reafons already related ; and it being a kind of Holiday to
him,

him, for he found nothing there was to do, he
was sat in the Corner of a Hall or Parlour
buried in a profound Meditation, when his
Mistress came into the Room, and even close
to him without his seeing her.

This Woman, out of the Overflowings of
her Gratitude, thought she ought not to keep
the honest Slave one Moment in Ignorance of
his good Fortune, and giving him a little
Pluck by the Arm, *James*, said she, *you would
not sit in that disconsolate Posture, if you knew
what was going to be done for you.*

The Astonishment he was in at this Saluta-
tion, took from him the Power of making any
Reply to it, or asking what she meant, all he
could do was to rise and bow, tho' with a great
deal of Confusion.———*I see you are surprized,* said she, *but I won't keep you in Suspence two Minutes; only tell me what is the
Thing you most wish for in the World?* That is a
Question, Madam, easily to be resolved, answered he, *Whoever is in the Situation of a
Slave, must certainly have the Hour of* Freedom *most at Heart. And I, of all who ever
had that Name, have perhaps,* added he with
a Sigh, *the strongest Motives to desire and languish for the Arrival of it. Languish then no
more,* resum'd she with a Smile, *the Hour you
thought some Years distant from you is at hand,
—it is not impossible but even to morrow may
produce it.*

As the Chevalier had experienced this Woman's Good-nature in many Instances, he
could not suspect she would go about to deceive

ceive him; yet was the Intelligence she gave him so wonderful, so little to be expected, that he knew not well how to indulge a Transport which had so little Appearance of having any solid Foundation.————*What is it you tell me, Madam?* cried he.————*By what Miracle can such an unhoped Event be brought to pass? There needs no Miracle,* answer'd she, *whatever is wonderful in it you yourself alone have wrought.————Ask me no further Questions; but be assured I do not deceive you when I tell you that you will not only receive your Freedom in a few Days, but also that you may have the Satisfaction of thinking that 'tis to your own Virtue and Discretion you are indebted for it. Mystery on Mystery,* cry'd the Chevalier, *how, Madam, can I flatter myself with such a Hope, who have done no more than is the Duty of a Slave? All Slaves, perhaps, would not have done as you have done,* reply'd she; *but I will not suffer you to leave us without knowing for what Reason we are grateful.————I know you are prudent enough not to mention what I am going to say, and will therefore inform you, that your Master and myself overheard your Conversation just now with* Maria, *and as that shewed us how well you merit our Esteem, so our conferring on you what you think most valuable, will also shew you we know how to requite an Obligation.*

The Chevalier now no longer at a Loss for what she meant, nor doubtful of his Happiness, was divided between a modest Confusion at the one, and Rapture at the other, and throwing himself on his Knees, and kissing

her

her Hands.——*O Madam! cry'd he, you are too good, and if it ever comes in my Power, I will return this Bounty with somewhat more than Prayers and Blessings. Thank your Master,* returned she, *but make no mention of the Discourse we have had, till he shall inform you of this Alteration in your Fortune.*

With these Words she went out of the Room, leaving the Chevalier in such an Extasy of Joy as cannot be well expressd'd. That heavy Sadness which had been of Years Duration, and by long Habitude seem'd to be a Part of his Nature, one Moment dissipated. The Pleasure of his Heart gave double Lustre to his Eyes, and Sprightliness to every Feature. Had *Maria* now seen him, she would have adored instead of loving him, and the Gaiety which now reign'd through his whole Frame might possibly have made him less indifferent to her Charms; but the careful Parents took Care he never more should come into her Sight while he remained with them; neither did he in the least desire it, wishing from his Soul she might overcome a Passion so unhappy for herself, tho' it had proved so beneficial to him.

No Opportunity for his going offering immediately, he staid in the House, and was used with Kindness enough, especially by his Mistress, who looked on him as a Prodigy of Temperance——but every Day seem'd tedious to him, till he got on board, and on his Way towards *Europe.* His Imagination painted out to him the Confusion his wicked Uncle would be in at his Return, and the Pleasure he should take in *forgiving,* after having *reproached* him

for

for the Injuries he had done him——the Satisfaction he expected his Return would afford to his Parents after fo long an Abfence—— and laftly, the Methods he would take for improving himfelf, and retrieving as much as poffible the Time he had loft. With thefe pleafing Vifions did he beguile Impatience, till his Mafter told him he was going the next Day to *Dover,* a great Seaport Town in the County of *Kent,* and that he fhould take him along with him. Tho' he had never heard from his own Mouth that he intended to put a Period to his Slavery, yet did he not in the leaft doubt it, as his Miftrefs had affured him of it; and fuppofing, with good Reafon, that the Time was now arrived, paft that Night, which he imagin'd was the laft of his Bondage, with the moft pleafing Ideas. In the Morning he went to pay his Refpects to his Miftrefs, who confirm'd his Hopes, by telling him that her Husband had heard of a Ship, and had agreed for his Paffage; but, faid fhe, he will not fay any Thing to you of his Defigns till you are out of *Newcaftle,* becaufe he would excite no Muttering among the other Slaves. This was too plaufible to be fufpected, and the Chevalier looked already on himfelf as a Freed-man. He ask'd if he might be permitted to take Leave of *Maria,* who he heard was fomewhat recovered of her Indifpofition; but her Mother thought it would be improper, and he forbore to prefs it.

With a chearful Heart did he attend his Mafter from *Newcaftle,* fuppofing every Step brought him nearer to the Place where he

fhould

should receive his Liberty; but his Example may be a Warning to every one not to build too much on Promises, or think themselves se-cure of any Thing till they have it in Posses-sion, lest falling at once, as he did, from their high-raised Expectations, they become more miserable than ever, by so much the more as they flattered themselves with being happy.

The avaricious Proprietor of our Noble Slave had either never any real Intentions, or soon chang'd them, of relinquishing his Right over him, without an adequate Consideration. He thought it highly proper indeed he should be removed from *Maria*, but was far from be-ing of his Wife's Opinion, that his Conduct on her Account deserved so great a Recompence as the Value of near five Years Service; there-fore had all this Time, instead of enquiring for a Ship, as he pretended to his Wife, been lay-ing out for a Master to whom he might re-sell him; and having, by Letter, agreed on the Price with one at *Chichester*, he took the Trouble of conducting him himself, not caring to trust him with any of his other Slaves, for Fear they should speak of it at their Return, and he should not only have the Reproaches of his Wife for having deceived her, but also that *Maria* knowing where he was, might be tempted by her Passion, which he found was extreme, to carry on a Correspondence with him, or it may be even run to him. As he had not any Notion the Slave had been made acquainted with what he had pretended to his Wife, he had nothing to apprehend either from his Reproaches or Despair, when he should
find

find himself affigned over to a new Mafter.

But how did the Chevalier's Heart exult at the Sight of *Dover* Port, and the Shipping he faw there! and what was the Surprize, when he found his Mafter paft not only thro' that Town but the whole Country without ftopping! Tho' the Awe in which the Slaves in *America* are kept, prevents them from fcarce ever fpeaking to their Mafters, except to anfwer any Queftion asked them, or deliver a Meffage, yet could not the Chevalier refrain his Impatience fo far as not to remind his Mafter, that he had thought the Place they juft now quitted was intended to be the Extent of their Journey. *What Concern is that of yours?* replied the other furlily, *your Bufinefs is Obedience.* This filenced any further Enquiry, but raifed fome troubled Emotions in the Breaft of the Chevalier, which utterly took away all his late Vivacity.

They travelled on till they came into the County of *Suffex,* and ftop'd at a Houfe about feven Miles fhort of the City of *Chichefter.* The Chevalier, whofe Perplexity increafed, followed his Mafter into the Houfe; where having waited fome Time in an outer Room, he was called, and learned the Certainty of his Fate, by being transferred, with all the Forms ufed on fuch Occafions, to the Perfon who owned the Houfe and Plantation they were now in.

Let any one now for a Moment imagine themfelves in the Chevalier's Place, thus cruelly deceived, thus raifed to Hopes of Freedom only to make Slavery more infupportable, and then

then, and only then, they may be able to conceive what it was he felt at a Difappointment
fo fhocking.   He look'd on his old and new
Mafters alternately with fuch Fury in his Eyes,
as threatened Vengeance on the one, and denoted little Willingnefs to pay Obedience to
the other.   *Is this,* cried he to the former, *the
Effect of all the Promifes were made me?*————
Is it thus you reward the Fidelity you praifed?
————*Treacherous ungrateful Man!* continued he, raifing his Voice, *you have made
over the Right you had to me*————*I am now
no more your Slave, and may take that Satif-
faction on you that my Injuries demand.* With
thefe Words he flew at him, and feiz'd him
with fo ftrong a Gripe, as, had they not been
feparated by him who was now entituled to
command him, the Father of *Maria* might not
perhaps have ever been able to return to *Newcaftle.*

He was after this forced out of the Room,
but the Perfon who had bought him imagining
by this Behaviour (as he was ignorant of the
Provocation) that he was of a turbulent Difpofition, was little pleafed with his Bargain;
but the other finding by what he faid, that either his Wife or fome one fhe had told it to,
had flatter'd him with the Hopes of Freedom,
made him more fatisfy'd, by affuring him that
the Slave was ordinarily tractable enough, but
had been inflamed with idle Stories; and then
related to him, how for a fmall Service he had
done, he had promifed his Wife to fet him at
Liberty.————*This, I fuppofe,* continued he, *fhe
has*

has been so foolish as to tell him, and the Disappointment makes him mad.

The Chevalier saw him no 'more while he' tarried at *Chichester,* Care being taken to keep him out of the way of a Person so justly incensed. Abating this new Addition to his Vexation, he had now a milder Servitude than any he had known since his Slavery. His present Master being of a more humane Nature than either *Drumon* or the Father of *Maria*; and when he came to hear his Story, testify'd an extreme Compassion for him, and used him in so kind a manner, that the whole Family gave him the Title of the *Favourite.* But what served most to alleviate his Melancholy, was being allow'd two or three Hours in every Day to read, and Books lent him by his Master for that Purpose. As he was a Man of more Learning than most of his Calling, he had a Collection of very good Authors both *Latin* and *English,* but the Chevalier had not the Happiness of understanding any thing of the former, so was obliged to content himself with the latter, or with some Translations; but by this Means made himself very much Master of the Particulars of those Transactions which he had learned in the general, through the Care and Good-nature of that old Slave before mentioned, at his first Master's.

His Provision here was also much better than what he had been formerly allow'd, and his Tasks of Work so easy, that scarce could what he did be call'd a Slavery, and he went through it more as an *Exercise* for *Health* and *Pleasure,* than a *Labour* of *Necessity* and *Compulsion.*

'Tis

'Tis certain indeed, that since he was to remain a Slave for the Time prescrib'd by the Magistrates on his last attempting to escape, he had great Reason to be satisfy'd with this Change of Masters; and so much did the good Nature of this win upon him, that in upwards of three Years not all his Impatience of returning to *Europe* had made him entertain one Thought of quitting him till the Expiration of his Time, tho' some Efforts had been made to persuade him to it by one who afterwards run away and never was taken. Possibly could he have foreseen what was to ensue, he would have taken his Advice, for his kind Master shortly died, and the Person who succeeded him not being a Lover of Business, sold great Part of the Plantation and several of the Slaves, among whom was the Chevalier.

By a whimsical Turn of Fortune he fell to the Lot of a Person of *Newcastle* County, within a Mile of the Town of that Name, and almost in Sight of that very House where he had suffered so many Troubles on the Score of his rival Mistresses, and been so ungratefully rewarded by the Father of one of them. As they were conducting him to his new Home, he happen'd also to pass by the Side of that River where poor *Turquois* had put a Period to her Life, and the Remembrance of that unhappy Adventure, join'd to other Reflections, render'd him exceedingly melancholy.— *O! said he to himself, I fear I am now going to pay dearly for the Tranquility I enjoy'd at* Chichester: *My cruel Fate not content with subjecting me to Slavery, and exposing me to*
Sale

Sale-like the Beasts of the Field to the best Bidder, is continually tossing me from Place to Place, only to make me taste Variety of Woes, else why am I destin'd to return to one, the Memory of which is irksome to me, and where I can see nothing but what will add to my present Miseries by reminding me of the past.

With these and such like interior Expostulations, did he arrive at his new Master's, who used him, tho' with less Kindness than his last, yet with more Gentleness than his two former ones ; and tho' his Life could not be said to be easy, yet it was supportable. Having a little Curiosity to hear what was become of *Maria,* he was inform'd by those he ask'd concerning her, that she had had a Child by one of her Father's Slaves, and by the Laws of that Country, was afterwards obliged to marry him ; that they were gone to live in a distant Part of the Country, where her Father had bought them a small Plantation ; and that since this Misfortune had happened in their Family, he was grown so peevish and quarrelsome, that no body would keep him Company. The Chevalier was too generous not to be sorry for *Maria*'s ill Conduct ; but his Concern was very much alleviated by the Contentment it gave him, that a Person who had used him so ill as her Father had done, had also some Share of that Anxiety he so little knew how to pity in others.

He now also found that the Story of *Turquois,* the Love she had for him, her Jealousy of *Maria,* and the Motives of her unhappy End, were now known to the whole Country, and

and was warned by some of the Slaves to beware of her two Brothers, who they told him had vow'd his Destruction. As he was not unacquainted with the revengeful Disposition of those People, he slighted not the Advice given him on this Score, and avoided as much as he could being alone in any unfrequented Place.

All his Care, however, had been in vain, and he must inevitably have fallen an innocent Sacrifice to the Manes of that *Indian* Maid, if Providence had not interposed in his Defence.

After having lain in wait for many Months, as they afterwards confess'd, without finding any Opportunity to execute their cruel Purpose, they had almost given it over, when Chance presented what they had vainly sought. The Chevalier happening on some Occasion to stay behind his Fellow-slaves one Morning, and knowing the Business he had to do that Day required Expedition, to make the greater Haste to overtake them ran through a Forest, which was a shorter Cut to the Field where they work'd than the Way he usually went. Here he was met by the two *Iroquois*, who both at once fell upon him: He defended himself as well as he could against their united Force, and neither of them being arm'd any more than himself, and he having his Back against a Tree, they struggled for a considerable Time without being able to get him down. One of them at last bethinking himself of a Knife he had in his Pocket, pluck'd it hastily out, and aim'd to stab the Chevalier with it in the Belly,

Belly, but he had the Dexterity to wreath his
Body so, that he broke the Force of the Blow,
receiving only a flight Wound on the Hip, but
could not do this without giving his other An-
tagonist so much Advantage as to get his Leg between his, and by that Means threw him; and
him who had struck at him at the same time
catching up his Knife again, was going to cut
his Throat while the other kneel'd upon his
Breast and kept him down.

Just in that Point of Time arrived some Persons, who being in search of a fugitive Slave,
suppos'd to have conceal'd himself in that Forest, had seen this unequal Combat at a Diftance, and before the fatal Knife could do its
Work, seiz'd on the Hand that held it, and
drag'd the Assassins off. One Instant produced
both the Danger and Relief——not less swift
than Lightning, and equally amazing to the At-
tackers and Attacked, each being too much taken up to perceive the Interruption till they
felt it.

These People belonging to a neighbouring
Plantation, knew both the Chevalier and those
who set upon him, and some of them supported him, being weak with struggling and
the loss of Blood which issued in great Abun-
dance from his Wound; and others forced the
disappointed *Iroquois* along with them before
a Justice, where the Chevalier's Master being
sent for, and the *Indians* Attempt plainly
proved, it was decreed that as the Wound they
had given was not dangerous, they should only
pay a Surgeon for the Cure, and his Master for
the Time it was supposed it would take up,
and

and that the Father of thefe two Defperado's,
with another Man of Credit fhould be bound
in a large Penalty for their civil Behaviour for
the future. All this being done, ended an adventure which had like to have brought thefe
Memoirs into a very narrow Compafs.

Tho' there was nothing dangerous in the
Hurt the Chevalier had received, yet he had
loft a good deal of Blood and was very much
bruifed, which kept him weak and unable to
do any Work for more than two Months. ——
Neither the Surgeon nor Mafter much haftened
his Recovery, the one being well paid for his
Attendance, and the other for his Time.

During this Ceffation of bodily Labour the
active Mind of our illuftrious Slave was not
idle—not the minuteft Accident of his unfortunate Life but came frefh into his Memory;
among the reft, that fignificant Dream I made
fo copious a relation of was ftrong in his Head,
and as he had ever look'd upon it as a kind of
Prognoftick of his future Fate, he could not
help thinking, that tho' his Slavery was near
expired, there wanting not a Year of the Time,
which whatever he endured he refolved to do
nothing to prolong, yet he doubted not but
after that he would find his Difficulties and
Dangers; and tho' he could not form any
Guefs of what Nature they would be, yet it
was reafonable to fuppofe an Uncle who had
done fo much to remove him, would not give
over his Endeavours either to take away his
Life, or to render the remainder as wretched as
the paft. Sometimes again he flatter'd himfelf
with more pleafing Imaginations, he reprefented

this cruel Uncle as repenting of what he had done, receiving the News of his safe Return with Tranfport, confeffing the Faults he had been guilty of, and conducting him to a Father who would endeavour by all poffible Acts of Tendernefs to make him lose the Memory of what he had fuffer'd. His Mother was much lefs in his Thoughts, becaufe at parting from her he was too young to retain the leaft Remembrance of her; yet having heard fhe was extremely beautiful, he would fometimes picture out a fine graceful Lady hanging over a long loft Son, and melting into Tears of maternal Joy and Fondnefs——the Welcomes of Tenants, Dependants, and Servants, blended with the gay Shew of Equipage and the Pomp of Titles, would now and then force their Way into his youthful Fancy————but all thefe pleafing Ideas were tranfient————no fooner form'd than vanifh'd————and his Apprehenfions of the *worft* that could befal him took Place of the two fhort-liv'd *beft*.

Hope is indeed a charming Paffion, the only real Friend of human Thought————it beguiles the prefent Mifery, robs Misfortune of its Force, and makes the Breaft that harbours it happy and ferene amidft a Sea of Cares; and if at laft found to be delufive, nothing at leaft is loft by it, but fo much Time from Woe. Had the Chevalier indulg'd it more, the Hurt he would have fuftain'd by the Difappointment would not have been adequate to the Satisfaction while it lafted.

It was doubtlefs a good deal owing to the various Agitations of his *Mind*, that his *Body*

G   con-

continued so long feeble, and to an Accident, which when he was grown a little better, might well retard his Recovery; for though it related not immediately to himself, the Generosity and Integrity of his Nature made him take Part in it, and involved him in fresh Difficulties and Dangers.

Having not been out of Doors in so long a Time, and the Weather extremely hot, he fancy'd the fresh Air would revive him, and on a *Sunday* Evening, taking with him *Plutarch*'s Lives, which his kind Master at *Chichester*, knowing how much he delighted in Books, had made him a Present of, he went into a Field adjacent to the House, and sat down by the Side of a Hedge under the Shadow of some tall Trees, to which this Division of certain Grounds belonging to two different Persons was join'd. He had not read many Pages before his Weakness making him a little drousy, he reclined his Head upon his Arm, and fell into a Slumber, in which he continu'd till the Sun had entirely withdrawn his Beams; on perceiving it was dark when he awoke, he was about to rise and go home, when the Sound of Voices very near him gave him a kind of Curiosity of knowing on what they were discoursing, especially as he thought the one was that of his Master's Wife, and the other of one *Stephano*, a Slave belonging to the next Plantation. The first Words he distinguish'd we spoken by his Mistress, and to this Effect *Are you sure*, said she, *the Master of the Boy won't betray us ? No, no*, replied he, *I know him well enough—he will do any Thing for his*
terest

*terest——if we but get the Money, we are se-
cure enough of every Thing else; but if we wait
till the Sum your Husband now has in the
House is laid out, as we did once before, we
shall find a Friend no where. Well,* resumed
she, *you shall have no more Occasion to upbraid
me on that Score——you know I have it all in
my Possession, and will take Care to leave none
of it behind me, nor nothing else that I can
carry that is of any Value——But then,* added
she, *if the Wind should turn, and we be detained in the Harbour, what would become of
us? You are always raising Difficulties,* said
he, *the Wind cannot turn so but we may get
off in some other Port; and if there be any
Danger of our Bark being search'd, give the
Captain a Piece of Money, and we shall have
his Boat to put us on Board some other Vessel,
or at the worst we may row over to the* Iroquois. *I have done with my Objections,* answered she, *but if after I do this you should
prove false, 'twould break my Heart. You
ought not to doubt my Love,* answer'd he, *since
I run as great a Risque as you, and would not
venture for any thing, but to have the Possession
of you entirely to myself.* In speaking this he
endeavour'd to enforce her Belief by other Proofs
of Tenderness, and she seem'd so well convinced by them, that she made no farther Hesitation, so it was agreed between them that she
should make her Escape that Night, the Wind
then being favourable, and blowing a strong
Gale, the Bark he told her was ready to sail,
the Captain apprised of their coming, and ready
to put off the Moment they came on board.

The

The Chevalier was ftruck with the utmoft
Horror at this Difcovery: He had heard that
the Woman who thus wrong'd and treache-
roufly confpir'd to rob her Husband, after having forfeited her Reputation in the Country
where fhe was born, had come over there in
hope of making her Fortune, and had done it
effectually by marrying one of the richeft Planters in the whole Country, who doted on her
with an Extravagance of Fondnefs: He had
alfo been an Eye-witnefs that fhe feem'd on
her part to outvy him in all the Proofs he gave
of a more than conjugal Affection; and now
to find all was Diffimulation and Artifice, and
that not content with injuring him in her Perfon, fhe alfo liften'd to the Infinuations of the
Villain who had feduced her, fo far as to quit
for ever fo good a Husband, and to deprive
him of all his Subftance in her Power, was
fomething fo fhocking to the honeft Soul of
him to whom it was thus accidentally reveal'd,
that he knew not prefently what Courfe to take
to prevent fo monftrous a Defign being perpe-
trated——At firft he thought of running
to his Mafter, and acquainting him with all
he had heard; but then he confidered, that
they would doubtlefs deny every Thing, that
the blind Love his Mafter had for his faithlefs
Wife would induce him to believe her as Innocent as fhe pretended, and in that Cafe he
fhould be deem'd an Incendiary, and accordingly punifh'd. Yet could he not refolve to
fuffer this Robbery to be committed, the
Thoughts of knowing and not preventing the
Villany, feem'd, in his Opinion, to make him
accef-

acceffary to it ; and all the time the guilty Pair were employ'd in their Endearments, was he debating within himfelf in what manner he fhould proceed.

At length they feparated, the Slave to prepare what yet remain'd neceffary to fecure their Flight, and fhe to return to her Husband, in order by fome new Deception to hinder his Surprize at her lying abroad that Night, or making an immediate Purfuit. As the Chevalier faw her pafs along, a fudden Thought came into his Head, which feem'd to him a happy Expedient: Without ftaying to deliberate, he ran haftily after her, and fhe fuppofing it was her Lover, who might poffibly have forgot fomething he had to fay, turn'd back ; and it being not light enough to difcern any Objects, farther than in the Grofs, fhe could not be undeceiv'd, and cry'd, *What now, my dear* Stephano! 'Tis *not* Stephano, *Madam,* anfwer'd the Chevalier, *but one who, perhaps, has more real good Wifhes towards you than even that favourite Slave.* The Tone of his Voice now convincing her fhe had been miftaken, put her into a terrible Confufion ; but not imagining he was fo well acquainted with what had paft, thought to take away any Sufpicion he might have, on meeting her alone in the Dark, by affecting an Air of Unconcern. *What is it you,* James? faid fhe, *that is not the way for you to get well again to be out in the Night Air.*——*Where have you been, pray?* *Where I have heard what very much aftonifhes me,* replied he ; *yet what, I hope, my Knowledge of may be a means of preventing, and you hereafter have reafon to thank Providence for making*

me

me the sole Witness of what it will be your own Fault, if I make any Use of to your Disadvantage. What is it you mean? cry'd she—*you are mad sure*—go home prithee, and go to sleep. *Na,* Madam, said he, till I have convinced you I am more desirous of your Happiness than you are yourself. But not to keep you in Suspence, know, that Chance has made me Master of your dearest Secret——I have heard all the Conversation between you and Stephano, therefore can be no Stranger to the Design this Night was to have been put in Execution; but I beseech you, Madam, to consider what you are about: If I should conceal the Matter from my Master, which neither Justice nor Conscience will permit me to do, if you persist in it, and you should even be able to avoid the Pursuit which will be made after you when once you are miss'd, which there is also little Probability of, how will it gall your Soul hereafter to reflect what a happy Situation you have quitted, what a Husband you have wrong'd for the Sake of a, perhaps, ungrateful Slave; for it is my Opinion, that the Man that is unjust can never be generous, or have one good Quality worthy a Woman's Love.

The Agitations this Woman was in all the Time he was speaking were so violent, that they were very near throwing her into a Swoon. —She supported herself as well as she could by leaning on some Timber which had been cut down the Day before, and was piled up, but was not able to make any Answer for some time, and the Chevalier had all the Opportunity he could desire to make her sensible both of the Danger and Shame of the Crime she was

going

going to commit. At laſt, *Say no more, James,* *for Heaven's Sake,* cry'd ſhe, burſting into Tears, *I now ſee and tremble at the dreadful Precipice on which I ſtood this Moment, and will turn my Back upon it for ever.—If you will be ſo good to keep the Knowledge of my Fault a Secret, I will ſwear to you by every Thing that is ſacred, never to repeat it, and will alſo make you all the Gratifications in my Power.*

O! Madam, reply'd the Chevalier, *if you preſerve inviolate the firſt Part of your Promiſe, it will entirely acquit you of the laſt ; and I ſhall think myſelf highly recompenſed in ſeeing you continue in a Condition which depends wholly on yourſelf to make happy. As for my Secrecy, be aſſured my Tongue ſhall never give the leaſt Utterance to what my Ears have heard.*

Whether it was this generous Behaviour that had the Effect upon her, or whether ſhe was before inſpired with ſome ſecret Liking of his Perſon is uncertain ; but ſhe immediately began to give him Teſtimonies that *Stephano* had not engroſs'd her whole Heart. *Since,* ſaid ſhe, *you are ſo well acquainted with my Fault, let us ſit down a While, and I will relate to you the Means by which I was drawn into it—Perhaps,* continued ſhe, leaning her Hand upon his Arm, *you will find more to pity than condemn me for.*

With theſe Words ſhe in a manner compelled him to ſit on ſome Planks which lay ſcattered off the Pile, and having placed herſelf very cloſe to him, ſhe told him, That being one Day alone, *Stephano* came in on ſome Buſineſs from his Maſter, and having this Op-

portunity

portunity forced her to his Will, and that she afterwards fearing to lose the Affections of her Husband, if he should know what she had suffer'd, tho' against her Inclination, she had ever since been obliged to yield herself to him, lest her Refusal should provoke him to divulge it: And that the same Apprehensions had made her also consent to go with him, he having, she said, often threaten'd to expose her if she would not quit *Pensilvania*; which, weary of his Slavery, he was resolv'd to run all Hazards to get out of himself.

The Chevalier, in spite of his little Knowledge of the World, had too much Penetration to give Credit to this Story: The Expressions she made use of in some Moments to *Stephano*, were more convincing to him that she was neither displeased with the Rape nor the Ravisher, than any thing she could say to the contrary; but he forbore letting her know his Sentiments on that Occasion, thinking it best she should imagine herself believ'd; and told her, that, in his Opinion, it would be little regarded what a Slave should say on her on that Score, and earnestly exhorted her never to be prevail'd upon to think of wronging her Husband any more in the manner she had intended. This she promised with many Asseverations, and concluded with saying, *I now see the Baseness of depriving him of any Part of his Substance, and if ever I should be tempted to a Thought of wronging him in his Bed, it would not be* Stephano *I should make choice of.*

These last Words, pronounced with the most tender Air, and accompanied with a kind of

lan-

languishing Loll upon the Shoulder of the Chevalier, made him sensible she was far from being a real Convert to Virtue, whatever Disgust she might have for her late Project, or the Person who was to have been her Partner in it. Unwilling however that she should explain herself more fully, he asked in what manner she would behave to that Slave, who 'twas like would grow desperate on his Disappointment? On which she told him, that if he would carry a Letter from her to him, which he should see before sealed, that she would invent an Excuse which she doubted not but would pass current for the present, and that afterwards she would endeavour to break off with him by degrees. The Chevalier was far from approving the Method she proposed, and told her that he would readily be the Bearer of what she wrote, but thought it more adviseable to let him know at once that she repented her past Conduct, and would never see him more. But this she would by no means be persuaded to, pretending still a Fear of what he might accuse her of; so he gave over insisting upon it, but resolved in his Mind to observe her very carefully, and if he found she relapsed into her former Folly, to make no Scruple of revealing all to his Master.

They went home together, she thinking it would look most natural to tell her Husband she had met him as she was returning from some Visits she had been making. But the little Way she had to go she behaved to him with such Marks of Kindness, as left him no Room to doubt that it was in his Power to succeed

Stephano,

Stephano, without making any use of that Violence she had accused him of. But this Discovery, instead of flattering his Vanity, or Inclinations, on the contrary gave him a good
deal of Uneasiness: Not that he was by Nature cold and insensible of Love, had a proper
Object presented itself; but tho' this Woman
was young and extremely handsome, the Vile-
ness he discovered in her destroyed all the Effects her Charms might otherwise have had on
him; and he besides foresaw many Inconveni-
encies would arise to him, if she were in reality inclined to favour him as much as her present Behaviour denoted.

These Cogitations kept him from sleeping
much that Night, and in the Morning as soon
as his Master was gone out to look over his
Slaves, he was called for and bid to go into his
Mistress's Chamber, where she shewed him a
Letter she had just wrote to *Stephano*, and bid
him read it, which he did, and found it contained these Lines,

To STEPHANO.

AN unexpected Accident has frustrated our
Designs at present——my Husband heard of
a Bargain, so took the Money out of my Hands
soon after I came home, in order to lay it out
this Day——I hope my not being able to acquaint you with it sooner, has not occasioned
your doing any thing that may give any Suspicion of what we had agreed upon——I got a
Hurt in my Foot last night, and fear I shall
not

not be able to walk fo far as our Rendezvous for fome Days.—Farewel.—Burn this before the Face of the Perfon that brings it, or I fhall think you do not mean fair to

                                        Yours.

It was in vain that the Chevalier endeavoured to prevail on her either to write in a different manner, or not at all; fhe was obftinate and found fo many Excufes, which the above Letter fhews fhe was not barren in inventing, that he was obliged to let her feal it as it was, and according to his Promife went and delivered it to *Stephano,* who muttered fomething to himfelf after he had it, and then ftruck Fire and fet a Match to it. When it was confumed, *Tell her,* faid he, *what you have feen me do; that's all.*

She indeed expected no other Anfwer than this Proof of his Obedience, and told the Chevalier that fhe was very well fatisfied with what fhe had done, and would engage to find fo many Pretences of avoiding him that he would at length grow weary of looking after her, and break off of himfelf; *which,* faid fhe, *is the only way to prevent his blabbing any thing of what has paft between us.* He feemed not to difcredit what fhe faid, and was going out of the Room; but fhe called him back, and gave him out of her Clofet a Slice of rich Cake and a Glafs of Cordial Water; and during the Time he ftaid, which was no longer than Civility required, both looked and talked to him in a Fafhion, which fully convinced him fhe was fo far from being a

                                        peal

real Penitent, that she wished for nothing
more than to repeat her Crime.

He now found, that instead of recovering
her to Virtue, as he had hoped, by his generous Proceeding, he had only changed the Object of her guilty Flame, and that she was
wholly incapable of Remorse, he began to repent he had not acquainted his Master with
the Disposition of a Wife, which, sooner or
later, he fear'd, would bring both him and
herself to Destruction.—He would also have
regretted his having discovered the Design she
had plotted against a Husband to whom she
had such great Obligations, but he thought he
should offend Providence by it, who had made
him the Instrument of preventing it. His own
Mind was however rendered extremely uneasy
by it.—He thought it his Duty to keep a
watchful Eye over his Mistress, in order to
hinder her from seeing that Seducer of her Virtue, and at the same Time to avoid all Occasions of being alone with her himself; but this
last was much the hardest Task: He being
always in the House, and his Master frequently
abroad, she was continually giving him some
new Proofs of her Affection, if the vicious
Inclinations she was possest of can deserve that
Name: His only Resource was not to seem to
understand her Meaning, which she indeed
spoke but too plain; his Stupidity, as she imagined it, vexed her to the Soul, and the Difficulties she found in making him more sensible,
heightening her Desire to do so, she at Length
threw off all Decency, all Shew of Modesty,
and told him that she loved him: Alledged in
her

her Excuse the Disparity of Years there was between her and her Husband⸻that having married him only for Convenience, it was not in her Power to take any Satisfaction in Embraces which Necessity alone had made her yield to receive; and that tho' she acknowledged all Gratitude was due to him, yet that was not a Passion sufficiently strong to bridle another to which Youth is incident⸻In fine, as she had Wit inferior to few, and Cunning superior to most, she made use of such Arguments to prove, that to gratify an Inclination which it was impossible to subdue, was at most but a venial Transgression, a pardonable Error; that, he has since confest, he was in some Measure half ready to acknowledge the Force of them in the Way she wished. But such a Propensity was too transient either to render him Guilty or her Happy, and was succeeded by a still greater Detestation of her Impudence, which deformed one of the most beautiful Faces in the World, and made even her Wit nauseous and offensive; whereas had either been the Ornaments of Modesty and Virtue, he would almost have adored them.

He one Day spoke so plain to her on those Heads, that she burst into Tears, and went out of the Room without making any Answer to what he said: This he took for a good Sign, and was in Hopes that beginning now to have a true Sense of her past Errors, she would amend: Especially as he had seen *Stephano* very much lurking about the House, and could not discover that she even attempted to go out to him; but whether this was

owing

owing to her Shame of the Folly she had been
guilty of with him, or to her new Paffion for
himfelf, he could not be certain. He thought
however, that he fhould not fully difcharge
that Duty he had fo well begun, if he fuffered that Fellow to be on the Watch for an
Opportunity, which fhe in fome unguarded
Moment might again permit him to make ufe
of, therefore went out to him and asked him
who it was he wanted? and what Bufinefs he
had there? To which the other anfwering in
a furly Manner, hot Words rofe between them,
and were foon follow'd by Blows.——*Stephen*
being robuft, and the Chevalier not having yet
recover'd his former Strength, had much the
worft of the Combat; and had not fome People paffing that way put an End to it, juft as
his Antagonift had got him down, he had
doubtlefs fuffer'd much more: He was very
much hurt, and obliged again to keep his Bed.
——His Mafter hearing of it, imputed the Quarrel only to fomething between themfelves, and
little imagined how great a Share his Honour
had in it; but his Miftrefs, who knew it well,
came frequently to enquire how he did, exprefs'd the greateft Concern at his Misfortune; and one Day brought him in a Mefs of
Soup, which fhe faid fhe had prepar'd for
him herfelf, and would be a great Reftorative.
Having that Moment taken fomething, he defired fhe would fet it down, and he would eat
it foon; on which fhe placed it on a Table by
his Bed-fide; but being call'd haftily away to
fome one that had Bufinefs with her, he forgot it; and happening to fall afleep, a Cat
came

came in, and attracted by the favory Smell
jumped on the Table, and presently emptied
the Bason that contained this precious Viand.
—On his awaking he bethought him of it,
but presently saw what had happened, by the
Cat being still there, and liking up some Drops
which had fallen, in setting it down—This he
would have thought no more on, had not the
poor Animal immediately swelled up to more
than twice her usual Size, and after foaming
at the Mouth, and giving all the Signs of the
most terrible Agony, fell down dead in the
Room.

What contrary Ideas must now crowd themfelves at once into his astonished Mind; a
mingled Gratitude and Admiration for the Divine Being who had so miraculously preserved
him from a Danger he had not the least Suspicion of, and the most consummate Horror at
finding a Woman capable of so black a Crime
as the Murder of an innocent Perfon, who so
far from having injured had conferred the highest Obligations on her.—The intended Mischief
and the Escape were both obvious; he saw the
fatal Effect of the one on the poor Cat, and
felt the other in being alive himself to bless the
Goodness that had saved him.—A long time
did these Meditations take him up, and had
doubtless employed him longer yet, had not
one of the Servants coming to ask if he wanted any thing, interrupted them.

He now began to confider in what manner
he should behave: He had sometimes a mind
to endeavour to rise and seek his Mistress, to
reproach her for her Design upon him; but
not

not doubting but she would deny it with an
Assurance which he found she never wanted,
and fearing that it would be in vain to attempt
exciting any Remorse in so hardened a Heart,
he judged it better to avoid her Presence.———
Reflecting afterward, that when she should
come to know the Disappointment of her intended Revenge, she might possibly take other
Measures to accomplish it, both Nature and
Religion bade him provide as well as he was
able for his Defence.———His Master was
abroad on Business, and not expected home
hat Night, he knew not therefore what she
might attempt when the Family should be in
Bed, and he alone, and exposed to all her Fury
could inspire her with———He therefore, when
it grew toward Evening got up, and having
fastened his Door with a Bolt which happened to be on it, dragged afterwards whatever he
could find in the Room, and set against it for
his better Security.

His Mind was notwithstanding too much
confused to admit of Sleep to enter his Eyes,
tho' the House seemed buried in a profound
Silence, 'till at once he heard a sudden Sound
of many Voices, all undistinguishable by reason of their being at a Distance, tho' he thought
too within the House; but soon the Noise
grew louder and more near, and he was more
astonished than affrighted when he heard his
Master cry high above the rest, *Drag her,
tear her if she will not move.*———He then
had Courage to jump out of Bed, and pluck-
ing away his Barricadoes unbolted the Door,
where the first Object he beheld coming towards

wards his Room was his Master, and two or
three Slaves hawling his Mistress, half naked,
down the Stairs. As he was so too, he ran
back to wrap something about him for Decency's Sake; but his Master prevented him,
and said, James, *go to Bed again, and if you
are honest, reveal at once all you know of this
most wicked Woman————this shameless Adul-
teress, whom I have this Moment taken in my
own Bed with a Slave.———She accuses you of
having betray'd her to me————you, therefore,
are not ignorant of her Perfidy.————Speak
now the Truth, and I will pardon your revealing it no sooner.* It would have been as ro-
mantick, as well as unavailing, to have attempted to conceal a Crime the Chevalier
now found she was detected in, and therefore, without any Hesitation, he unravel'd the
whole iniquitous Scene he had discover'd between her and *Stephano* in the Field, the Motives that induced him to hide her Shame, and
the Promises she had made, on his doing so, to
correct her Conduct for the future; stifling no
Part of what he knew, excepting that which
related to the Passion she pretended for himself; and concluded with producing the dead
Cat, and the Means by which she had been
destroy'd.

The Master listen'd with a Mixture of
Astonishment and Horror to what he said, and
casting his Eyes furiously on his Wife————*O
thou vilest of all Creatures,* cry'd he, *thou
would'st not only have robb'd me, but would'st
have murder'd this poor Man, for having prevented it.————I wonder my own Life was*
safe,

safe, too much in the Power, as well as my Fortune and my Honour, of such a Fiend as thee. She spoke not all this Time one Word, nor lifted up her Eyes; and he made them bind her, naked as she was, with strong Cords, and then locked her into a Room alone, the Key of which he kept himself; but placed two Slaves at the Door to prevent any Attempt that might be made of rescuing her. When he had seen this done, he retired to another Chamber, rather to meditate than sleep.

Several of the Servants staid with the Chevalier to ask further Particulars of this Affair, and he having done his best to satisfy their Curiosity, they, in their Turn inform'd him that at Midnight their Master came home, and being let in by one that heard him at the first Knock, and lighted him to his Chamber, *Stephano* was found in Bed with their Mistress; that their Master running to his Closet for a Pistol to shoot him, the Villain took that Opportunity of jumping out of the Window, and that the Fall had broke his Neck.

The Remainder of that Night past over in Reflections occasion'd by the late Adventure, and early in the Morning the fair Offender was carried before a Magistrate, and from thence to the County Prison, where she was to wait the Arrival of some other Justices soon expected, to take her Trial. Every Body believed her Sentence would be Death, because the Adultery was committed; and the Robbery of her Husband, and Murder of the Chevalier *James* disappointed, only by the Interposition of Providence;

vidence. Her Husband, wrong'd in the cruel manner he had been, could not endure the Thought of seeing her Execution, and 'twas imagin'd brib'd the Jailer to affift her to make her Efcape; for fhe got not only out of Prifon one Night, but fafe on board a Veffel which fail'd with her the fame Moment, and fhe was never heard more of in *Penfylvania.*

This Affair made a very great Noife, and the Conduct of the Chevalier received all the Praifes it deferved——His Mafter, fenfible that it was his Peace of Mind he had confulted, in rather endeavouring to convert than expofe a Woman he knew was fo dear to him, became afterwards extremely kind to him ; but the Chevalier himfelf was very thoughtful for a long Time, he compared the Difpofition of this Woman with that of his Uncle *Richard,* and found they were infpired with the fame wicked Spirit; and it feemed no lefs ftrange than fhocking to him, that Human Nature could fo far degenerate.

At Length however, his recovered Health and wonted Strength enabling him to go about other Occupations than thofe of *Thought,* he went chearfully to his accuftom'd Work, in which he continued till the full Expiration of his Time of Servitude, without any other ill Accident happening either to retard or hinder his being made free.

Thus had this young Nobleman, born to an ample Fortune and illuftrious Rank, lan-guifhed full thirteen Years in the moft painful and laborious Bondage that can be endured—expofed to all manner of Hardfhips, Difficulties,

ties and Dangers; but now the Time was come to put an End to his Misfortunes on that Side the Globe, and give him an Opportunity to try what Reception he should find in those Parts where he had Reason to expect better Usage. Let us, therefore, leave him setting out for a Place he had so long languish'd to behold, and cast our Eyes a-while on the odd Figure his cruel Uncle made in the Dignity he had assum'd.

He might, indeed, be justly compar'd to the *Jay* in the Fable, pluming himself and strutting in the *Peacock*'s Feathers; for tho' he was high born, and had been allow'd a suitable Education, yet his Soul was not the least a-kin to Nobility; and, instead of true Grandeur, either in his way of thinking or outward Behaviour, he had only a certain mean Pride; whenever he went about to ape the Man of Consequence, he did it with so ill a Grace, as excited rather the Contempt than Reverence of all that saw him.

Having, as has been already related, taken on him the Title of Baron *de Altamont* immediately on his Brother's Decease, he began to blaze in all the Pomp of his borrow'd Dignity, without considering how small a Revenue there was to support it; for though the late Baron could dispose of the Estate only for his own Life, yet he had so encumber'd it with Debts, for the Payment of which the Chevalier was engaged, that the gay Equipage he at first set up was soon retrench'd, and he found himself in such very low Circumstances, as obliged him to solicit the Government for a Pension,

in

in which he had better Succefs than he merited, and was ordered an Allowance of fix-
teen hundred Crowns *per Annum*, till the
Eftate fhould be clear'd; but this not being
fufficient for his private Extravagancies and
Debaucheries, he bethought himfelf of looking
out for a Wife with a good Fortune. To this
End he left *Altamont* and return'd to his own
Country, in the Weftern Parts of which he
found a Lady, who to her great Misfortune
gave Credit to the Vows he made her of a moft
tender and faithful Paffion : Her Relations
being plain-bred People, who had not converfed much with the Great-World, tho' of a
very good Family, faw not any thing to object
againft either in his Manners or Character, fo
that the Match was concluded in a fhort Time.
He lived with her in the Country for a few
Months; and then, pretending Bufinefs, came
to Town, taking with him the beft Part of her
Fortune : Having foon run through it, he went
down again for the Remainder; but here a
moft unlucky Accident befel him, and he was
accufed of a Crime, which, whether guilty or
not, he really merited the Punifhment of for
thofe he had committed againft his innocent
Nephew.

Not many Miles diftant from his Lady's
Seat, two of his Servants were taken up for a
Robbery on the Highway; being found guilty,
they impeached their Lord, on which, notwithftanding his Dignity, he was feized, carried to Prifon, and laid in Irons. No Proof
however being brought againft him befides the
Oaths of thefe Fellows, which it feems was
not

not sufficient to convict a Man of Quality, tho' either singly would have hang'd a meaner Person, he was acquitted; but the Affair made so great a Noise in all that Part of the Country, that he lost all the Respect he had there.

Soon after this the old Count *de Anglia* died, whose Title and Possessions devolving on the Heir of *Altamont*, as next of Blood, this pretented Peer began to think himself the Minion of Fortune, and blown up with his new Dignity, render'd himself more ridiculous than ever: He so over-acted the *Great-Man*, that his *real Littleness* was visible even to the most shallow Capacity, and he never attempted to inspire *Awe* but he excited a *Sneer* instead of a *Submission*. This he had too much Cunning not to see, but Self-love not permitting him to imagine the small Regard paid to him, especially by his Inferiors, was owing to any thing in himself, he would sometimes fall into such Fits of raging Passion, as were little different from Madness.

He had indeed some more material Occasions for Discontent; the late Count having never loved him, he took Care, since he could not deprive him of the Title, to deprive him as much as was in his Power of the Means of supporting it with Dignity, and bequeath'd not only all his personal Effects, but also very considerable Portions of the Estate to other Relations who he thought more worthy of it. On this Count *Richard* had Recourse to some Gentlemen of the long Robe, who gave it as their Opinion, that the late Count had no Right to make such a Testament; and pursuant to their

their Advice, he commenced many vexatious Proceſſes againſt the Claimants, which having once enter'd into, he could not eaſily diſentangle himſelf from. As he heartily hated to part with any Money except for the Gratification of his looſer Pleaſures, or to make a Shew in the World, the Sums continually drain'd from him on this Account put him beyond all Patience — every *Fee* he found himſelf obliged to give threw him into Agonies, and the Sight of a *Chancery Bill* was a Dagger to his Heart.

Finding himſelf thus without Love, without Reſpect on the one Side, and teaz'd with perpetual Importunities on the other, he left the Care of his Affairs to a Perſon he could confide in, and croſſed the Sea, determin'd to live for ſome Time at his Barony of *Altamont*, which being a cheap Place, he might repair the Damages theſe expenſive Law-ſuits had done his Eſtate. He had not however ſo much Command over himſelf as not to make a Stop at the Capital in his Way, that being a Place where he knew he could indulge his Inclinations, ſuch as they were, at a very low Price. But here it was he found what he never knew before, or had believed it was in Nature to inſpire him with; I mean an honourable Paſſion, in which he had no View of Intereſt. He happen'd on a Viſit he made to the Lady of a dignify'd Clergyman to meet a young Perſon whoſe Charms ſo ſtruck him at firſt Sight, that he thought himſelf the moſt miſerable Man on Earth in having already diſpoſed of thoſe Vows to another, which could alone entitle

title him to any Hope of poſſeſſing her; but as he had the moſt active and ready Invention of any Man breathing, he preſently bethought him of giving out that his Lady was dead. The Mother of the Chevalier *James* having reſign'd her unfortunate Life juſt before his Departure, Decency had obliged him to wear Black on that Occaſion, and the Mourning-Habit he arrived in, correſponding with his Pretences, every Body believed him a Widower.

That poor Lady, whoſe real Death gave a Colour to this Pretence, had all this Time led a moſt melancholy Life: The News of her Husband's and Son's Death reach'd her at the ſame Time, and tho' according to all Circumſtances that Part of this Intelligence that was real, had not great Effect upon her, yet the fictitious one occaſioned ſuch Agonies as threw her into a lingring Diſorder, which at laſt ended her Days. As ſhe had for a long Time lived unloved and unreſpected, ſo ſhe died unpitied and unregretted, and was bury'd in a Manner little befitting the Rank ſhe once held in the World, or ſhe indeed deſerved.

So little Excuſe do the ſlighteſt Errors ſometimes find, while greater ſhall paſs uncenſured by the World, and reflect no Obloquy on the Perſon guilty of them! how weak the Judgment therefore that is built on Rumour, or guided by Appearances!

The young and beautiful *Anadea*, for ſo the preſent Object of our Count's Affections was called, might however be eaſily deceived by the Pretences of a Nobleman who ſeemed to languiſh for her with the moſt tender and ardent
Paſſion.

Paffion : *Simplicius,* her Father, was a very honeft and wealthy Merchant, had good Senfe ; but, without Guile himfelf, fufpected it not in others, and faw with Pleafure the fair Profpect his beloved Daughter had of making her Fortune fo much above what he ever could have expected for her, fo that the Count *de Anglia* found no Difficulty of obtaining Permiffion to vifit her ; fhe received his Addreffes as they were authoriz'd by her Father, with Sweetnefs ; and if fhe found nothing in him to infpire her with a violent Paffion, fhe looked on that he profeffed for her as an Honour which fhe could not too gratefully acknowledge.

Thus for a Time did every thing go on in a fmooth Channel, and Count *Richard* had not the leaft Room to fear the Succefs of his Defigns ; 'tis certain indeed that had they been carried on with fomewhat more Privacy, they had not met with the Impediment they did : But the intended Marriage between fo great a Man and the Daughter of *Simplicius,* becoming the general talk, there were not wanting fome who took the Liberty of faying to all her Friends, they wifh'd the young Lady was not going to be made as miferable as fhe expected to be happy. On this a farther Enquiry was privately made into the Count's Character, and many aftonifhing Accounts of his Debaucheries, ill Management, and ill Humour were daily brought to the Family of *Simplicius.* Dazzled with the Grandeur of Equipage and Title, and deceived by an exterior Profeffion of Honour ; at firft they faw not the Vices hid beneath fo fair a Covering, but general Report,

H   backed

backed with very ſtrong Circumſtances, now making them more cautious, the virtuous Father reſolved to be aſſured there was a thorough Reformation of Manners before he conſented to the Marriage, flattering as it was in Appearance: He would not however raſhly reject ſuch an Offer, but behaved with ſomewhat more Coolneſs to the Count, and order'd her Daughter to do the ſame, ſometimes pretending ſhe was abroad when he came, or that being indiſpoſed, ſhe could not receive his Viſit. This Alteration was viſible enough to the impatient Lover, and fearing ſome Accident might intervene to diſcover the Deception he had been guilty of, preſſed more eagerly than ever for the Completion of his Wiſhes, and became at laſt ſo very importunate, that *Simplicius* was obliged to anſwer him in this manner: *My Lord*, ſaid he, *I am as ſenſible as I ought to be, and as any Man of my Circumſtances can be, of the Honour of your Lordſhip's Alliance, but I ſee no Occaſion for hurrying up the Affair——my Daughter is yet very young, and Perſons of her Age are uncertain in their Affections—— I therefore think it would be better to wait, till a more perfect Knowledge of your good Qualities has fixed in her thoſe Sentiments, which are neceſſary make you both happy.*

It is not to be doubted, but that a Man ſo bent on the Gratification of his Paſſion as was Count *Richard*, ſaid every thing he could to make *Simplicius* more compliable, but the Merchant was reſolved, and all his Rhetorick had no Effect :——After this he uſed his utmoſt Efforts to prevail on the young Lady to marry him

him privately ; he complained to her of the little Sense she had of his Passion : Accused her Father of forgetting in Age the Warmth by which Youth is instigated ; and swore he could not live in so cruel a Suspence. What her Heart felt on this Occasion I will not pretend to say : but this was evident, that whatever Tenderness she felt for him, the perfect Obedience she had for her Father's Commands exceeded it.

Finding the same turn of Mind both in Father and Daughter, and that though his Addresses were far from being rejected by either, yet that they equally wanted to gain Time, he began to suspect that they had received some Intelligence of his Lady's being living, and therefore waited till they should be more certainly informed as to that Point.——He knew very well that by sending to *** they would easily be convinced of the Truth, and as that would be the total destruction of his Hopes, had recourse to a Stratagem, worthy of himself, to assure the Accomplishment of them.

He employed two Fellows, who were Dependents on him, to watch her wherever she went, till they should find an Opportunity to seize on her, and bring her to him, and they executed their Commission with Facility enough. After waiting two or three Days without Time and Place concurring with the Enterprize, they saw her just at the Close of Day go out of her Father's with only a little Foot-boy to attend her ; she was going to make a Visit at a Friend's House three or four Streets off, and had Occasion to pass through a pretty dark and narrow Passage in her Way to it ; here they

stopped

stopped her, and one of them putting his Handkerchief to her Mouth to prevent her crying out, forced her along with him to the Extremity of the Alley, where a Hackney-Coach happening to be, he thruft her into it. The other all the Time kept the Boy in the Place where they firft met, that he might not fee what was done with his Lady, and when he thought his Companion had carried her off let him go, and made the beft of his Way to the Count's, where he found the Prize they had been in Chace of, was juft brought in before him.

It would be in vain to go about to reprefent the Father's Agony when the Boy's return informed him of this Rape, or the Daughter's Terror, firft in finding herfelf in the Power of a Man fhe knew not, and afterwards in that of one who had fo violent a Paffion for her, and who fhe might well think wculd not have proceeded thus far without having fome Defign againft her Virtue.

Simplicius privately omitted nothing to difcover the Ravifhers; but as he little fufpected Count *Richard* was the Perfon, endeavour'd to conceal what had happened from his Knowledge; and when he came to vifit her, as he did the very next Day, in order to prevent all Thoughts from arifing on his Account, he was only told that fhe was gone to pafs a few Days with a Relation a little way out of Town. Every thing thus favouring his Defigns, he kept the young Lady exceeding clofe, but treated her with the extremeft Refpect, laying the Blame of what he had done intirely on the Force of his Paffion, and the cruel Delays he

had

had met with in his honourable Pretensions;
but all he could say was effectually to remove
her Apprehensions: She wept Night and Day,
and still entreated him to let her return home.
This he told her was the only thing he could
prevail with himself to refuse her, as she had
asked it without Hope of being granted, she
could not be surprized her Petition had no
better Effect, yet she still continued to renew
it, perhaps for the sake of Form; for by degrees her Apprehensions grew less formidable
than they had been, and she became more easy.
She had always looked on the Person of the
Count with favourable Eyes----as she had not
conversed much with any of her Sex, she saw
not in his Behaviour that want of Delicacy
which some Ladies would have despised him
for---In fine, she rather lov'd him than hated
him----Then his Quality had Charms for her
which she could not resist, and his Excess of
Affection she thought demanded some Return.
She began to repent her having paid too great
an Obedience to what now seemed to her the
Caprice of a Father; and had the Count now
pressed her to Marriage without his Consent, she
doubtless would have yielded. But this subtle
Lover perceiving the Advantage he hourly
gained over her, evaded any Discourse of that
kind, yet still continu'd to tell her he could
not live without her — that she was the only
Woman he ever did, and ever could love; and
ply'd her incessantly with Oaths, Tears, Prayers, mingled with the most hyperbolical Encomiums on her Beauty---Would sometimes,
as if he knew not what he did, and was transf-

H 3

ported

ported out of himself, snatch the most ardent Kisses from her Lips and Breast; then feigning he condemned his Passion as guilty of too great Presumption, fall on his Knees imploring her Forgiveness. ——The Pardon granted, he again offended; and then again repeated the Offence—still every time encroaching farther, till he arrived at the most dangerous Liberties.——Angry she was, but, alas, her Resentment was short-liv'd: He had the Artifice by new Submissions to alleviate new Transgressions, and became more emboldened as she grew more softened —— that timid Modesty, which is one of the surest Guards of Virtue, by degrees wore off; and by being accustom'd to pardon those tumultuous Marks of his Passion, she began to think they stood in need of none, and by her Eyes confessed she was not displeased with them: He watched the melting Moment, and to one Freedom added greater still, till he pursued his Temerity to the full Gratification of all luxurious Love can covet.

It may, perhaps, seem strange that a Man of his Humour, and having the Object of his Desires so fully in his Power, should not without any Ceremony have seized at once the Joys he languished for, and saved himself the Trouble of these Artifices which but Step by Step made him the Master of them. With any other Woman he doubtless would have acted in that manner; but he really loved *Anadea* with a Passion which would not suffer him to be content with Favours from her obtained by Force, and in which her own Inclinations had not some part.

She

She after this proposed to him what he had often done to her, being united for ever by a private Marriage; but tho' he loved her still, he was now in the Possession of all she could give him, and found no Necessity for Forms to secure it to him without some other Consideration. He therefore told her, that as her Father was extremely rich, that it would be for their mutual Advantage to oblige him to give a Portion with her, which might clear his Estate of some Incumbrances at present on it, through the ill Conduct of the late Baron, and the unkind Testament of the Count. These two Articles, which she knew to be Truth, made her readily promise to join with him in any Method that might gain her Father's Consent.

Count *Richard* was extremely glad to have brought her to this Point; and as he was in reality so much distressed for Money, that he would have married any Woman with a Portion, he chose to have it with *Anadea* rather than any other. That which was once necessary for his *Passion*, was now so for his *Interest*; and he went about obtaining it by ways pretty extraordinary, but which seemed to him most likely to succeed, and which are not greatly to be wondered at in a Man of his Arrogance.

He prevailed with *Anadea* to write a Letter of his dictating to her Father, the Contents of which were as follow :

H 4

To

To Monfieur SIMPLICIUS.

Moft dear and Honoured Sir,

IT is with Shame, tho' not Repentance, I
confefs my Tendernefs and Gratitude for
my dear Count got the better of my Duty to
you, and all other Confiderations whatever.——
That Coldnefs you commanded me to treat him
with, on Surmifes which I am convinced had
not the leaft Foundation of Truth, had like
to have been fatal to us both——neither of
us could fupport it, and we agreed to throw off
that cruel Conftraint——My pretended Rape was
with my own Confent, only a feign'd Force
was ufed to take off all Sufpicion from my
Lord, to whom I directly went, and have ever
fince continued with him : As all this was
done only with a view of engaging your Confent to what you have no reafon but to embrace
with Joy, I flatter myfelf you will no longer
refufe it, fince in doing fo you will render for
ever miferable her who wifhes to be hencefor-
ward

Your *moft obedient Daughter,*

ANADEA.

This he inclofed in another from himfelf,
the Words whereof were thefe :

To

To Monſieur SIMPLICIUS.

SIR,

AS you are not yet old enough to forget the Warmth of thoſe Deſires incident to Youth, that Remembrance will, I dare anſwer, influence you to pardon both your lovely Daughter and myſelf—If what we have done can be called a Crime, I beg you will reflect it was wholly owing to your cruel delaying that Union we mutually deſired. I had a ſincere Inclination for your Alliance; the Flame I had for *Anadea* was no leſs pure than her own Virgin Thoughts; yet you, as my dear Girl has ſince inform'd me, on ſome idle Stories invented, perhaps, by thoſe who envied you, wanted Time to conſider whether I were worthy of the Bleſſing I aſpired to——I mention not this to reproach you, I have too much Reſpect for the Father of my *Anadea*; but, Sir, it was a ſtrange and ill-tim'd Caution, and, were I of the Temper of ſome Men, might have proved the Ruin of your Daughter; but I ſtill love and adore her, have a Regard for you, and for my own Honour. —I wiſh nothing more than to call her mine by thoſe Ways which Heaven has ordain'd; but as I am at preſent circumſtanced cannot marry without ſome Money—I ſhall deſire no more than what the Exigence of my Affairs juſt now require, and what you can very well afford to give her without any prejudice to your other Children. Five thouſand Crowns will be of infinite Service to me at this Time, and as you must be certain, nothing but the extremest Passion could induce a Man of my Quality to marry with so trifling a Dower, you may be as certain that nothing but a pressing Occasion could make me ask any thing at all of you. Consider then, Sir, how we stand at present—your Daughter's eternal Happiness, Reputation and Peace of Mind depend upon your Answer; and do not by an ill-judg'd Resentment, which would neither avail you nor prejudice me, slight the Offer I now make—— What is done can never be undone—it lies on you to render it the Glory or the Infamy of your Family, and I doubt not but you will have good Sense enough to choose the former of these two, and also to believe, that in leaving it to your Option, I acquit myself both to God and Man of all Blame in this Affair. The sooner you resolve, the sooner your Daughter's Character will be cleared from all Aspersions which may be thrown upon it; and as I desire her Vindication equal with my own, I shall think every Hour an Age till I am her lawful Husband, which Tie will bind me to stile myself,

Your most obedient Son,

as well as humble Servant,

R. DE ANGLIA.

Let any one who is a Parent judge what *Simplicius* must feel at the Receipt of these two Letters.

Letters. To find that the Count *de Anglia*, who had profeſt ſo honourable a Paſſion for his Daughter, was the Raviſher who had ſtole her, and that by her Confeſſion ſhe had been acceſſory to her own Rape, were ſuch equal Matters of Aſtoniſhment to him, that it is hard to ſay at which he wonder'd moſt. That Grief too which had never left his Heart ſince the Loſs of *Anadea*, was now greatly heigh-tened by perceiving that ſhe had loſt even the Shame of her Condition, and durſt not only avow it, avow it to a Father who, ſhe knew, deteſted Infamy much more than Poverty, but alſo mention it as a trivial Error, a Fault ſhe even pretended no Repentance for. All this was ſo ſhocking to his honeſt Nature, that he could ſcarce ſupport it; but however, taking Prudence for his Guide, tho' he had much leſs Tenderneſs for his Daughter than before this Accident happened, yet he ſtill had too much for the Reputation of his Family, not to be willing to repair it, if by any means he could——

He was ſtrangely divided in what manner he ſhould proceed: He had been lately told, by ſeveral People that the Counteſs *de Anglia* was really living; others, deceived by the Report the Count had cauſed to be ſpread, aſ-ſured him ſhe was dead——It would require Time to be aſcertained of the Truth, and the Honour of *Anadea* would ſuffer no Delay—— She might poſſibly become pregnant, and Marriage after that would be ineffectual to re-trieve her Fame; beſides the Count's Mind might change, and ſhe was then inevitably loſt.

It

It seemed also unlikely to him, that a Person of so high a Rank would expose himself so far, whatever other Vices he might be guilty of, as to marry a second Wife while the former was in being, who could not long be kept in ignorance of the wrong done to her, and would doubtless assert her Right, to the Confusion of her perfidious Husband: It therefore seemed best to him to comply with their Request, and give both the Money demanded of him, and a free Pardon for what was past ; yet being willing to have as little as possible to reproach himself with on this Occasion, he required the Count to give his Oath before a Magistrate, that there was no Woman living that had any Claim to him as a Husband. Alas! he little knew that the Person he had to deal with considered the most solemn Vows no more than Words of course, and would have made and broke ten thousand for half the Sum he now expected. He went with the same Unconcern that Innocence itself could have done on such an Occasion, and in the presence of several of the Friends of *Simplicius* took the most sacred Oath that Words could form, that he was never married but once, and that the Lady to whom he had been thus engag'd was no longer in the World.

This done, *Simplicius* paid him five thousand Crowns, and the Marriage was solemnized in a very publick manner, many Relations of the Bride being Witnesses of it ; after which, for till she was a Wife, the still anxious Father could not be prevailed upon to see his Daughter, he gave them both his Blessing, and wished them lasting Happiness, tho' as he since fince declared he little expected they would find it. He lived not however to fee the fad Reverfe in the Count's Behaviour, or the Miferies that afterward befel his Daughter; but his Family had fufficient Reafon to regret the Alliance, and to be afhamed of what at firft they had looked on as an Honour.

For fome Years fhe was treated with the Refpect due to her fuppofed Dignity; and the Count continued to have that regard for her; that having fome Reafon to fear his firft Wife might be troublefome, he employed a Perfon, of whofe Fidelity to him, and good Underftanding, he had Reafon to be convinced, to treat with her, and offer her a pretty large Sum of Money to quit all Claim to him. That poor lady being left in a very indifferent Condition at his parting with her, and now knowing him too well to wifh to live with him any more, wifely accepted the Propofal, and gave it under her Hand never to moleft him with any Woman whatever.

As the Count never before had any Children that he could depend on were his own, and had now three by *Anadea*, it may be fuppofed they contributed not a little toward preferving his Affection for their Mother; but the natural Inconftancy of his Nature at laft prevailed, he grew weary of the Charms he had once fo much adored : He not only wrong'd her Bed with Women of the moft abandon'd Characters, but alfo treated herfelf as a common Proftitute.—As a Sanction for his own profligate Behaviour, he accufed her of having been falfe to him — grew by degrees to deny her even

Clothes

Clothes and Pocket-money.——abuſed all her Relations, pretended they carried on her Intrigues; and at laſt went ſo far as to deny his Marriage with her, tho' it was impoſſible for any thing to have better Teſtimonials. What brought him to uſe her with this Height of Barbarity, was a ſtrange Affection he had taken for a Woman who had not any Qualification to recommend her to a Man of the leaſt Share of Senſe or Delicacy in his Pleaſures; but was Miſtreſs of a conſummate Impudence, and, 'tis ſaid, made the Price of her Favour his ill Uſage of his Wife. Whatever it was, happening to come home one Evening more early than was his Cuſtom, and finding his Wife abroad, he enquired where ſhe was gone, and was told the Chariot was ordered to her Brother's; on which he went directly thither, fell upon her in the groſſeſt Terms, quarrell'd with her Brother, ſearched the Houſe for a Gallant he pretended ſhe came to meet there, drew his Sword upon the Servants, and behaved like a Man bereft of Reaſon; when in reality this Paſſion was all put on, and only the Prelude to his turning her out of his Houſe for ever, which he did that ſame Night, without ſuffering her to take any of her Jewels, Trinkets, or even wearing Apparel, but what ſhe had upon her Back.

On this cruel Uſage ſhe complained to the Biſhop of the Dioceſe, who was her very good Friend, and at whoſe Houſe it was ſhe firſt had the Misfortune to ſee him : He aſſured her of his Protection, as did alſo ſeveral other Perſons of the greateſt Diſtinction. The Count

was

was highly condemn'd by every Body, and some there were who took the liberty to speak pretty sharply to him on this Account, which so enrag'd him, that he sent his Footman to her with a Message by word of Mouth, importing, That if ever she dared to complain or even mention their Separation as an Act occasioned by any thing but her own ill Conduct, he would turn her Children out of Doors, and declare them Bastards. To this she return'd for Answer, That she was entirely free from all Apprehensions on that Score, for he very well knew she could prove her Marriage. This so incensed him, that he obliged the same Messenger to go back and tell her, She would find herself no more than a Concubine, for he had another Wife who had a prior Claim. Such a Menace, which to make good he must proclaim himself the basest and most perjur'd of Mankind, made her conclude he was really mad, and that she ought not to feed his Frenzy by any further Replies.

After this there was nothing of Ill he did not accuse her of being guilty of, tho' perhaps few Women have fewer Vices or more Virtues than this unhappy Lady; but her own pathetick Words can best express her Character, in a Letter she wrote to a Gentleman who had been a Receiver of Rents to the Baron *de Altemont,* as also to her own cruel Lord. It was in Answer to one from him, condoling her on this unhappy Turn in her Affairs.

To Monsieur AMICO.

SIR,

HOW great a Cordial Pity is to Diftrefs,
your obliging Letter has convinc'd me——
Many there are who feem'd to *idolize* me in
Profperity, now throw *Contempt* on my *Affliction;* but thank Heaven I have a Soul capable of difdaining fuch ungenerous Treatment——yet they fee the Injuftice which has
brought it on me more plainly than you can
do at the Diftance you are——But you indeed
are better acquainted with the Temper of my
perfidious Lord, and therefore may with the
greater Eafe acquit me in your Mind of the
Crimes he has the Barbarity to accufe me of.
——O Sir, what Words can paint——nay, what
Heart but mine that feels it, can conceive the
Calamity I labour under !——to be turn'd out
of Doors, ftript of every thing, abandon'd to
the Charity of my Friends even for Bread,
would be the leaft of my Troubles, were they
not inflicted on me by a Husband——a Husband
whom I have loved with the moft tender and
fincere Affection.——But to be torn from my
Children, to have thofe dear Babes expofed
to the cruel Ufage of a Wretch who triumphs
in their Mother's Place, this is what I can
fcarce fupport; yet is not this the worft,——my
Reputation, dearer to me than Husband——
Children——all the World——my Reputation, Sir, is ftruck at——the moft innocent
Actions of my Life cenfur'd, and reprefented as Crimes, fuch as I never had even
                                                          an

an Idea of. ——You have been Witneffes of my Behaviour for fome Years, have feen with what Submiffion I have borne all the perverfe Humours of my Lord——how little I regarded any Company but him——how happy I have been whenever I faw him pleafed————how much I have endeavoured to divert him when difquieted——In fine, it was my whole Study to render him content——and now to be thrown off——vilify'd——fcorn'd, turn'd out to Beggary and Shame, was ever any beloved Husband fo unjuft, fo inhumane! was ever any faithful Wife fo truly miferable!—— What I fhall do, I know not——both am I to commence a Profecution, yet how fhall I avoid it without giving room for the World to believe me as ill as I am reprefented——If he has another Wife, as I am apt to believe he faid but too true in that, for Heaven's fake inform me of it——you who are in the fame Kingdom cannot be ignorant of that Fact—— your Advice will be Charity to a helplefs, friendlefs, innocent Woman, who never knowingly did hurt to any one in the world, yet who is made by him, who ought to be her Protector, the moft forlorn Wretch breathing. —— Continue to commiferate my Condition, to pray for me, and to write to me, who, in what State foever I am, can never be but the Friend of fo honeft a man. There yet may come a Time in which I may more teftify my Gratitude, till then, accept the Thanks of

Yours fincerely,

A. de Anglia.

Nothing

Nothing could be more deplorable, and indeed more critical, than the Case of this injured Lady. The Count now openly declared he was never married to her, tho' besides the Register, there were yet many living Witnesses who had been present at the Solemnity——Easy was it for her to prove herself his Wife, but then she trembled for her Children, who were entirely in his Power, and whom, if he turn'd out, she had do means of supporting. And then again, should it be true, as she now much feared it was, that there was a prior Wife in being, she could have no Claim even to the Title or Name she now enjoy'd, and her Children would be proved illegitimate, tho' born in Wedlock and of a virtuous Mother——both she and them, tho' innocent, must have borne all the Scandal of Guilt, without any other Recompence than the poor Satisfaction of recording Infamy on a Man who seem'd dead to all Sense of that as well as of Honour, choosing either indifferently, as it served his Avarice or the Gratification of his sensual Appetite. These Considerations oblig'd her to lie still under her load of Woes, while the inexorable Count was so far from pitying, that he seem'd to take a malicious pleasure, or at least in flattering that of his Mistress, in glorying in the Wrongs he did her, and making her Distress the daily Subject of the most scurrilous Mirth in all Companies.

That shameless and wicked Woman for whose sake the unfortunate *Anadea* had been thus treated, did not however long triumph in her successful Mischief : he grew as weary of
                                               her

her Impudence as he had been of the other's
Modesty, but she bore not her Fate in the
same manner; after he had put her out of his
House and forbid her ever entring it more,
she came in his Despite, would burst into the
Room when she heard Company was with
him, overturn the Tables, reproach him with
having promised her Marriage, and call him
by such Names as he indeed deserved, tho' not
from her.———A Termagant by Nature, and
audacious by a low Education, she regarded
neither Threats nor Blows, both which she return'd with so much Force, that sometimes
the Servants were obliged to come to the Af-
sistance of their batter'd Lord. He got her several times put into the House of Correction;
but she was no sooner at Liberty than she renewed her Affronts, would frequently break
his Windows, and raise such Mobs about his
Door, that his House seem'd rather a common
Brothel than the Dwelling of a Nobleman.

To get rid of this Plague, as well as of the
daily Remonstrances made him by all the
sober part of his Acquaintance on *Anadea's*
account, he prepared to leave that Kingdom
and return to *****; but before he did so, he
was in a manner compell'd by the Bishop and
some of the Nobility, who join'd with that
Prelate in so good a Work, to settle Pensions
on the three Children, who were all Daugh-
ters, he had by *Anadea*, but could not be prevail'd upon to see their Mother or do any
thing for her. What a Complication of unprecedented, barefaced Cruelty, Ingratitude and
Perjury, was there shewn in his Behaviour to
this

this Lady ! But it feem'd, as if flufh'd with the Succefs of his unnatural Defign againft his Nephew, he had fince not thought it wort his while even to diffemble the leaft Propenfit to *Good*, but went on in a continued Series o all manner of Crimes, without the leaft Regard to Decency or Reputation.

Soon after his Return to that Kingdom of which he was a Native, he gave an Inftance of Mean-fpiritednefs, which is fcarce to be equal'd among the loweft Rank, I hope much lefs among his own. He received Intelligence from the *Weft* that the Countefs *de Anglia* his firft Wife was dead, and that by her prudent Management of the Sum he had given her in order to prevent her from difturbing him in his new Choice, joined to the Acceffion of fome Legacies from Relations, fhe had left behind her to the Amount of between five and fix thoufand Crowns, on which, greedy of getting that Money into his Poffeffion, he pofted down directly, and took out Letters of Adminiftration to that Wife whom he had renounced and abjured in the moft folemn manner.

Strange Example of mingled Meannefs and Effrontery ! who but himfelf would not have fcorn'd to have deprived the furviving Relatives of that poor Lady of that Pittance her Frugality had faved, perhaps to recompence at her Death thofe who had been kind to her in Life ? ——Who but himfelf would not have been afhamed to have feen any of thofe who were of the Kindred, or even of the Acquaintance of a Lady he had fo greatly wronged ?
But

But this must be said of him, that his *Pride*
never hinder'd him from descending to any thing
by which he could be in the least a Gainer;
nor his *Modesty* from imagining that every
thing he did was becoming him.

In this manner did the titular Count *de Anglia* disgrace the Dignity he had assum'd,
while the real Owner, amidst all the Toils of
a cruel Slavery, lamented nothing so much as
the want of Opportunity to improve those Talents he had received from God and Nature,
that he might do honour to it. But the Time
was now at hand when the Contrast between
them should be seen, as well as those dark
mysterious Projects brought to Light, by
which the artless Innocence of the one had
been betray'd, and the Treachery of the other
so long successful.

The Chevalier *James*, now no more a Slave,
took his Passage in a Merchant's Vessel to *Jamaica*, where being safely arrived he found a
Fleet of Ships of War riding in the Port ; as
he heard one of them was shortly to set sail
for *Europe*, he enter'd himself on board it as
a common Sailor, having neither Money nor
Recommendations to be received in any other
Capacity ; but he had been too long inured to
Labour to think this a Hardship, especially
when it contributed to bring him each Moment nearer to the Place he so much had
wish'd to see.

He had not been many days on board before
he observed one of the Officers look'd very
earnestly upon him whenever he happen'd to
come in his Way ; and he also imagin'd he had
                                        seen

seen a Face resembling that of this Gentleman,
but could not recollect when nor where; till
the other put him out of all Suspence on this
Score.

He was on the Forecastle with some others
of the Ship's Crew, when he heard a Voice
from the Quarter-deck cry, *Here! — you Sailor in the blue Jacket.* None present having
such a one but himself, he ran immediately to
the Person who call'd. *What is your Name,
honest Friend?* said the Officer. *James de
Altamont,* reply'd the Chevalier. He then
ask'd him if he were not at a School he nam'd
to him. At which Question the Chevalier
look'd more earnestly upon him, and now remembring him, *Yes, Sir,* reply'd he, *I was at
that School you mention, and if I am not very
much mistaken, you are* Chavigny, *who was
there at the same time.* At these Words the
Officer lifted up his Hands and Eyes in token
of Astonishment. *Great God,* cry'd he, *what
Miracle is this! if you are* James de Altamont,
*Son to the Baron of that Name, how happen'd
it that you so long since were reported dead?—
Where have you been conceal'd?——Why so
long lost to the World?—By what Chance does
your Uncle* Richard *enjoy your Title and Estate
while you are in this Station?* The Chevalier,
who at the beginning of these Exclamations
was endeavouring to restrain some Tears just
ready to start from his Eyes at the Remembrance of the Barbarity excercis'd against him,
was rouzed to a kind of Fury at the latter
part of them. *My Uncle* Richard, *the Monster,*
cry'd he; *he enjoy my Title and Estate! Is
then*

then the Baron dead? The Officer then told him that he was, and the Time in which he died; which the Chevalier finding correspond exactly with that in which he was trepan'd to Slavery, made him cry out, *O Heaven, can there be such Villiany in Man!* The Officer then made him come into the State-Cabin, and having heard all his Adventures in the same manner as they are here set down, recounted to him those of the Chevalier *Richard,* now call'd Count *de Anglia,* as he had heard them reported by the general Voice ; in which the Chevalier *James,* in spite of the little Acquaintance he had with the great world, found so much to despise, that he could not forbear frequently interrupting the Narrative, by saying, *Is it possible a Man who has had the Advantages of Education can descend to such mean Actions!*

The Conversation between these two lasted a considerable Time, and the Officer assur'd him he would speak to the Captain that he might make his Voyage in a different manner from what he expected when he came on board. He was going immediately out of the Cabin to perform his Promise, when recollecting himself, *Hold,* said he, *now I remember the young Chevalier* James de Altamont *had a very particular Mark about him, which I have often taken notice of when we happen'd to wash together——not that I doubt you are the Person, the Lineaments of your Face and the Account you give of your self, assure me of it ; but if you have that Mark, it may serve to corroborate the rest, and be a Conviction to others as well as myself.* The Chevalier immediately

mediately ſtript and gave him the ſight of this
indelible Proof, which the other no ſooner beheld than he embraced him, ſaying, *There*
needs no more———you are the real Chevalier
James de Altamont—*the true Count* de Anglia!

With this he went directly and made the
Captain acquainted with this ſurpriſing Story,
who being of noble Blood himſelf was the
more affected with it——He alſo was no Stranger to the Character of the preſent Court,
and it therefore ſeem'd to him not the leaſt
improbable that he ſhould have been guilty of
ſuch an Action ; he deſired the Officer would
bring this injured Nobleman into his Cabbin
that ſame Evening, being willing to hear
from his own Mouth ſome farther Particulars
of his Sufferings.

The Chevalier's Friend gladly obey'd this
Injunction of his Captain, and it was now
our new enfranchiſed Slave found himſelf
treated like what he was, not what he appeared: The Officers of the Ships of War of that
Nation theſe were, as they are the Defence
and Glory of their Country by their Bravery,
ſo are they the Honour of their Court by
their Humanity and Politeneſs : The noble
Commander liſtened to a Tale ſo full of
Wonders with Admiration ; and when he
ſometimes interrupted the Chevalier in the
Courſe of it by ſome Queſtions, which teſtified his Curioſity of being informed of the
minuteſt Circumſtances of his Life, he always
intreated his Pardon for it. Nor was this
Behaviour owing merely to Complaiſance.
The Adventures he heard, tho' delivered in a
plain

plain Manner, without any Ornaments of Language to excite the Paffions, being dictated by Truth, and uttered with a Boldnefs infeparable from it, ftole more effectually into the Heart than the moft elegant Fable could have done. ——The Captain and all prefent *admired* the *Virtues* and *pitied* the *Hardfhips* of the illuftrious Sufferer: Every one feemed to emulate the other in fhewing the Senfe he had of both; but young *Chavigny*, for fo was he called, who had been School-fellow with the Chevalier, was quite tranfported with having been the lucky Difcoverer of him.

'Tis not to be doubted but that the Chevalier, new excufed from all the Duties for which he had entered himfelf on Board, paft the Night in a manner widely different from what he had done for a long Series of Years—His Repofe would now have been perfectly Tranquil, had it not been a little difturbed with the Reflection that all the Misfortunes fo commiferated by Strangers, had been brought upon him by thofe of his own Blood—it troubled him to think that in afferting the Rights of his Birth, he muft expofe and bring to Confufion the Brothor of his Father; and that a Family of which he had heard fo honourable Mention made, muft have a lafting Blemifh caft upon it by the vile Practices of one fo near a-kin to him—were thefe the Sentiments of a Slave! Could a Delicacy like this be expected from one thruft out from his Infancy and expofed to all the fervile Officers, Labours and Hardfhips of the moft bafely born!——where had he them?——Not from Education —not

I   from

from Example——— not from Conversation——— Heaven alone inspired them, and supplied every other Want, in order to make him worthy of enjoying the Dignity he was born to inherit.

His Virtues and Misfortunes which had acquired him these new Friends, made them more solicitous to serve him than generally those are of a longer standing ; and every thing so much contributed to prosper their Endeavours, that it seemed as if Fortune repenting of her Cruelties to the Chevalier, was now resolved to attone for them by being no less lavish in her Favours.

The Admiral who commanded the Fleet, was a Gentleman whose Character must suffer by any Description given of it ; yet it is impossible to make mention, or even to think on him, without touching on some of those great and amiable Qualities which make him seem as intended by Heaven for an Example of the true Dignity of human Nature———Inflexibly Good!——superior to Temptation——too Brave to be awed——too wise to be deceived——Justice and Glory were the sole Aim of all his Actions; and when he judged of others, it was not according to Prejudice or appearances——ever a steady Friend to Virtue though in Rags ——an implacable Enemy to Vice though clad in all the Pomp of vain luxuriant Pride.——— Zealous in his own Duties.———Stern, but not cruel to those he found remiss in theirs——— nothing was capable of souring him more than Flattery and Ostentation: He looked on both as Indications of a mean, a weak, or wicked Mind; and if ever he discovered a Peevish-

ness

nefs of Humour, it was when any one attempted to gain his Favour by Wordinefs or
exterior Shew.

To the Prefence of this Hero, who may be
truly faid to have rival'd, if not out-done (Circumftances confidered) all thofe of *Greece* or
Rome, did the Captain think proper to introduce his Noble Sailor. Early therefore in
the Morning he ordered out the Long-boat,
and went aboard the Admiral, to whom he
recited the whole Hiftory of the Chevalier
James de Altumont, and intreated Leave to
bring him. There was little need of Intercef-
fion; the Admiral had given an attentive Ear
to what was faid, and found by the Courfe of
fuch unprecedented Adventures, fo much in-
nate Generofity, Fortitude, and Patience in
the Perfon who paft through them, that he
was no lefs defirous of feeing him than the
other that he fhould do fo. This obtain'd
the Captain return'd well-pleafed to his own
Ship, and acquainted the other Officers and
the Chevalier with what he had done. The
perfect Knowledge every one there had of the
Admiral, made them affured he would not
defire to fee a Perfon whofe Conduct he did
not approve; and that he would not approve
without teftifying it by fomething more than
Words, in which he was always much more
fparing than in *Actions.* Thefe generous Officers had a Satisfaction in this thought, almoft equal with what the Chevalier felt himfelf: Among them they equipp'd him in fomewhat a better manner than the Habit he came
on board in; and the Time perfixed by the

Admiral for bringing him being arrived, he went with the Captain and *Chavigny*, who it was thought proper should go as a Witness for him, to wait on that illustrious Man, whose Name and Deeds were too much celebrated in those parts of the World, not to have fixed with Admiration a Mind so inquisitive after great Actions as was that of the Chevalier.

His Reception was more obliging than, perhaps, he would have met with if in Possession of the Title and Estate of *Anglia*; because there was a Pity joined to the Regard due to his Birth, which gave a double Softness to Complaisance itself: He had the Honour to be told by one who well knew how to distinguish, that there was more Praise belonged to him, who, by the Strength of his Virtue, knew how to bear Afflictions well, than to him that conquered Kingdoms by the Force of his Arms; *because*, said he, *the one is owing wholly to himself, and the other he is indebted for to the Courage of his Troops,*

On the Repetition of his Misfortunes, for the Admiral would needs hear them from his own Mouth, the manly Tear started into the Eyes of that great good Man, particularly when he mentioned the Distresses of his infant Years; and though he said nothing on the Behaviour of the Chevalier *Richard*, yet all his Gestures shewed how abhorrent it was to him.

When they were about to return to their own Ship, the Admiral desired he would draw up a Memorial in Form and present to him, which he would send a Copy of, in order that

that when he arrived at that Place where he could only hope Relief, his real Quality and unhappy Cafe might be known before he appeared there in Perfon.

This was doing all that could be done for him at fo greet a Diftance; and the Chevalier received the Obligation with all the Demonftrations of a moft fincere Gratitude. It was indeed too material an Article to be delayed, and the Captain made his Secretary that fame Day draw up the Memorial, and on the next delivered it to the Admiral, who fent it away immediately by a tender, and at the fame time feveral Letters to his Friends, as did alfo the Captain, and fome other of the Officers, with an Account of this remarkable Paffage.

The News of the Chevalier *James de Altamont* being living, and on his Return, arriving fome time before himfelf in both thofe Kingdoms where his Eftates lay——the falfe Count *de Anglia* had Reafon to be alarmed—he knew not which Way he fhould proceed, nor whofe Advice to ask——he feared being betrayed by the *bafe* part of his Acquaintance, and could not flatter himfelf that the *honeft* would ferve him in fo black an Affair. He was one Day alone, full of difturbed Meditations, when *Amico* came in, that *Amico* to whom the unfortunate *Anadea* had wrote fo melancholy an Account of her Situation; but as this Gentleman will bear fo great a Share in what remains of thefe Memoirs; it will be neceffary to give fome part of his Character.

I 3

He

He was well born, had a liberal Education, and a very great Capacity for Bufinefs: He had been extremely ferviceable to the late Baron, and alfo the prefent Count, in many intricate Affairs into which their Inadvertency had plunged them. He was never backward in his Endeavours to do good, and always zealous for the Caufe he promoted, but then he was ftrictly juft, and would be well affur'd before he undertook any thing, that he fhould have nothing hereafter to reproach himfelf with, or give occafion for others to do fo. He had known the *Altamont* Family feveral Years; and had a regard for them, in particular for the prefent Count, whofe Perfon he loved, though he hated his Vices, which he had not fcrupled frequently to reprimand him for, in a manner which he would have taken from no Perfon in the World lefs capable of ferving him; but he had fuch continual Occafions for his Affiftance, that he durft not difoblige nor break Acquaintance with him. *Amico*, 'tis certain, knew him a bad Man, but looked on his Vices as proceeding more from the Arrogancy and Impetuofity of his Nature, and the Example of fome profligate Perfons he converfed with, than from a confirmed Propenfity to any thing that was wile; and ftill hoped that Time and Experience would reform him. This worthy Man had heard, as well as others, that a real Heir to *Altamont* and *Anglia* was foon expected; and as at his firft Acquaintance with the Baron he had heard him mention a Son he had, which he had been obliged to conceal on the Account of
raifing

raifing Money by Leafes, as already mentioned, he had, fince the prefent Count's Affumption of thofe Titles, often afked him in Converfation, though without any Sufpicion of the Truth, in what Place, and of what Diftemper his Nephew died? and he now remembered, though when it happened he did not take Notice of it, that the Count always gave very flight Anfwers on that Head, and waved all Difcourfe of it as much as poffible. The Report there now was about Town very much furpriz'd him, and brought him to the Count in order to engage him to be more explicit on that Affair.

I hear ftrange News, my Lord, faid he, *what Perfon is this who is coming from Jamaica to call in queftion your Lordfhip's Title?* while he was fpeaking, he obferved a deadly Palenefs overfpread the Count's Cheeks; but recovering himfelf as well as he could, *I know not,* replied he, after a Paufe, *who or what the Impofture is; but an Impofture he muft be.* ———*I hope,* refumed the other, *your Lordfhip has had convincing Proofs of the Death of your Nephew, the young Chevalier* James? *Yes, yes, to be fure,* cried the Count, ftill more confufed.

Amico did not like the manner in which he looked, and willing to be more afcertained, put feveral pretty clofe Queftions to him concerning the exact Time and Place of that young Nobleman's Death; and at length went fo far as to tell him, that if he could not be very particular as to that Point, and find fufficient Vouchers for it, all the World would

look

look on this young Person as the lawful Heir, and himself no other than an Usurer. This so nettled the Count, that the Rashness of his Temper got the better of his Dissimulation, and he threw out at once a Design which he had then but roughly form'd, and too undigested to pass on a Man of *Amico's* Penetration. *Why then*, said he, *if you must know the Truth, I do not believe my Brother ever had a Son.* —————— *Ever had a Son!* cry'd *Amico*, surprized beyond Measure. *No*, resumed he, *not by his Wife.* —————— *And this Fellow that is coming over, if he is my Brother's Son, must be by one who was a Servant in the Family. But was there not a Son acknowledged by the Baron as egitimate?* demanded *Amico*. *My Brother, you know, was a weak Man*, said the Count; *but this is an Imposture, I tell you. It behoves your Lordship to prove him one*, cry'd *Amico*, very gravely, *as well as call him so; or your Affairs will be but in an indifferent Situation.* —————— *I do assure you, the World is strongly prepossest in his Favour. The World are Fools then*, said he, peevishly; and then began to talk of something else.——————*Amico* would fain have renewed the Conversation, but he artfully evaded it, and Company coming in, reliev'd him for that Time.

This good Man, however, could not be easy; he heartily wish'd the Count might be innocent, but very much fear'd he was the contrary: The more he heard of the Chevalier *James*, the more Reasons he had for believing he was that Son of whom he had heard the Baron speak, and whom he would have taken
home,

home, had he not been too much influenc'd by the Perfuafions of his fecond Wife *Helena* and her Relations. He had indeed heard his *Legitimacy* queftion'd by *them* on the Score of his *Mother*, but had never heard the leaft mention that he was born of any other than the *Baronefs* ; and the Count's now afferting, that he was not *her* Son, look'd very dark and fufpicious.

The wicked Count in the mean time having well confider'd the Scheme he was to go upon, found he had no other Game to play than boldly to deny that the Baronefs had ever been a Mother ; and remembring that his Brother had a Child by one of his Servants, he refolved to pafs the Chevalier for that Boy on whofe Milk the Chevalier was nourifhed : Having invented feveral Circumftances to give the beft Glofs he could to this improbable Story, he fent for *Amico*, and pretending now to fatisfy that Curiofity he had exprefs'd when they were laft together, repeated it to him, and added many Oaths and Imprications as a Confirmation of the Veracity of what he had faid. *Amico* knew not well whether he ought to believe or to rejeft the Account, therefore made but little Anfwer, and was determined within himfelf to fufpend his Judgment till he fhould have farther Light into the Truth.

At length that Ship of war which contain'd the Chevalier *James*, fafely arrived at her intended Port, and he had the Satisfaftion now to find himfelf in one of the fineft Kingdoms in the World, and that where lay the greateft

Part of thofe Domains he was the lawful Heir of. He made all imaginable hafte to the Capital, and having recieved his Difcarge from the High Admiral of the Navy, made it his next Bufinefs to enquire after thofe who were of his Father's Acquaintance. He was fo fortunate as to meet in a very fhort time with *Amico*, who no fooner had heard of his coming, than he had an Impatience to fee him. On being inform'd of the Time and Manner in which this young Nobleman had been fent to *America*, he no longer doubted the Treachery his wicked Uncle had been guilty of to him; but fearing to be too precipitate in an Affair of fuch Confequence, he would not fhew the Conviction he had within himfelf, but fpoke in this manner to the Chevalier. Sir, faid he, *I am inclinable to believe what you fay is Truth, and if I were even to be deceived fhould have no Reafon to be afhamed of my Credulity, having the Example of fo great and wife a Man as that Admiral whofe Credentials you bring; but it is my way never to affert any thing without having the moft fubftantial Proofs.——I will therefore make you an Offer, which, if you are the Perfon you pretend, it will not be for your Intereft to refufe—What I mean,* continued he, *is this, that you will put your felf under my Protection, and remain at my Houfe, where every thing convenient fhall be prepared for you, while I go to the Province where you were born, and procure fuch Teftimonials as may be convincing to the whole World as well as myfelf, that you are the real and lawful Son of the late Baron* de Altamont, *and born of the Baronefs*

his

his Wife——On this you may depend, added he, *that if I find you such, I will omit nothing that may forward your Establishment in those Rights derived to you from* God *and* Nature ; *but if, on searching into the bottom of this Mystery, you should be proved an Imposture, I shall be no less implacable in pursuing your Punishment.*

The Chevalier was extremely ready to put all his Hopes and Expectations on this Issue; but being too young when he was removed from *Altamont* to remember any Persons there, he told *Amico* he must be obliged wholly to his own Endeavours to find out the Testimonials which were necessary. This the other was sensible of, but thought to bring a Matter such as this was to Light, was very well worth all the Pains it would cost him, and therefore having taken the Chevalier home with him, began to prepare for his Journey.

The Count in the mean time no sooner heard that his injur'd Nephew was landed and come to the Capital, then he had his Spies in every Corner, to observe where and to whom he went: He could not therefore be ignorant that he had not only seen *Amico*, but was even a Lodger in his House; and as that Gentleman came not now to visit him as he was wont, doubted not but he had espoused the Cause of the Chevalier against him: This very much perplexed him, because he knew his Zeal and Integrity wherever he pretended a Friendship: but much more was he alarmed, when his Emissaries brought him Intelligence that he was about to take a Journey to *Altamont*. As
he

he had reason to dread the Informations that
might be gather'd there by a Person of *Amice's*
Sagacity, he began to call about in his Mind
for the Means of preventing his going, and being able to find no other, he caused him to be
arrested for an imaginary Debt, of a very large
Sum, and while he was in Confinement difpatch'd two or three of his Creatures to the
Province where the Chevalier was born, with
Orders to endeavour either to deter or buy off
all those who might be Evidences for him.

It was but two Days before *Amice* found
Bail and regain'd his Liberty, after which he
immediately set out; the Count's Agents however having got the Start of him, were busy in
executing their Commission, as he heard after
his Arrival.

As the Count himself had mention'd to him
the Name of the Woman whose Son he pretended the Chevalier was, he thought he could
not at first addrefs to a more proper Person;
to this end having enquired her out, he went
to a House of Entertainment near the Place
where she lived, and sent for her; but the
Messenger not finding her at home, he bethought himself of examining the Church Register in order for the Nativity: The Clerk
not being in the way, the Sexton hearing a
strange Gentleman had sent, came to ask what
Commands he had, saying he had been an old
Parishoner, and could inform him in any thing
he wanted to know as well as the Clerk or
even the Parson himself. *Amice* then question-
ed him about the Birth of a Son of the late
Baron *de Altamont*, and told him he wanted
to

to fee the Regifter. On which the Fellow readily anfwer'd, *that he remember'd the Birth of the young Baron very well, but could not be pofitive as to the Day of the Month; and that there was no Regifter kept there.* This troubled *Amico*; but as it was unavoidable, muft content himfelf with fuch Evidences as were to be had. The Sexton then added, that one *Juggan*, a Woman that lived hard-by, might poffibly remember the exact Time, becaufe fhe had nurfed him. *Amico* imagining that fhe would more readily come if this Fellow went to her, after having won his Heart by feveral Glaffes of good Liquor, defired he would do him that friendly Office as to bring her. The Sexton prefently ran to her Houfe and found her at home, but in a very great Terror, the Occafion of which was this:

Two Men, the Emiffaries which the Count had fent down, had been with her that fame Day, and having been very inquifitive concerning the Birth of the Chevalier *James*, to which Queftions fhe had anfwered with Truth and Integrity, they told her fhe was a Mad-woman, that there was never any fuch Child as the Chevalier *James*, and that it was her own Son, and no other fhe had nurfed. This Difcourfe ftrangely amazed the Woman, and fhe cry'd out, *What! will you perfuade me I had not the fweet young Baron to my Breaft a whole Year and a half, and did he not ftay under my Care for two Years more——long after my own poor Baby died?* On this one of them told her, that if fhe talk'd at this Rate the Count *de Anglia* would have her taken up and punifh'd;

nish'd; and the other pulling out a Purse of Gold, cry'd, *Don't be your own Enemy Mrs. Juggan, my Lord makes you a Present of this, and will take Care of you as long as you live, if you will be of our Party, and swear you know of no Child the Baron had by his Wife* ——*besides,* added he, *it will do no good to say otherwise, for if there was any such Child he is dead long ago.* Ill take none of his Money, interrupted she, *nor I wont forswear myself for him nor a better Man*——*if my young Lord is dead, God rest his Soul, but I'll never deny him.* She spoke this with such an honest Assurance, that they despaired of gaining her over to their Purpose, so went muttering away. They had not long been gone before she began to think there was somewhat more than ordinary in this, and resolved to be seen no more by them if they should come again; so that on seeing the Shadow of a Man at the Door when the Sexton knock'd, believing they were return'd, she was just runing out of the House thro' a Back-door, that led into the Fields. The Man having just open'd the Door, for it did not happen to be lock'd, ran after her, and pull'd her back; *What is the Master,* Juggan? said he; *did you think I was coming to murder you?* No, reply'd he, trembling, *but I did not know but that somebody else might.* The Sexton laughed at her Fright, and then asked her to go along with him to a Gentleman that wanted to speak with her about the Chevalier *James.* This redoubled all her Apprehensions she doubted not but it was one of those who had been with her, and imagin'd she saw

a Knife

a knife already at her Throat.——The Sexton
affur'd her that the Perfon who wanted her
was a very fober good natur'd Gentleman, and
giving fome Defcription of him, which fhe
found different from the others, fhe at laft con-
fented, on condition he would not leave the
Room all the time fhe was there.

She foon, however, loft all her Fears a
Sight of *Amico*, and the manner of his Behaviour to her ; and prefently perceiving he was
not of the Count *de Anglia*'s Party, made no
Scruple of relating to him in what manner
fhe had been both tempted and menaced by
fome Perfons fent from him. *Amico* was not
furprized at the Account fhe gave of this Affair, and the Simplicity with which fhe told it
would have convinced him, if he had not been
fo before, of the Reality of the Chevalier
James's Claim : He ask'd her many Queftions
concerning the time of his Birth, which fhe
well remember'd, even to the Day of the
Week and Hour in which it happened.——She
told him alfo, that the Child fhe had by the
Baron, was born a little before the Baroneffes's
Arrival at *Altamont*, and that had he lived he
would have been about a Year and too Months
older than the Chevalier : And on his interro-
gating her on the Death of her own Child, fhe
anfwered without any Hefitation, that he died
fuch a Day, was burid at fuch a Place, and
even mentioned the Perfon of whom fhe bought
his Winding-fheet ; for in that Country all
are buried in Linnen. Having thus given all
the Satisfaction he required, and even more
than he expected, fhe asked him in her turn,
the

The Meaning of the Chevalier's Birth being
now called in question, since he had also been
dead a great many Years: On which *Amy*
removed the Mistake she had been in, gave
her the Motives which had induced the Baron at first to spread that Report, which the
Chevalier *Richard* afterwards confirm'd to
bring about his own ambitious Ends: and af-
sur'd her, that he was still living, and now
going to claim his Right. The poor Woman
was transported with this Intelligence, but
found she had more Reason than ever to be in
fear of the Chevalier *Richard*; (for she could
not, after hearing this, prevail on her self to
call him *Count*) as he had done so much to
gain the Title, it was highly probable he
would do yet more to secure it, and as he
found they could not make her a Friend, put
it out of her Power to be his Enemy; one Moment she rejoiced for her Foster-Child's Life,
the next she trembled for her own. *Amy*
suffer'd this Apprehension to settle it self in her
Mind, and when he perceived it had wholly
gain'd on her Timidity, which indeed she had
reason enough for, he told her that he would
take care she should not suffer for her Fidelity
to her young Lord, for she should go with
him to **** and be provided for as well as
himself. But he added, that he hoped she had
uttered nothing but the exact Truth; for she
must swear to all she had said before a Tribunal which was incapable of being imposed
upon, and if she swerved in the least Article,
would be sure to punish the Fallacy with a
great deal of Severity. The honest Creature
melted

melted into Tears at this feeming Doubt, and protefted that every thing fhe affirm'd was ftrictly true, that fhe would take a thoufand Oaths of it, and would not forfwear herfelf for the whole World.

Amico was forry to have given her this Concern, and comforted her as well as he could for it, by telling her, as fhe did not know perhaps the Nature of a Court of Judicature, efpecially fuch as fhe would appear before, and thefe were Facts which happened fome time ago, it was neceffary to prepare her, that fhe might confult her Memory, and neither add nor diminifh through Miftake or Forgetfulnefs.

After this they enter'd into farther Confultation how they fhould proceed for the Service of this injured Nobleman. *Juggan* faid, there were feveral Perfons in that Neighbourhood who could atteft the Truth of his Birth as well as herfelf; and it was therefore agreed fhe fhould talk to them of it as in a carelefs manner, and without the leaft mention that any Perfon was come into the County in fearch of Witneffes. This fhe fo well managed, that one who had been a Servant of the Family, and in the very Room when the Baronefs was deliver'd, declared the Matter in the Prefence of feveral People; another that had been fent by the Baron himfelf to acquaint an intimate Friend then in the Country, that his Wife had brought him a Son. In fine, tho', as it may be reafonably fuppofed in fuch a Space of Time, many who knew of the Chevalier's Birth were either dead or removed from that

Part

Part of the World, yet there were still a Cloud
of Witnesses remaining. *Amico* thought two
besides *Juggan* were sufficient to take with
him; and if Necessity required more, the
others might be subpoena'd afterwards. But
he took the Pains to hear what every one of
them had to say apart, and found their Testimonies agreed so exactly with each other, that
it was demonstrable their Words were dictated
by Truth.

Those two material Witnesses which he
thought proper to take with him, settled their
Affairs, as well as *Juggan*, in order for their
Journey; but during the Time the Preparations they had to make took up, the before-
mentioned Emissaries of the Count *de Anglia*
were constantly after *Juggan*, they spared neither Promises nor Threats to engage her to go
with them and make Oath, that she knew of
no Son that the Baron *de Altamont* ever had
by his Lady, and that the Person who was
call'd the Chevalier *James* was born of her
own Body; but she remain'd unmoved with
all they could say to her, any farther than to
be sometimes in most terrible Frights of their
doing her some mischief, and would never stir
out after it grew dark, nor go alone in any unfrequented Place.

The Count *de Anglia* was of that particular
Character, that he never took it into his Head
to undertake any thing, but he concluded it
done. Having put *Amico* under Confinement,
as I have already said, and sent Persons over
in order to corrupt the Honesty of *Juggan*,
he look'd on the Thing as compleated, and
had

had the Folly to tell all his Acquaintance, that he should foon prove the *Pretender* (for fo in Derifion he called the Chevalier *James*) an Impofture; for he had a Woman who would fwear he was her own Son. He judged of others by his own bad Heart, and doubted not but the Offers he had caufed to be made to her would bring her eafily into his Party. This Security heighten'd his Mortification when he received Letters from thofe Agents he had employed for that Purpofe, with an Account of the ill Succefs they met with, and alfo that *Amico* was there, very bufy in finding Witneffes, and that he had frequent Meetings for the Intereft of the Chevalier *James*, with feveral of the chief of that Province.

Our titular Count went now roaring about like a mad Bull, exclaiming againft *Amico*, inventing Millions of Falfhoods to blacken his Charafter, and threatning all who efpoufed the Caufe of the Chevalier with the fevereft Punifhments; but what did this Rage and Malice avail! It ferved to render him the Contempt of thofe of his own, and the Deteftation of all Degrees; for whether he had, or had not, any real Right to the Dignity he poffeft, he fo ill became it, that none except thofe whofe Penury, or natural Depravity of Manners, made them his Dependents or Companions, but would have feen him fall without Pity.

This, however, his Vanity kept him from forefeeing, and the good Opinion he had of his Perfon and Parts made him take that common Complaifance, which the Rank which

he

he at prefent held in a manner enforced from
the World, for a real Liking and Good will
towards him; and this very Self-fufficiency and
Conceit, occafioned him very frequently to do
things, which inftead of creating an Efteem
only ferved to render him more ridiculous.——
In a word, he was too much in Extremes,
and made ufe of fuch Hyperboiles in his Expreffions, as deftroyed all the Credit he attempted to gain. Thus in endeavouring to
blacken the Character of *Amico* he expofed his
own, by uttering Falfhoods of that Gentleman,
fo very palpable and abfurd, that the moft ordinary Capacity could not be impofed on by
them: But the Lofs of a Perfon whofe Friendfhip had in many Refpects been very ferviceable
able to him, and the Apprehenfions how much
the contrary his prefent Enmity might prove
in a Circumftance on which no lefs than his
All depended, was not the only Misfortune
which made him fuffer in his Mind fome part
of that Anxiety which ought to be one of the
Confequences of Crimes like his; and which,
had it proceeded from Remorfe, as it did from
Rage and Difappointment, would have deferved its Share of Compaffion.

A little before the unexpected Arrival of the
Chevalier *James*, being high in Spirits, and
exulting within himfelf that he had fo eafily
got rid of one Wife and buried another, he
began to think of getting a third, whofe Fortune might repair thofe Damages which inceffant-
fant Law-fuits and private Debaucheries had
done to his Eftate.

Arabella, the Daughter of a wealthy Merchant

:hant lately deceafed, was the Lady he fixed
his Eyes upon for this happy Purpofe.———
She was very lovely, had an unblemifh'd Reputation, and what far outweigh'd in the Balance of his Opinion all her other Charms,
was the Miftrefs of a large Fortune in her
own Poffeffion.——As fhe had been kept extremely clofe during her Father's Life, and
was herfelf of a Temper too referved to fee
much Company, he had the more hope that
the Amorous Pranks he had been guilty of had
not reached her Ears, as they had done thofe
of fome others who on that Score had rejected
his Addreffes. This made him fo fecure of
gaining her, that before he had even mention'd
a Word of his Intentions to her, or even been
in her Company, he began to calculate the
Ufe he would make of her Fortune, the Expence this Addition to his Family would be
to him, and the frugal Manner in which he
would oblige her to live. —— Having found
means to be introduced to her Acquaintance,
he foon declared his Pretenfions ; and becaufe
Difparity of Years fhould be no Bar to his Defigns, he affumed all the Gaiety, or to give it
a more proper Name, all the Foppifhnefs of
Youth in his Air and Drefs, and made his
Court with the Paffion and Vigour of a Lover
of Twenty-one, tho' he was then turned of
Fifty-five. But *Arabella* was far from being
enchanted either with his Perfon or Behaviour :
The *one*, tho' not ugly, had nothing in it agreeable to her Fancy ; and in the *other* fhe perceived fuch an Inconfiftency, as fhe had too
much good Senfe not to laugh at rather than
approve. His Quality and the Rank he could
give

give her in the World were Things however not to be despised, and had she not heard some Rumours concerning both the Legality of his Title and Pretension, 'tis possible all rest might have been more tolerable to her.

So strong is the Desire of Precedency in that Sex, that it often gets the better even of Love——many a Woman has rejected the Man she *like* and for the sake of two more Horses in her Coach given herself to one she *hated*. Many a one to appear with greater Splendor in the *Day*, has sacrificed the *Night* to Diseases and old Age:

Arabella however was not of this Class, and had perhaps as small a Share of Vanity as any of her Age and Sex, but yet enough not to be offended at the Eclat of being solicited in Marriage by a Man of the Count *de Anglse's* Quality; and to this alone must be imputed the Encouragements she gave his Visits; for after a while, being better acquainted than he imagined with his Character, she only waited a proper Opportunity to dismiss him in a Fashion that would be most mortifying to him.

As he was one Day more importunate with her to fix the Moment of his Happiness, she very gravely told him, that she could think of no such Thing without the Approbation of her Guardians: For tho' by her Father's Will she was left sole Mistress of herself and the Fortune he thought fit to bestow on her, and they had no Power either to compel or restrain her Inclinations, yet she knew them to be such wise and honest Men, that she was resolved to engage in no material Affair, much less in that

OR

in which the Happineſs or Miſery of her
whole future Life depended, without having
previouſly conſulted them. — *Therefore* added
ſhe, *if your Lordſhip thinks fit to communi-
cate your Intentions in my favour to them and
ta my Mother, to whom I owe that Regard,
their Judgment ſhall be the Standard and the
Rule of mine.*

Any body as well as he might indeed have
taken this for a conditional Conſent, and not
ſuppoſing they could poſſibly be ignorant of
his Addreſſes to her, thought ſhe had already
prepared them, and that now he had no more
to do than to declare himſelf to them to obtain that Sanction, which he imagined ſhe in-
ſiſted on only for the ſake of Form, and to
ſave the Bluſhes it would have coſt her Mo-
deſty to beſtowed herſelf on him of her own
Accord. With this Opinion he had no reaſon
to make any Heſitation in complying with what
ſhe ſaid, ſo readily told her that he would
wait immediately on them. *No, my Lord,*
reply'd ſhe, with an Air of the greateſt Reſpect, *I cannot ſuffer you to deſcend ſo much beneath your Dignity as to go to them——I will
invite them to dine here to-morrow, and after-
word take an Opportunity of leaving you together to diſcourſe on the Affair.*

This Conſideration in her was ſo perfectly
calculated to flatter his Pride, that he paſt the
Night in the moſt aſſured Expectation of having the Poſſeſſion of a fine Woman and a great
Fortune confirmed to him the next Day.

Accordingly he went the next Day with
all the Chearfulneſs of a Bridegroom: He
found

found her Mother and the Gentleman she had
mentioned already there: A very elegant Entertainment was prepared, after which she
withdrew as she had told him, and he began
to declare his Pretensions in a formal Speech
he had studied for that Purpose.

They suffered him to go on without offering to interrupt him; but by their Gestures
affected to be very much surprized at what
they heard; and when they found he had concluded all he had to deliver on that Subject,
If I did not know, said the old Lady; *that my
Daughter had too much Duty and Affection
for me, as well as Regard for these experienced
Friends of her Father to offer to impose upon us,
I should think all your Lordship has been saying
was a Contrivance between you to make your-
selves Diversion at our Expence.* How Madam, cry'd the Count, more astonished at her
Words than she had pretended to be at his, *Do
you imagine I would presume to rally in this
Company, and on such a Subject?*——*Has the
charming* Arabella *never made you acquainted
with the honourable Passion I have for her?
No really,* my Lord, answered she, with a dis-
dainful Toss of her Head, *and am sorry to find
their is any thing serious in what you have been
entertaining us with; for tho' I know your
Lordship is a Peer of two Kingdoms, I can
scarce believe it probable you have Interest in
either to bring* Bigamy *into a* Law, *without
which it is impossible for you to have an honourable Passion for my Daughter.*

This was sufficient to make the Count
know they had some Intelligence concerning
Anadea,

——des, on which, with his ufual Artifice he began to confefs himfelf guilty of a fmall ——e, in order to feem innocent of a greater he faid he was forry indeed to remember, that there was a certain Lady whofe Reputation had fuffer'd on his Account; but that the Scandal happened merely through her own Inadvertency in putting too much in the Power of a Confidenf, by whofe Treachery the Affair between them had got Air; but made a thoufand Affeverations that he had no farther Concern with the Lady, whom he fuppofed they might have heard fome mention of, and that there never was the leaft Intentions of Marriage on either Side.

When he had given over fpeaking, one of the Guardians to *Arabella* pulled fome Papers out of his Pocket, and prefenting one of them to the Count, *See there, my Lord,* faid he, *an Excufe for our Credulity; and wonder not after this, that we fhould believe you married to a Lady you took fuch uncommon Methods to obtain.*

Not all the Count's Audacity could keep him from changing Countenance at the fight of this Paper, which he prefently found was a Copy of the Affidavit that *Simplicius* had expected from him before he would confent to his Daughter's Marriage, with the Name of the Magiftrate before whom he had made it. Much ado had he to refrain from tearing it before the Faces of thofe who produced it as a Witnefs againft him; but hoping ftill to recover his Credit with them, he only threw it from him with an Air of Contempt, cried

K   it

it was a vile Piece of Forgery—that *Anadea,* herself would clear him of it; and had the Effrontery to say he would write to her for that Purpose; and they should soon be convinced of the Truth.

Your Lordship shall not need be at that Point, reply'd the other coldly, *I have here a Letter from a Right Reverend Prelate, with one inclosed to him from the Lady herself, testifying what Part she has in you——so that all further Enquiry would only be loss of Time——I think this is a sufficient Conviction.* With these Words he took out two other Papers, and read as follows:

The BISHOP's *Letter.*

SIR,

AS you desire me to acquaint you with what I have heard concerning the Marriage of the Count *de Anglia* with a Lady of this City, I conclude you have some particular Reasons for this Enquiry, and therefore take upon me to assure you he was lawfully married to the Daughter of a rich Merchant, called *Simplicius,* about fifteen Years since—The Ceremony was publickly performed, several of my Friends were present; and he not only acknowledged her as his Wife to all the World, but she also took her Place at Court as such—They have always lived together, have several Children, and he was looked upon as a good Husband, 'till a vile Woman seduced his Affections; after which he used her very ill, and at length

totally

totally abandon'd her. ———— It has been credibly reported here, that he had another Wife in your Country ——— of that you are the best Judge; but I am certain he has one here.——— I have just received a Letter from her, which I send for your further Information; and shall be glad it may be of service to you, or any of your Friends, and am,

Yours, &c.

The Countess DE ANGLIA'S Letter to the Bishop.

My Lord,

NOthing but Afflictions such as mine, which are sure the greatest ever Woman felt, can apologize for the repeated Troubles I give you; but as your Lordship vouchsafed to interfere so far in my unhappy Affair, as to constrain my unjust Lord to allow a Maintenance for our Children, I cannot help acquainting your Lordship, that it is so ill paid that I am in continual Apprehensions for the Usage they may receive on that Account from the People they are with, who I find are extremely Necessitous ——— Though I am denied the Privilege of seeing them, a Cruelty sure unprecedented to a virtuous Wife and tender Mother, as I have ever been, I make it my Business to enquire daily how they are; and yesterday my Brother brought me this unwelcome Intelligence ——— I am persuaded to appeal to the Legi-

flature;

flature; but if it should be true that he has a
prior Wife, the Certainty of which I cannot
learn, I fear I should be able to get but little
Justice either for my self or Children —— I once
more take the Liberty to intreat your Lordship's Advice, whether to apply to a Court
of Judicature here, or wait till one above,
who best knows my Wrongs and the Miseries
I sustain, shall think fit to right me, or revenge
my Cause. I have the Honour to be,

With all Submission and Veneration,

Your Lordship's most unfortunate Servant,

A. DE ANGLIA.

To conceive what Confusion, what Distraction the Count felt at so full a Detection of
his Crimes, one must be guilty of some Part
of them, so can only judge by his Behaviour
that it was in Proportion to the Cause. —— He
stamped—he raved, cried it was a Plot upon
him—denied every thing; but in so wild a
manner, and mingled with such horrid Curses
and Imprecations, as made the good Mother
of *Arabella* repent of having joined in taking this Method of putting him to Shame.—
The Gentlemen desired he would be more
moderate in his Expressions, since it was in
vain for him to think they were to be deceived by any thing he could say; and then
told him, that in Attonement for the ruinous
Design he had on *Arabella*, they should expect

pest he would not only forbear ever speaking
to her more, but also never mention her Name
as a Person he had ever been acquainted with——
To this he replied, That it was beneath him
ever to speak or think of any of them; and
with these Words, accompanied with a Look
full of Fury and Malice, he flung out of the
Room, leaving them to pass what Animad-
versions they pleased on his Behaviour.

This Disappointment, the Motives which
occasioned it, and the Shame, as well as the
ill Consequences he had to apprehend from
so plain a Discovery of Things he had imagined altogether unknown in that Kingdom,
made a perfect Hell within his Bosom; for to
what else can be compared so horrible a Mixture of unavailing Rage——enervate Malice
——Shame——Terror and Despair?

In a happy Reverse of all this did the true
Count *de Anglia* pass his Days in the Absence
of *Amico* : He knew his Cause was good, and
had nothing to fear from any thing that worthy Friend should be able to discover concerning it.——The Desire he had of improving
his Mind, having engaged the other before
his Departure to provide him Persons proper
to instruct him in some of those Accomplishments, it was necessary for a Person of his
Rank not to be ignorant of; he kept extremely close to his Studies, and seldom went
abroad; when he did, it was in Company of
a Gentleman named *Macario*, whom *Amico*
had brought him acquainted with, and who
being possest of all those Qualities the Chevalier was ambitious of attaining, render'd his

K 3. Con-

Conversation a kind of School for him, since
there were few things he wanted to know, that
the other was not capable of informing him of.
As Theatrical Entertainments are not only the
moft elegant Diverfion, but also if on well-
chofen Subjects, and wrote with Spirit, are
very pretty Improvements to thofe, who,
like the Chevalier, had been deprived of
greater, *Macario* would fometimes take him
with him to the Play-houfe; but then he always firft confulted the Bills, and never fuffer'd him to be a Spectator of any loofe or
idle Scenes: Hiftorical Reprefentations were
thofe he look'd upon as fitteft for him, and he
always took care to point out to him thofe
Places where the Poet had either adhered to
the Truth of Facts, or fwerved from it, the
better to illuftrate his Piece: And this Caution fhewed the good Senfe of him that gave
it, fince without being perfectly well read in
the Hiftory itfelf, one might form a wrong
Judgment of paft Tranfactions, or at leaft be
confounded in our Ideas of them, by the real
and the fabulous being thus blended.

The Chevalier was very much pleafed with
many of thefe Performances, but infinitely
more at the auguft Affemblies he beheld at
Court, and in the Heart of the Capital on
fome particular Days: The Aftonifhment
which Objects fo new and fo dazling at firft
excited in him wearing off by Degrees, he
confidered that all his exterior Magnificence
ought only to diftinguifh an interior Worth;
and therefore Perfons thus ornamented, fhould
make it their whole Study to excel in Wif-
dom

dom and Virtue thofe of whom they had the Advantage in Appearance ; and was forry to find by fome Accounts, that the *Great* did not always think it a Duty incumbent on them to be equally *Good.* He often expreft himfelf in this manner to *Macarie,* who charm'd with Sentiments fo truly noble, fo rare to be found even among thofe who make the moft fair Profeffions, and fo little to be expected in a Perfon train'd up in that unhappy way the *Chevalier* had been, conceiv'd fuch an Af- fection for him as we do not often meet with between thofe neareft in Blood.

In this agreeable and laudable Mixture of Study and innocent Amufement, we will leave for a while the principal Subject of our Hif- tory, and return to *Altamont,* where the ge- nerous *Amico* was labouring for his Friend, and expofing himfelf to Dangers he had not apprehended, and which it was with infinite Difficulty he efcaped.

He fet out with *Juggan* and two other Wit- neffes for the next Sea-port, but the Wind not being favourable, they were obliged to wait there for fome Days; in which Time, fome Perfons whom fhe had not thought of men- tioning to *Amico,* hearing on what Account he had taken that Journey, came and volun- tarily offered their Depofitions; fome of which he contented himfelf with taking before a Ma- giftrate, and others he found fo very material, that it would be neceffary thofe that made them fhould appear in Perfon; which they were ready to do, and accordingly agreed to be of his Company. All they had now to do

K 4 was

was to pray for a Wind, which still continu'd averse to their Impatience, and there was not the least Appearance of a Change when *Amico* received this Letter by the Post.

To Monsieur AMICO.

SIR,

THE Regard you shew for Truth and Justice in espousing the Cause of an unfortunate Nobleman, makes it the Duty of all honest Men to wish well to your Endeavours, and give you all possible Assistance; and at the same time renders you too formidable to the Enemies to Right, not to subject you to all their wicked Malice can contrive.——Providence has just now, by the strangest Chance in the World, discovered to me, that there is a Scheme laid to put you and the Witnesses you have with you under Confinement. I know not on what Pretence; but imagine, that as you are a Stranger where you are, it may be of ill Consequence, at least it would be a Delay of the Business you are at present engaged in, so give you this Advice, that you may take what Measures you shall judge most proper to frustrate this Design.——As I am not certain this will reach your hand, you'll pardon my not subscribing my Name, and be satisfied with knowing that it comes from one who wishes well to the real Heir of *Altamont,* and is,

Your sincere Friend.

Th

This Information had fo much Probability of Truth in it, that *Amico* thought he fhould be to blame if he neglected it ; and therefore got a Boat, and removed with his Witneffes by Night from that Town to another, about eight Miles down the River, where the *Brig* he had agreed with for their Paffage was to take them up. But all the Secrecy and Precaution he made ufe of in this Affair was in vain : Thofe who had form'd the Plot againft him, arrived at the Place he had quitted the next Morning after, and foon got Intelligence not only of his Departure, but alfo where he was gone, and immediately purfued him. Finding they had not been deceived in the Directions given them, they gave an Information to the Governor of the Fort, that he was come there to enlift Men for foreign Service ; on which he was taken into Cuftody with two of the Witneffes, the others happening at the Time he was feiz'd to be walking to view the Town, and hearing what had happened, conceal'd themfelves till they fhould know the Event.

He was not a Prifoner above two or three Hours before his Pockets being fearched, and his Papers examined, the Governor found he was not employed on any military Affairs.--- Minutes of Family Tranfactions----Affidavits of a Birth----a Death, &c.----with the cautionary Letter juft inferted, and fome others of his own private Bufinefs, being fufficient Teftimonies of his Innocence in what he was accufed of, he was fet at Liberty, as well as thofe taken with him. Judging by this of

what

what thofe Agents, of one who was a Foe to all Goodnefs, were capable of doing, he thought it not fafe to continue in a Place where they were ; left finding themfelves fruftrated in this Defign, they fhould attempt fome other Mifchief againft him, fo removed from thence in the moft private manner he could to a little Village on the Sea-coaft, where he had not been many Hours, before the Ship arrived, and dropped Anchor in order to take in fome Parcels apointed to be left there.

Here he acquainted the Captain of the *Brig* with the Danger he was in, and told him he would make him a Prefent of twenty Crowns over and above what he was to pay for his Paffage and thofe who were with him, if he would fail the next Morning, and keep to Sea till they could make their Paffage. This he readily agreed to, and all the Witneffes, to the Number of eight or nine, were put on board. *Amico* did not embark with them for this Reafon ; A Friend having heard of the clandeftine Practices againft him, came down in his own Boat on purpofe to advife him of it, and it was judged more fafe for him to go in that very Boat the fame Night, to the Mouth of the River, and there wait for the Ship, which when once under Sail would foon overtake them, than to go on board her at that place.

This Expedient, tho' it preferved him from one Danger, plunged him into another——the Wind immediately fhifted————the gathering Clouds gave fome Prefages of an approaching Storm——the Captain of the *Brig* found it impoffible to weigh Anchor, and the generous

Amico

Amico with his Friend found themselves on a
very troubled Sea in a small Boat, and no Appearance of any better Accommodation : But
Heaven was too just to suffer them to perish in the Cause of Virtue ; just as they were
beginning to despair of any Relief, they saw
at some Distance a small Bark standing out to
Sea, to which they made up with all their
Might, and having hail'd her, found she was
bound to the same Kingdom, tho' a different
Port than *Amico* designed for, so went immediately on board her. His Friend could not be
prevail'd on to accompany him ; for being accustom'd to the Sea, and the Wind which hindered the *Brig* from coming out, favouring his
Return, he went back, glad that the Enterprize
he had advised had succeeded so well.

Amico arrived safe, but having his Heart on
the Witnesses he had left on board the *Brig*,
made what haste he could by Land to the
Place he hoped to meet them, and was there
eight Days before the Vessel came in.——He
was standing on the Beach when he saw the
Long-boat thrown out, and several Sailors on
board it make all the way they could to
Shore ; on their landing, one of them seeing
him, made a Sign for him to retreat ; at which,
tho' greatly amazed, he drew back some Paces;
the Fellow went towards him, but still waved
his Hand for him to go yet farther ; which he
did till he came to a little Turning ; the
other then coming up to him, said, *Sir, my
Captain charged me to find where you were
lodged, and desired you to keep close, for we have
Men on board that he is afraid have no good*

Intentions toward you. Poor *Amico* was a little surprized, as thinking he was not like to be safe any where; but not so much, as to hinder him from enquiring after those he had left in the Ship: The Sailor told him they were all well, but thought it proper to stay on board either till Night, or till those Persons were gone; but desired he would appoint where they should come to him. *Amico* then gave him Directions where to conduct them on their landing, and went immediately to his Inn, and gave Orders that if any Persons, but such as he described, enquired for him, to say he had been there, but was gone.

By this means he avoided whatever Mischief was intended for him, as some there was 'tis evident. The Captain afterward inform'd him, that just as he was ready to sail two Men came on board as Passengers——that they had been very inquisitive after a Person they told him they expected to have found there, and seem'd much surprized at the Disappointment ——that they had been extremely troublesome to the Witnesses during the whole Voyage, and pretended to rally them on the Reasons of their taking it —— and that he had been obliged to make them keep in their Cabbins in order to preserve Peace in the Ship. This was sufficient to convince *Amico* he was not yet out of Danger; he was glad, however, he had once more got his Witnesses with him, and thinking a long Stay in the Place he now was, would render it impossible for him to avoid the wicked Contrivances of his Enemies, he hired Horses for four of his People, and a

Coach-

Coach-and-Six for himself, *Juggan*, and two others, and set out very late at Night for the Capital, where in three Days they arrived, having travelled through By-roads, and such as none could imagine they could have passed in a Wheel-Carriage.

Amico soon after had Reason to believe the Caution he had taken was not unnecessary nor on a vain Surmise, for he received various Informations that he had been way-laid in three different Roads, his Person and the Company he had with him describ'd at all the Inns, and the most particular Enquiry made after them, by Persons who were afterwards seen at the Count *de Anglin's*, and who it was known were supported at his Expence.

But the toilsome and dangerous Task his Honesty had engaged him in thus happily ended, he thought himself well rewarded for it by the Pleasure he took in the meeting of the Chevalier with those Persons he had brought from *Altamont* —— *Juggan* in particular was sometimes ready to throw herself about his Neck and embrace him as her dear Foster-child —— at others to fall at his Feet and testify the Submission due to the Son of her Lord and Patron —— Yet in the midst of these Transports, which the first Sight of him inspired, she cryed out to those who accompanied her —— *Hold, let me be well assured I am not imposed upon myself, nor shall impose on others* —— *I gave Suck, 'tis certain, to a Son of the Baron and Baroness* de Altamont, *but how can I say this Gentleman is that noble Babe? Can I remember his Face in so long a Time, and such a*
Difference

Difference of Age? No, and if I should pretend to it, you might have Reason to call my Integrity in Question——but, Neighbours, you have often heard me say, that that Infant was born with a peculiar Mark, which if this Gentleman can show, then I will suffer Death rather than deny him for the Heir of Altamont, born of the Baroness, and the same whom all of you have seen a thousand Times, both at my Breast and in his Mother's Arms.

The Chevalier on hearing these Words, immediately convinced her that she had not been deceived, by uncovering that part of his Body where Nature had imprinted this happy Token, as pre-ordain'd to baffle all the wicked Plots the Art of Man could form against him.

This was sufficient to make the good Nurse and every one present melt into Tears of Joy, and bless the Divine Goodness, who by Means least taken notice of, often brings the greatest Events to Perfection, and disappoints all human Efforts to the contrary.

All the Contrivances form'd to render Amico's honest Endeavours fruitless being thus happily disappointed, and as much ascertain'd as human Evidence could make him, that the Claim of the Chevalier *James* was no Chimera; he consulted with some of the most able of the long Robe, and proper Measures were presently taken for that injur'd Nobleman to assert his Birth-right, which few, if any, now question'd: but as Forms of Law must be observ'd, an absolute Decision could not be soon expected.

Indeed, whoever considers these *Memoirs*
with

with any Attention, will find thro' the whole
Courſe of them, that nothing ſerved more to
confirm the Validity of the Chevalier *James's*
Claim, than the very Meaſures Count *Richard*
took to deſtroy it——Firſt, would any Man of
Quality, nay, any private Gentleman, who
knew himſelf the lawful Poſſeſſor of an Eſtate,
ſit tamely down, while another pretended to a
better Title, and even commenced a Proceſs a-
gainſt him for an unjuſt Detainer of his Right?

Secondly, If there was nothing he dreaded
the Diſcovery of, why did he take ſuch Pains
to prevent the Truth being ſearch'd into?——
Why were ſuch dark and unwarrantable Methods put in Practice to prevent *Amico* from
going to *Altamont ?*——Why were Tempta-
tions uſed to corrupt the Integrity of ſome ?——
Why Dangers menaced,——nay, even Miſchiefs undertaken, to deter others from revealing what they knew ?

No, this would never have been the Caſe, if
Count *Richard* had not been conſcious the
Ways by which he aſſumed the Dignities he
enjoy'd were ſuch as would not bear the Light.
——None ever could accuſe him either of Indo-
lence or Tameneſs where his Intereſt was concern'd, and whoever had, without the ſtrongeſt
Foundation, laid any Claim even to the leaſt
Part of what he was in Poſſeſſion of, would
have ſoon found the ſevereſt Effects of his Reſentment——What then would he have done to
find the whole invaded?——would he not on the
firſt Notice of ſuch a glaring Forgery have
cauſed the Impoſtor to be ſeiz'd?——have forced
him to produce Proofs of his pretended Wrongs,

or made him suffer the Punishment the Law
inflicts on Fraud and Calumny? Even guilty
as he was, had not his Cunning in this material
Point deserted him, he might, by taking a Method quite different from what he did, have
screen'd himself for a time, and kept the Cen-
sure of the World a while suspended——nay,
who knows but it might have deprived the injured Chevalier for ever of the Means of af-
serting his Birth-right, by rendering him, a
Stranger as he was, incapable of raising either
Friends zealous enough to espouse his Cause,
or Money to carry it on.

But all-seeing Heaven, who hates Injustice,
would not suffer that cruel Usurper of another's Right to proceed in a manner which
might secure him the Possession, and for his
greater punishment render'd him accessary to
his own Shame and Confusion.

But now the time arrived when our Chevalier was to experience different Inquietudes
than what he yet had known——such as he had
before had no Idea of, and had only beheld
the Effects of in others with Surprize. His
dear Friend *Macarie* having been a little indisposed, was advised by his Physicians to go
a little way out of Town as the best Means for
the Re-establishment of his Health: This
Advice he could not be prevail'd upon to take
without the Chevalier would accompany him,
and accordingly they went together to an extreme pleasant Place about seventeen Miles from
the Capital. They happened to be lodged
just over against a House, where, from some
or other of the Windows, or passing in or out,
they

they saw every Day a young Lady whose Beauty could not but attract their Admiration: To the most regular and delicate Features in the World there was added such a perfect Innocence, as gave her a kind of an angelick Sweetness.—*Macario* would often cry out, *What a lovely Creature she is!* but the Chevalier had no Words to express the Sense he had of her Charms— his Heart, by having been so long insensible of the tender Passion, felt it now with double Force—he was all Confusion when she appear'd—all Sadness when she was withdrawn—his Eyes were continually attach'd to the Place where he might hope to see her, and yet when she was there durst scarce look up to her.—So great is the Awe which *Love*, when it is real, inspires, that indeed it may be said to be the only Characteristick which distinguishes the *feigned* from the *sincere.*

Macario was a Man of Gaiety, and tho' far from being a Libertine, had often felt the Pains and Pleasures of that Passion: He often discovered the Effects this young Lady's Beauty had on the Chevalier; and by a little rallying him on his new Sentiments, first made him sensible himself of the Nature of them——he now knew and confessed he loved, and that it was impossible for him to live without the Hope of one Day being in Possession of the adorable Maid. *Macario* was a little troubled to find his Passion of a more serious Nature than he had imagined, because, tho' he was ignorant of the Condition of the Lady, it was easy for him to perceive she was not of a Birth suitable to that of her Lover. This he sometimes

times remonstrated to him, but in vain ; for, as the Poet says,

Love either finds Equality, or makes it.

Every thing seemed to conspire to indulge his Inclinations, some Relations of the young Lady having heard his Story, were desirous of being acquainted with a Person who had experienced such strange Adventures ; he was invited with *Macario* to one of their Houses. The Object of his Affections was there. His Misfortunes had inspired her with a generous Pity, and that Prepossession made her treat him with more Softness than she was accustomed to use towards Strangers.——The obliging Manner in which she behaved, both heightened and flatter'd his Passion ; and she found something in his Person and Deportment, that very much added to the Concern she before had for him——This Interview made him so wholly her's, that from thenceforward he took no other Pleasure than in meditating on her Perfections, and she became so interested for him, that she could form no Wish but that of seeing him as happy as she thought he deserved to be.——Being now acquainted, whenever they met, as frequently they did by Accident, they walked together, and entered into Conversations which shewed they were far from being indifferent to each other, yet without any Declaration of Love on either Side, 'till one Day talking of the Wrongs had been done him, the fair Object of the Chevalier's Affection said to him, *Indeed I shall be apt to turn Free-thinker, and impute all*

the

the Accidents of this World to Chance, if Merit, such as your's, should have any thing left to wish for. Ah, Madam, answered he with a deep Sigh, *you know not, perhaps, the Extent of my Wishes, and when you do, I fear, will think them too presuming to deserve Success.* She was young and altogether unexperienced in Love, yet the Tone of his Voice in uttering these Words, and the Look he gave her at the same time, made her not far from guessing what was meant by them, and brought a modest Blush into her Face. They were both silent for some Moments, he not daring to explain himself more fully, nor she to desire it; and when they renewed the Conversation it was on a different Topick —— so fearful is Love, so bashful is Virginity, that neither have the Courage to reveal what each languishes to make known.

The Chevalier, however, after this became somewhat more bold, and by degrees declared to her, that in spite of the great Views he now was in pursuit of, she alone engrossed his whole Attention—that all his expected Grandeur would be nothing to him without she consented to share it with him; and that all the Miseries he had sustained in Slavery, had never given him half those Pangs he now endured in the Apprehensions that his Passion was not acceptable to her. These Professions, which it was easy for her to perceive were dictated by the Heart, and accompanied with the strictest Honour and true Respect, being often repeated, and every time with greater Ardour than before, at length obtained from her this.

Con-

Confession, That tho' the Addresses of a Person of his Rank to one of her's was too great an Advantage to be refused, yet she esteemed him infinitely more on the Account of his Merit than Quality, and all the Compliance he received from her, he must believe himself indebted for chiefly to them. In fine, as their Love was mutual, so a small Space of Time brought on mutual Declarations; till neither attempted to disguise any part of that Tenderness they were equally inspired with, nor to give each other all the Testimonies of it that Virtue and Innocence would admit.

It cannot be doubted but the Friends and Relations of this young Beauty were highly satisfy'd with the Offers made to her by the Chevalier; but *Amico*, to whom *Macario* imparted by Letter all that passed, was not so well pleased: He thought the Chevalier should wait for the Recovery of his Birthright before he entertain'd any Thoughts of Marriage, and came down into the Country on purpose to dissuade him from a Step which to him seem'd imprudent—But to what Use are all the Arguments that Reason can suggest against a Passion such as filled the Breast of this young Nobleman! He listened to all that both *Amico* and *Macario* alledged, could not deny the Justice of what they said, but was not to be gain'd over by it—to think of delaying his Happiness was a kind of Death to him—he knew not what Accidents might intervene to rob him him for ever of it; *and then*, said he, *let who will take the Coronets of Anglia* glio and Altamont ——— *The Recovery of my Birthright without her, would only serve to make me more conspicuously wretched.*

With such like passionate Expressions did he silence these Gentlemens Remonstrances; and as they had not the least Objection to make to the young Lady's Person, Character or Accomplishments, which were such as might become the highest Rank in Life, they ceas'd opposing his Inclinations, and *Amico* return'd not to the Capital till he had seen a Marriage solemnized, in which *Hymen* could justly boast of joining those Hands whose Hearts were closely united. After which that generous Friend left the happy Pair at the House of one who was a near Relation of the Bride, and accompany'd by *Macaria*, came back in order to prosecute what he had so well begun.

The Chevalier now thought himself repaid by Heaven for all the Hardships he had undergone: So serene was his Mind, so perfect his Contentment, that he scarce gave a Moment to the thoughts of recovering his Birthright; and when he did, it was only for the sake of his dear Wife. He found in her all those Virtues, for the Reward of which Dignity was originally instituted, and which alone can render it either beneficial or amiable to Mankind——It is not in the Blaze of Jewels, the splendid Equipage, the number of Attendants, or the Pomp of Titles, that true Greatness consists, but in the well executing the Power of doing Good, in being faithful Stewards of the Treasures Heaven thinks fit to deposite in their Hands ——in setting Examples

of

of Hospitality and Benevolence, and in treating their Inferiors in the same manner they
would wish to be treated themselves if in
their Place.   How few alas! consider this!
—— How apt are we all to keep our Eyes
continually bent upwards, envying and aiming
still at a superior Sphere, without once
deigning to look down on that beneath us;
much less examine the Worth it may contain.

All these Reflections coming frequently into
the Chevalier's Mind, he could not help
sometimes entertaining his fair Companion
with them; and the Answers she made testifying how sincerely her Thoughts agreed with
his, made him see she would no less adorn by
the Beauties of her *Mind*, than by those of
her *Person*, that high Station he hop'd soon
to place her in.

It was in a Felicity which might make the
greatest Enemies to Marriage, wish to partake the same that this amiable Pair past several Months: Equally loving and beloved,
they were all the World to one another; and
when at any time they were apart, engaged in
different Companies, it was but to return
with greater Ardour to each other's Arms,
and to relate with pleasure all the little Accidents which had passed during their Separation; for where there is a true Affection,
nothing is a Secret, and the most minute Adventure of the darling Object becomes a
matter of Importance.

They had their Visitors, their Circle too,
not composed of Flatterers and Sycophants,
such

fuch as ufually haunt the Drawing-Rooms of Perfons in Power, but plain and honeft Hearts, who came to congratulate their prefent Happinefs, and fincerely wifh'd to fee their Virtues fhine in a higher Sphere.

The manner in which they now liv'd, had indeed fo much Sweetnefs and Tranquillity in it, that had not the Chevalier believed it a Duty incumbent on him to affert thofe Rights given him by God and Nature, he would fcarcely have wifh'd to exchange it for the noify Splendor and continual Hurry, which he faw at the Houfe of thofe of his own Rank. He often faid, that in fpite of all the Hardfhips he had endur'd, he had more Contempt than Vengeance for his cruel Uncle, fince he muft certainly be a Man of a very weak Judgment, who could forego his Peace of Mind, break through all Laws, and even throw off Humanity merely for the fake of acquiring the Reputation of being what he was not, and enjoying what he in reality wanted not, and might have been infinitely more happy without. Not that the Chevalier was without Ambition, or was that cool Stoick fome who heard him fpeak in this manner imagined ; bu this Ambition confifted in his performing well the Part he was born to act in the World, and had too much laudable Pride not to defpife any Man who affumed the Character of another : In what he thought his own Province, no body exerted themfelves with more Vigour, or teftified a greater Share of Spirit ; and as he was careful not to *give* the leaft Offence, fo he was not of a Temper to *receive* it tamely. With

With how much Satisfaction could I dwell upon this Scene of Bliss, this Interval, as one may call it, from those Calamities the Chevalier *James* was pre-ordain'd to suffer! But it was, alas! too short, and afforded too little Variety of Adventures to take up much time in the Description of; the dreadful Purport of his Vision was not yet fulfill'd; but now his Sun of Joy at once withdrew — the gathered Cloud, charg'd with unnumber'd Woes, was ready to burst upon him; and Fate's worst Terrors hung suspended over his Head. —— Dangers he least foresaw or apprehended, encompassed him. — What all the Malice of his Enemies could not bring about, a cruel Chance accomplish'd, affording Matter of rejoicing to them; Grief and Confusion to his Friends, and to himself the extremeft Anguish, Horror and Bitterness of Heart. Now did his malevolent Stars pour in full Cataracts their Venom down, and shed at once the Mischiefs they had so long threatened, and which Slavery, Imprisonment, and Fears of Death, were but imperfect Samples of. Since this had in it all in one, and the Addition of yet worse.

Among the Diversions of the rural Life he now was in, Shooting might be accounted his favourite one. He frequently went out with some or other of his Neighbours with him, and was seldom so unlucky as not to spring some Game,

One Day, mark'd out by Fate to be the most unfortunate of his whole Life, he went out alone, but happened afterward to meet a

Person

Perſon who liv'd near, and was Game keeper to a Perſon of Condition to whom that Manour belong'd; as they were walking together and diſcourſing on ordinary Affairs, they ſpy'd two Men fiſhing in a little River that ran through the next Meadow, which not being allowable for them to do, the Game-keeper jump'd over the Stile, and ran towards them, with an Intention to ſeize their Net, as it was his Duty; the Chevalier follow'd and came up with him juſt as he had taken one of them by the Collar, who had the String on his Wriſt, and refuſing to reſign it, there was ſome Struggle between them. The other Fellow, who, as it proved, was the Son of him who had the Net, ſeeing the Chevalier advancing, and not doubting but he would aſſiſt his Friend in taking it away, cut the String, and threw it into the River, then ran in himſelf, for the Water was very ſhallow, and drag'd it to the other Side. This the Game-keeper perceived not, being engag'd with the Father, but the Chevalier that Inſtant coming, ſtoop'd haſtily down to catch hold of the Cords, that trailed on the Ground, in order to pull back the Net; but in that Action the Gun he had in his Hand unhappily went off, and ſhot the Father dead—All this was done at the ſame time, and in one fatal Moment.

Horror and Amazement immediately ſeiz'd the Soul of the Chevalier—He ſaw the Fellow fall—The Report and Smoke that had iſſued from his Piece, which he had charg'd with Bullets, left him no room to doubt the fatal Accident—All his Faculties recoil'd—

L   He

He ftood like one transfix'd with Thunder
and no lefs incapable of Motion for a time,
than him, whom that mifchievous Engine he
intended only for his innocent Recreation had
deftroyed.

The Game-keeper was almoft as much a-
larm'd, and cry'd out, *O God! how has this
happen'd!* — but then hearing the young
Fellow, who by this time was got on the other
Side, call out to fome Men that were paffing
that Way, that his Father was murder'd ; and
feeing them about to crofs the Stream, he took
hold of the Chevalier's Arm, and rouzed him
from the Lethargy he feem'd to be in, faying,
*Sir,—Sir, the Man is dead—We fhall be pur-
fued—Let us endeavour to efcape—We have
no time to lofe.* O *where,* cry'd the Chevalier,
*where can I fly!—Wretch that I am—Where
hide me from the Guilt of innocent Blood.*
However, feeing the other run, he run too,
without even knowing that he did fo, or whither he directed his Steps, till he came to the
Houfe of one who knew him very well and no
lefs loved him—*I have killed a Man,* cry'd he,
*with a Wildnefs in his Countenance, which too
well affured the Perfons he fpoke to, that
what he faid was a fad Truth.—Let us conceal you, then, Sir,* faid they ; and prefently
led him to a retired Place which few People
went into, and there made him lie down.

The Game-keeper in the mean time having much more Prefence of Mind in this Adventure, fled to a Place where he remained
fafe from all the Purfuit that was afterwards
made. Thofe Perfons however, whom they
faw

&c. coming from the other Side of the River, made no Haste after them; for, not knowing but there might yet be Life, they first sent for a Surgeon, and it was some time before they got a Constable, and attempted any Search; so that the Chevalier might have been out of their Reach as well as the Game-keeper, had the Horror he was in at what had happened, given him the Power of reflecting what was best to be done for his own Safety. But so wholly was he taken up with his Misfortune, that he had not the least Thought of himself, and if not in a manner forced into that private Room before-mentioned, he had doubtless given no Trouble to his Pursuers, but waited their Arrival with that Fearlesness which real Innocence inspired.

On a Certainty that the Man was dead, the Alarm was presently spread through the Town, the Crowd gathered from all Quarters, and the House where the Chevalier was concealed, being one that he frequently used, it was the first they searched: The guiltless Delinquent was easily found; but in such a Condition as excited more Pity than Resentment in those who apprehended him. The Closeness and Darkness of the Place where he lay hid, heightening the Horrors of his Mind, had such an Effect over his Body, that he was fallen into a Fit: They put him into an easy Chair, and carried him into the open Air, which, with the Help of other Remedies, brought him to himself; but the first Use he made of his recover'd Breath was a most heavy Sigh——then, *O!* said he, *If any one among you is my Friend — have Compassion on what I feel, and kill me instantly — I desire not to live after being accessary to the Death of a Man who never offended me.*

Though it was impossible for any one, except the Son of the Deceased, to know exactly the Truth of this Affair; yet the Behaviour of the Chevalier, during the time he had been a Sojourner in these Parts, had given them so good an Opinion of him, that none could believe he would have wilfully been the Death of any Man, without an extreme Provocation, which the Words he spoke taking off all Suspicion of they concluded it must have been done by Accident.

Every Body endeavoured all they could to comfort him, but in vain: a thousand times he wished himself in the Place of the Deceased; and tho' he very well knew the Law could not touch his Life, yet he declared that it was impossible for him ever to enjoy any real Peace of Mind again.

He was in the midst of these Exclamations, when *Macario* entered the Room: He was come into the Country with an Intention to pass some Days with him, and arrived just as the Noise of this unhappy Adventure began. The Sight of that dear Friend made our disconsolate Chevalier burst into a Torrent of Tears———They held each other for some time lock'd in the most strict Embrace without either being able to utter one Syllable, and it is hard to say which seemed to feel the greatest Agony for some time, the Prisoner or the Person who came to console him

him. The latter, however, being foon after more fully inform'd of the Circumftances of what had happened, refum'd fome Part of his accuftomed Chearfulnefs, and would have perfuaded the Chevalier to do fo too—Reminded him that both Divine and Human Laws regarded the Intention, and it was according to that alone all Facts were to be judg'd —that as his Will had no part in the Accident, he would be acquitted by God and Man, and he therefore ought not to accufe himfelf, nor be dejected at what might have been the Chance of any Man as well as he.

All this the Chevalier was not ignorant of, but it had a double Influence over him when fpoken by a Perfon for whom he had fo great a Regard —By degrees he grew more calm than he had been, and fuffered himfelf to be carried before a Magiftrate without teftifying any thing more than that decent Concern which every honeft Man muft feel in having been the Caufe, tho' unknowingly, of the Death of his Fellow-Creature.

But what became of his dear and amiable Wife all this Time, what Words, what Arguments could have Force to moderate her Griefs ! —The dreadful Intelligence of her Husband's Danger, reach'd her almoft as foon as the Accident happened that had occafion'd it—She was running to learn from his own Mouth the Truth, but knew not where to find him, and when the News of his being in Cuftody arrived, fhe was unable to go to him —Impoffible it is to defcribe her Defpair, fo I fhall only fay it was conformable to her

Love

Love and Tenderness—She was deaf to all
Intreaties, all Persuasions, all Remonstrances—
She wept, she tore her Hair, nor had any
more Mercy on her lovely Bosom—She fainted
every Moment, she almost died between the
Arms of her Heart-broken Friends——That
little Dwelling lately the Seat of perfect Tranquillity and innocent Delights, was now a
Chaos of Confusion——Grief and Distraction
in the Face of every one that came into it,
which yet seemed heightened at their quitting
it by the little Success their Endeavours had
to assuage the Sorrows of that beautiful and
unfortunate Person they had come to visit.
Our Fears for those we love, magnifies every
Danger ; and as she yet had only heard her
Husband had killed a Man, without hearing
any of the Circumstances which might have
either alleviated the Crime, or removed the
Apprehensions of the Punishment, it is rather
to be wonder'd at that she suffer'd no more
than that she suffered so much.

It is uncertain however, to what Extremi-
ties she might have been reduced, if *Macario*,
who had left her in these Agonies, and who
at his parting from her was able to give her
little Consolation, had not return'd to her with
a more explicite Account of every thing. After the horrible Ideas she had form'd of Guilt,
of Shame, and the most ignominious Death,
to be told, that a Husband she so dearly loved
was not only innocent, but must infallibly
be pronounced so by the Arbitrators of his
Fate, was such a sudden Rush of Joy, as was
nigh depriving her of her Reason——She
asked

afked the fame Queftions a thoufand times
over —— conjured *Macario* to deal fincerely
with her, then entreated his Pardon for having doubted him —— as often bid him return
to his unhappy Friend —— then called him
back with fome new Meffage from her ——
incoherent in this Extafy of Joy, as before fhe
had been in that of Grief——fo violent had
been the Extremes of both, that it was aftonifhing, fo tender and delicate a Frame had the
Strength to fuftain fuch terrible Revulfions,

But Nature could not long have borne a
Rapture, fuch as the Safety of the Chevalier
excited, nor would indeed the Occafion fup-
ply it ——That rapid Whirl which the firft
Affurances which *Macario* gave her, was foon
abated by the Reflexion, that as innocent as he
was, he muft be under Confinement fhe knew
not how long — that fhe muft all that time be
deprived of his Society, and by the yet
more afflicting one, of the Difquiets fhe knew
he muft endure for having been the Inftrument
of this fatal Accident ; and fhe now funk into
a gloomy Sadnefs, which that faithful Friend
knowing would take up a good deal of Time
to diffipate, left her to the Care of fome Relations who were with her, and returned to the
Chevalier, whom he found juft going to take
his Examination before a Magiftrate,

The Depofitions being made, the only ma-
terial of which, was that of the Son of the
Deceas'd, and he not pretending to accufe the
Chevalier of any Malice, or even Defign in the
Affair; none had any Notion of his being in
Danger. In all fuch Cafes however, the Law

L 4   appoints

appoints a Trial, and the Magiftrate was oblig'd to fend him under Guard up to the Capital, where he was to remain in Prifon till the Time of his Hearing fhould arrive.

-What gladfome News was this to the inhumane Count *de Anglia*; 'tis faid that in fpite of the Parfimonioufnefs of his Nature, he even gave the firft Perfon who brought it to him four whole Crowns, a Sum fo valuable to him, that he would not have beftowed it to have faved the Souls of his whole Species from everlafting Perdition—He doubted not now but he fhould be able to order Matters fo as utterly to deftroy his Nephew's Competitorfhip, and put an End to his Pretenfions by the moft fhameful of all kinds of Death—So much did he exult, fo much imagine himfelf the Minion of Fortune, that it was not in his Power either to conceal his Satisfaction or fet any Bounds to it—He triumph'd even to a degree of Wantonnefs, and cou'd not content himfelf with knowing the real Owner of the Dignity he had ravifh'd and ufurp'd, languifhed in a miferable Prifon, without feafting his cruel Eyes with the malicious Pleafure of feeing him there, and infulting his Calamity.

With this fiend-like Difpofition he went to the Jail, and demanded to fee the Prifoner Chevalier *James*; but as it is the Cuftom not to permit any one to the Speech of Perfons in his unfortunate Circumftances, without they themfelves give leave, one of the Keepers went and inform'd him of this Gueft.

The Chevalier was amaz'd, as he had Reafon to be, at fo unparallel'd an Affurance; he
had

had thought a Man who was conscious of having so greatly injur'd him, would rather have taken all imaginable Care to have avoided the Sight of him, than have come to seek it; and as it was not probable that there could be any Good meant to him by this extraordinary Visit, he refused to receive it, and desir'd the Keeper of the Prison to tell him so.

This so highly incens'd the arrogant Count, that he order'd his Chariot to drive to the House of a Justice of the Peace, with whom happening to have some slight Acquaintance, he obtained a Letter from him directed to the Master of the Prison, requiring him to admit the Count *de Anglia* to the Presence of him who call'd himself the Chevalier *James de Al-tamont.*

On producing this Letter, and yielding to leave his Sword behind him, he was conduct-ed to the Room where his Nephew was confined, but that ill-treated Nobleman no sooner saw him enter, than he insisted on the Jailor's staying in the Room all the time he was there, ——giving as his Reason, that as he could not imagine a Person who had been the Author of all his Calamities, could be instigated to see him by any other Motive than that of adding to them ; so he could not answer for his own Temper in the Presence of one who had so highly injur'd him.

This Precaution was not unnecessary, for the Provocation he received was such as might possibly have excited a Man less warm by Nature, to Actions he might after have repented of.

L 5   The

The firſt Words the Count *de Anglia* ſaid to him were, *Are you the Wretch who takes upon you the noble Name of* Altamont, *and pretend yourſelf the Heir of a Family whoſe Dignities and Titles are devolv'd on me?*

To this the Chevalier reply'd, with an equal tho' more juſtifiable Haughtineſs, *I need not ask if you are the Monſter that uſurps my Right—too well I remember the Face of that deceitful Man, who, counterfeiting a Tenderneſs for my Youth and Innocence, under the Pretence of ſending me to an Academy, trepan'd me into Slavery, and did your utmoſt to make of me a Wretch indeed! but Providence,* continued he, in ſomewhat a lower Voice, *has diſappointed all your baſe Attempts—I am return'd, and—*

Yes, cried the injurious Count with a malicious Sneer, *you are return'd — return'd to take up your imagin'd Titles—I ſuppoſe you fancy yourſelf already in Poſſeſſion of them; and this is the Caſtle of the fine Count* de Anglia. *Look round, and ſee if it does not well ſuit your* Lordſhip's *State.* In ſpeaking this he pointed to the Iron Bars of the Windows; which cruel Inſult putting the Chevalier beyond all Patience: *Barbarous Man! ſaid he, You can find nothing here that is not infinitely better than you merit to enjoy; and, unhappy as I am, I doubt not but to live to ſee you reduced even lower than I am at preſent — a worſe Priſon than even this, befits and may perhaps be the Portion of Fraud, Perjury, and Oppreſſion, ſuch as yours.*

You

You ſhou'd have inſerted Murder too in your Catalogue of Crimes, replied the Count, with the ſame Diſdain as before, *and then indeed the World might believe I were as near of Kin to you, as you pretend I am.*

The Chevalier in this gave ſome Tokens that he ſhould not be long able to maſter his Reſentment, which the Maſter of the Priſon perceiving, and fearing the Effects, thought proper to remind the Count, that it was not generous nor becoming his Lordſhip's Rank to inſult a Perſon in Diſtreſs, and that Diſputes of this Nature were never permitted in the Place he now was; and added, that if his Lordſhip would not reſolve to behave in a different manner, he muſt inſiſt on his quitting it.

This Reproof agreed but ill with the Pride of him 'twas given to, but as he knew that thoſe ſort of People were abſolute in their way, and there were few times in which he could not command himſelf ſo far, as not to diſcover in his Countenance any Part of what paſs'd in his Mind; he ſeem'd not to take it at all amiſs, and only ſaid that if he knew the Vileneſs of that Fellow, (meaning the Chevalier) he would not think it ſtrange he uſed him in that manner. The other told him that he had nothing to do with any private Quarrels, he only pretended to keep Peace in the Priſon, and that if he had any Complaint againſt the Priſoner, or the Priſoner againſt him, they muſt both wait the Deciſion till he ſhould be diſcharged.

Diſ-

Discharg'd! cry'd the Count, *you mean till he is hang'd* — *Has he not kill'd a Man, and can you think he'll ever be at Liberty till the Gallows sets him free?*

Neither my Opinion, nor your Lordship's, reply'd the Jailor, *I believe, will be consulted in this Point—but every Man is free to think as he pleases.*

While the Count and Jailor were discoursing in this manner, the Chevalier had time to recover himself from that Hurry of Spirits, which the Sight and Behaviour of his Uncle had occasioned in him; and he resolved that whatever he should say to him for the future, he would answer with Unconcern; but the other put him not to that Test, for a little stung at what the Jailor had said to him, he thought proper to avoid all Occasions of further Admonitions, and turn'd out of the Room to go away.

The Jailor follow'd to restore his Sword, which, before he had suffer'd him to come up, he had oblig'd him to pull off — while he staid till the other had order'd it to be brought, he gratify'd some Part of the Spleen he was possest of in the most virulent Railings against the Chevalier, and at last asked him, why he did not put him in Irons. *I had no Orders for it,* replied the other, *and beside see no Occasion for any such Severity* — *'Tis no Severity at all,* cry'd the Count, *and I think you ought to do it.*

Could he have imagined the Person to whom he spoke had been so well acquainted with some of his past Transactions as in reali-

ty

ty he was, he scarcely would have talked before him in this manner; but it was his way always to conclude People were ignorant in whatever he wished they should be so; and though that Confidence had frequently turned to his Confusion, and subjected him to Affronts he might otherwise have avoided, yet was he still incorrigible——the Folly, or rather the arrogant Stupidity was ingrafted in his Nature, and he was not to be shamed out of it.

On his first mentioning the Chevalier's being laid in Irons, the Jailor fix'd his Eyes on him with a Look intelligible enough, had he not been too much blinded by his own obstinate Tenaciousness to observe it; but on his repeating the Necessity he thought there was for so doing; *Ah! my Lord,* said the other, *'tis a sad thing to be laid in Irons——does your Lordship know what it is to be laid in Irons?* I know, reply'd the Count, a little surprized at the Emphasis he gave these Words, *how should I know? but one may guess 'tis Part of the Punishment that is the Due of Murder. Ay, and of Robbery too,* resum'd the Jailor, *and the World is strangely unjust in censuring, if your Lordship does not more than guess how these Boots and Gantlets feel when they are well lock'd on —— I have been told, you knew the Weight of them in the* West, *though not for* Murder.

The Count now found he was catch'd, and there was no way to come off, so putting as good a Countenance as he could upon the

Matter

Matter—*Yes, indeed, said he, an impudent In-dictment of that Nature was once laid against me ; — but it was a malicious Prosecution every Body knew—and I was acquitted.*

Yes, said the other, flily, *I think your Lord-ship's Servants committed the Robbery and af-terward impeached you, either as their Compa-nion in it, or sharing the best Part of the Booty, I can't remember which.* No matter, answered the Count, *'tis a foolish Story, and not worth mentioning.* Yet *I have often thought of it,* said the other, *and the seeing your Lordship puts it fresh into my Head.* I could like, me-thinks, *to know the Particulars, if you would be so good as to inform me of them.*

To this the Count replied, that he remem-ber'd nothing of it; and was now in a great Hurry to take his Leave, but the other, who saw how it mortify'd him, found some Pretence or other to hinder him from going for a good while; but in what Discourse soever they had, he still introduced something of the Irons and the Robbery, till the Count perceiving the Motive of it, and not a little enraged to find himself the Jest of such a Fellow, flung away excessively disconcerted, and the Jailor return'd to his Prisoner and gave him a Detail of the Revenge he had taken for him on his Uncle. The Chevalier smiled, and could not help feeling an interior Satisfaction in any thing that gave Pain to a Person whose bad Quali-ties merited the Contempt and Hatred of all that knew him.

Amico and *Macario,* who came in soon af-ter, were made acquainted with the Story,
which

which afforded them as much Diverfion as the Circumftance and Place their Friend was in would permit; but tho' they carefully conceal'd every thing from him that might add to his Difquiet, yet they were very uneafy themfelves: — They found that his Confinement, and the various Reports this unhappy Accident had occafion'd concerning him in the Town, was a very great Damp to his Affairs———— fo eafy is it for Misfortune to check the Vigour of the warmeft Friends—Pity is a fhortliv'd Paffion when the Object of it once lofes the Profpect of better Times.——Few there are who do not naturally fhun thofe who ftand in need of their Affiftance, and fewer ftill who do not withdraw it when the hope of any Return ceafes—This, however, was not the Cafe of the Chevalier, none that knew him but loved him, and the Rumours which his cruel Uncle and his Emiffaries induftrioufly propogated, had an Effect only on thofe who were entire Strangers to him; but the Pains taken to render all good Wifhes fruitlefs, and Knowledge of the general Corruption of the Age, made his Friends fometimes tremble, left, innocent as he was, Means might be found to make him appear otherwife.

'Tis certain, indeed, the wicked Count left nothing unattempted for that purpofe: The Minute he was inform'd of the Chevalier's Misfortune, he employ'd one of his Agents to fend for the Son of the Deceafed, who had him lodged in his own Houfe and fed at his own Table. This was the Place where the Creatures and Dependents of that inhuman

Uncle had their daily Commons at his Expence; not out of Charity it may eafily be believed, but to affift and carry on his Defigns of all Kinds and by all Methods, no matter whether juftifiable or not———Their Bufinefs was not to *examine* but *obey*; and if any one of them happen'd to have a more tender Confcience than the reft, and but befitated to go through any dirty Work he was employ'd in, he was immediately ftruck off the Roll of Penfioners, and driven to feek his Eating at fome other Quarters.

These Wretches, as foon as enter'd into the Service of their munificent Lord and Patron, were carried into a Street famous for equiping fecond-hand Gentry, and immediately tranfmigrated from the *Beggar* to the *Beau*; at leaft they appeared fo in the Eyes of this poor Country-Fellow —He took them for fine Gentlemen and all they faid as Oracles —they feem'd to have a mighty Friendfhip for him, and to pity him for the Lofs of his Father, but were continually infinuating to him that he had been too favourable in his Evidence againft the Murderer — that the Man who call'd himfelf the Chevalier *James de Altamont* had certainly kill'd him with Defign, and that he was one of the greateft Impoftures and Villains upon Earth. Nay, one of them went fo far as to frighten him with his Father's Ghoft, if he did not do every thing in his Power to revenge his Death.

Thus was the Ignorance of this poor Creature work'd upon by their Artifices, to believe even contrary to what his Eyes had feen, and

and his Tongue declared, not only before the Magiſtrate who took the Depoſition, but alſo in the Preſence of ſeveral others, and indeed to every one who had aſk'd him any Queſtions concerning the Accident. And he now told theſe new Friends, that when the Chevalier came to be try'd, he would ſay other Things than he did before the Juſtice, and that no-body ſhould perſuade him to ſell his Father's Blood.

How! cry'd one of the Count's Agents, *were you offer'd any thing not to proſecute the Chevalier?* Yes, anſwer'd he, *he told me he was very ſorry I had loſt my Father through his Means, and that when he got his Eſtate, he would ſettle two hundred Crowns a Year upon me to make me Amends.*

But you refuſed to take it, I hope, ſaid one of theſe pretended Gentlemen. *Yes,* reply'd the other, *I ſtood out for four hundred, and he told me he could not promiſe that, for he had more People to provide for.*

This was no Invention of the Fellow's for the Chevalier had really ſaid, that in Conſideration of his Loſs he would make him that Settlement when it was in his Power; and this Effect of the Generoſity of his Nature would his Enemies fain have conſtrued into a Bribe, or a Perſuaſive to the Man to com-pound for Juſtice; but all the Attempts they made for this Purpoſe ſerved only to ſhew the Villany of their Intentions, and, with all People of Senſe, gave a Luſtre to the Charac-ter of him they endeavoured to defame.

How-

However, as the Man to whom the Chevalier had made this Promise, could not be fuppofed to have any true Notions of Honour, or
that Magnanimity which diftinguifhes the noble Soul, had himfelf taken it in a far different
Light than what it was intended for, it was
eafy to confirm him in that Opinion, by crying out againft the Bafenefs of tempting a Son
to renounce all filial Duty and Affection, and
to confent to fcreen the Murderer of his Father for a Gratification to himfelf: *At this*
Rate, faid one of thefe Incendiaries, *he might*
perfuade you to have killed your Father your-
felf---I wonder how he could look on fuch an
honeft Face as yours, and flatter himfelf with
the Imagination that you would not do Juftice to
the Afhes of him that gave you Being—it was
an Infult upon you, and methinks I hate him
for this Villany more than all the reft — to offer
to corrupt a young Man of fo much Integrity.

Ay, and fo much good Underftanding too,
added another. *Ah! Sir,* faid he, *you are*
pleafed to be merry with your humble Servant,
——*Not at all,* reply'd the Flatterer, *I don't*
know a more clever young Man——you will cer-
tainly make your Fortune.

The Brain of this poor Fellow was quite
intoxicated with receiving fuch Civilities and
Praifes from Perfons he took to be fo much
above him—he thought himfelf in another
World, and was fo tranfported, that they
might have made him believe any thing or do
any thing.

They told him one Day, that it was pity he
was

was not in some settled Way of Life, and that they would prevail on the Count *de Anglia,* who was a noble-spirited generous Gentleman, to provide for him; and accordingly, some Days after, said that they had spoke to him, and he had promised to make him a Present of eight hundred Crowns to put him up in some good Business, and that he might be sure of it, he would give him his Note for the Payment of so much Money after the Execution of the Chevalier *James: For,* said one of them, *it would be needless for you to receive it till then,--you cannot go about any Business nor attend to any thing, till you have done with the Prosecution, but as soon as that is over, the Sum I mention shall be yours; and, it may be, a great deal more.*

Wiser Heads than that of this young Country Fellow, might have been thus seduced; and the Manner in which he afterwards behaved at their Instigation, ought rather to be imputed to his Infatuation than any Propensity in him to Villainy or Corruption.

As he was the principal Evidence against the Chevalier, the most Pains was taken about him; but there were others also whom they endeavoured to spirit up, some of whom yielded to the Temptation offered them, and others saw into it and despised it.

Macario and *Amico* had Intelligence of all these clandestine Proceedings, and were not idle in taking every proper and justifiable Measure to ward off the Blow they were intended for; and tho' these Gentlemen had no Recourse

courſe either to Promiſes or Bribery, they ſoon
found ſubſtantial and credible Evidences to
oppoſe whatever fictitious ones the Count or
his Agents could muſter up for the Miſrepre-
ſentation of the Fact in queſtion— The moſt
material of which were from thoſe Perſons, to
whom the Son of the Deceaſed had immediately after it happen'd declared, that in his
Conſcience he did not believe the Chevalier
had any Deſign to kill his Father, and that
he was not in a Poſture, even to menace ſuch
an Action, when the Gun he had in his
Hand unhappily went off——The Surgeons
alſo who examin'd the Body, were Men of
too fair and honeſt a Character to be prevail'd
upon by any Temptation to pervert the Truth.
— Nor was the Magiſtrate, to whom the De-
poſitions were firſt made, capable either of
concealing, or giving a different Turn to the
Meaning of any Part of what was then ſworn,
and which muſt infallibly render every Thing
that could be trump'd up afterwards in Con-
tradiction to it, manifeſtly the Effect of Malice and Corruption. So that on the whole,
the Counſel conſulted on this melancholy Affair, who were not only the ableſt for their
Learning in the Laws of the Kingdom, but
alſo the moſt conſpicuous for an unbiaſs'd
Honour and Integrity, aſſured theſe anxious
Friends of the Chevalier, that they had not
the leaſt Ground for Apprehenſion — that
there was nothing could be alledged againſt
him that could poſſibly touch his Life, or even
give Occaſion for a Bluſh to riſe hereafter in
his Cheeks on mention of it.——*Let the*
guilty

guilty Man, the perfidious and cruel Uncle, take Shame to himself, said one of them who knew the bafe Practices the Count *de Anglia* had recourfe to in order to put an effectual End to his Nephew's Claim ; *the Infamy he endeavours to throw on the Heir of* Altamont *will recoil upon himself, and his Attempts to diftrefs him in this Point be of the greateft Service to him.*

Such an Affurance from a Mouth they knew incapable of uttering any thing the Brain had not well digefted, entirely diffipated all the Fears thofe had been in that heard it ; and *Amico* had the Courage to vifit the Chevalier's fair and difconfolate Lady, and confirm the Hopes he before had given her with much lefs Certainty than he had now to boaft of.

The Condition of that young Beauty was indeed truly worthy of Commiferation : withheld by her Friends and Relations from running to the Prifon where her dear Husband was confined, fhe form'd to herfelf the moft diftracting Ideas ; imagin'd that thofe who told her the beft News either deceived her or were deceived themfelves, and believed all the worft fhe heard. In fpite therefore of the known Integrity of *Amico*, he had no fmall Difficulty to gain Credit in a Point on which fo much depended.

But the Count *de Anglia,* whofe fanguine Difpofition made him always ready to believe every thing that footh'd his Wifhes, was, notwithftanding the little Reafon he had for it in Effect, very much elated at the Accounts given him by his Emiffaries, which tho' he found
they

they swelled. to exaggerate their own Dexterity in the Management of what they were intrusted with, yet he enough depended on what they told him, to make him flatter himself, that when the Trial came on so much would be sworn against the Chevalier, as would infallibly procure such a Sentence as would remove for ever a Person whose Claim none now called in question, except himself and those he had gained over to be his Instruments.

He stood indeed in need of the Consolation this Hope afforded him; for besides the Mortification he had received from the Kindred of *Arabella*, he had Intelligence that *Anadea* had resolved no longer to endure the Infamy he endeavoured to fix on her, and was preparing to assert her Right and prove herself his Wife——He heard also, that an eminent Tradesman was about to prosecute him! for having seduced his Wife; and finding that all these things being in every one's Mouth, he began to think it would be impossible for him to persuade any Woman to marry him, who was of any Condition or Fortune, which last he now stood more in need of than ever——His Law-Suits, with those Claimants to Part of his Estate before-mentioned not being yet determined —— the more alarming Process carrying on against him in behalf of the true Heir — the Debts he had already contracted, and those he was every Day contracting for the securing the little Interest he had, and answering the Demands of those who supported his bad Cause, had now rendered him so wretchedly

edly

edly Neceffitous, that he fcrupled not to offer
the moft exorbitant Premium, nor to defcend
to the meaneft Pretences for the raifing Money to defray the daily Expences he was obliged to be at.

O what is Greatnefs, when purchafed at the
Expence of all that can render the Poffeffor
defervedly refpected by the World, or eafy
in himfelf! In vain does the unjuft Afpirer
hope to cover his Infamy with ill-got Titles
and the Glare of Pomp, the bafe Ground-
work is vifible through all the tinfelled Out-
fide ——— _Man_ fees it with Contempt, and
Heaven with Abhorrence!

Of this Truth the Count _de Anglia_, it muft
be confeffed, was a notorious Inftance ——— his
Coronet neither procured him the leaft Efteem,
nor his Eftate, large as it was, Ceffation from
Difquiet ——— eternally affronted ——— eternally teized with the Importunities of his Creditors, his Life was one continued Hurry;
and to this perhaps was owing, that wanting
Time for Reflexion, he experienced not thofe
Racks which, at fome Moments, the moft
hardened want power to repel in a Confciouf-
nefs of Guilt.

The Day appointed for the Trial now drawing near, there was a great Debate among thofe
Gentlemen who were of Counfel for the Chevalier : Some thought it would be derogating
from the Dignity of his Birth to fubmit to
the Decifion of that Court before which he
was cited to appear, and that, as being the
Count _de Anglia_, none had a Right to acquit
or condemn him but the high Tribunal of his
Peers

Peers—Others were againſt his offering to alledge that Privilege, becauſe tho' born to the Title, he had not been in *Poſſeſſion* of it, and 'till he was ſo, could be looked on no otherwiſe than as a *Claimant*; for tho' his *Right* was undeniable in *Reaſon* and in *Juſtice*, yet as it was conteſted in *Law*, he was not properly the *Count*, 'till *Law* ſhould confirm to him that Title.

The Majority were of this laſt Opinion, and it ſeemed moſt juſt both to *Amico* and *Macaxio*; but the Chevalier himſelf would hear nothing againſt it: He deteſted every thing that had the Appearance of Shift or Evaſion; and how juſtifiable ſoever his Pretenſions were, to exert them on this Occaſion he thought would be conſtrued by his Enemies as a Fearfulneſs of his Trial; he therefore deſired they would offer nothing that would look like a Deſire in him of delaying it. *As I am* innocent *or* guilty, *ſo may I be* acquitted *or* condemned, ſaid he---*and I am ſo conſcious of the* one, *that I am impatient 'till I am cleared from all Suſpicion of the* other.

This put an End to the Diſpute, and inſtead of further Arguments they ſet themſelves to make proper Preparations for the Trial, which was to come on in a few Days.

The Chevalier's Enemies were however infinitely leſs eager for it than himſelf; for being well convinced it could not terminate to the Satisfaction of their Patron, they dreaded the Iſſue of an Affair which muſt convince him they had only deceived him with vain Expectations, and conſequently put an End to the

the Subsistence they received from him at present.

To prolong the Necessity of his Depen-
dence on them therefore as much as possible,
they found Pretences in the Prosecutor's Name
for petitioning the Court for a Delay of Trial
—This was twice granted, but on Condition that Chevalier *James de Altamont*, and
the Game-keeper, who had now surrendered
himself, should be admitted to Bail. A certain Proof how little they were supposed guilty of the Crime laid to their Charge.

The Chevalier now flew to the Arms of his
Beloved, who received him with an Excess
of Transport, though somewhat allayed by
the Apprehensions, which notwithstanding all
the Assurances had been given her, yet hung
upon her tender Heart—Her Soul was divided between Grief and Joy, and the fond
Tears she shed flowed equally from these two
Sources—She felt indeed a Pleasure which
no Words can speak, but then it was mixed
with Pain; and the more he endeavoured to
remove her Fears, the more she found him
worthy of them, and doubted the Permanence
of a Blessing such as she now possest in him.

At length the Day arrived which was to put
an End to all Suspence: No more Demurs
were listened to, and the Accusers and Accused ordered to appear. They obeyed the Sum-
mons, but the Agitations of both Parties were
just the Reverse of what is usual in Persons
of such Circumstances — the *Accusers* here
were the only anxious — the *Accused* were
decently composed and tranquil.

M

As-

As this Adventure, on the Account of the great Share the Claimant of *Anglia* and *Altamont* had in it, engrossed the Attention of the whole Town, the Concourse of People who came to hear the Event was prodigious——Few that had heard his Story but interested themselves in his Success, and even those who were most insensible of the Wrongs of others, were excited by their Curiosity to see a Person no less eminent for his Misfortunes than for the Dignity of his Birth.

But, O God! who will believe that among the Number of Spectators, the inhuman Count *de Anglia* was seated——yet so it was——Blown up with the vain Hopes his Emissaries had given him, he would not be prevailed upon to be absent from a Scene, the Catastrophe of which he expected would fulfil every Wish his wicked Heart had formed — beside, he imagined that if aught was wanting to assure the Ruin of his Nephew, his Presence would compleat it, by striking an Awe on the Friends of that abused Nobleman, and more emboldening those who should appear against him——Shallow Policy!——Here Malice overshot its Mark—not all the Merits of the Chevalier,——not all his Sufferings, could so much have influenc'd the Assembly in his Favour, as did this glaring Proof of the Barbarity of his Uncle. Every Heart anticipated the Judges Decree, and, without seeing him, pronounced him worthy of Life, worthy of Means to assert his Birth-right, and tear the Coronet from the guilty Brow of him whose Actions so ill became it.

He

He needed not, indeed, this Pre-poss.ssion, either to clear him from the Imputation of the Crime he was accused of, or shew he merited the Dignity he claim'd: His *Innocence* was sufficient for the *one*, and his *Behaviour* for the *other*; though it must be owned both appeared with double Lustre when compared with the vicious Disposition and arrogant Deportment of his Oppressor and Competitor.

Assoon as he was brought up with the usual Form by the Keeper of the Prison, the Court thought fit to distinguish him from common Criminals by ordering he should be placed within the Bar, which Mark of Respect galled Count *Richard* to the Soul, but afforded Matter of Satisfaction to every one beside.

All Eyes were fix'd upon him, while he seemed neither to despise nor court the Applauses he heard whisper'd of him through the Crowd—a sweet Composure sat on all his Features—grave, but not sad—spirituous, but not gay—the solemn Occasion engrossed, but not perplexed his Thoughts—the Presence of those on whose Decision his Life or Death depended, inspired him with Respect, but not with Fear; and he shewed rather like one who came to attend the Fate of another, than his own; but this Serenity received a sudden Interruption, when happening to turn his Eyes a little on one Side of him he beheld his merciless Uncle: At so unexpected a Sight he lost all his Presence of Mind, and cried out to one that stood near him — *Heaven! does that Prodigy of Wickedness come here too to insult me!— to render me, by*

M 2 *and*

an Object so justly hateful to my Eyes, incapable of making my Defence; and distracting my Mind with the Remembrance of what he has made me suffer.

As he spoke these Words with some Vehemence, they were heard by many others beside the Person to whom they were addressed, and passing from one to another through the whole Assembly, occasioned a general Murmur against the unparallel'd Cruelty and shameless Behaviour of the Count.

The Chevalier's Solicitor came up to him on this Occasion, and conjured him to consider his Uncle's Proceeding merited more his Contempt than Indignation; and not to suffer even this Provocation to transport him into a Passion, which however justifiable in another Place, would in this he now was be inexcusable.

Fear me not, reply'd the Chevalier, *I know both where, and before whom I am, and shall not do any thing that may assist that cruel Design which doubtless brought him hither.*

He had Time to say no more, the Court now calling to him, by the Name of the Chevalier *James de Altamont*, to answer if *Guilty* or *Not Guilty* of the Crime laid to his Charge, he replied immediately:

That tho' as Count *de Anglia* he might refuse to be judged by any but his Peers; yet, as he was conscious of his Innocence, and impatient to be acquitted of a Crime so unworthy of his Dignity, he readily submitted to the Decision of that Court he was before, and pleaded *Not Guilty*.

They

They then proceeded to examine the Witnesses, who, less embolden'd by the Presence of their Patron, than intimidated by that of the Chevalier, had not Consciences sufficiently hardened to alledge any thing material against him; and even in what they said contradicted themselves every Moment. The Artifices practis'd upon them were obvious to all present, and on some Cross-questions being put to them by those Gentlemen who were Counsel for the Chevalier, they could not avoid giving such Answers, as had not the Count *de Anglia* been lost to all Sense of Shame, must have made him immediately quit the Place; especially when the Chevalier being permitted to make his Defence, he modestly and in the most pathetick Manner apologiz'd for want of proper Expressions, *Having*, said he, looking full upon his Uncle at the same time, *been deprived of an Education suitable to my Birth, by the unparalleled Cruelty of those whose Duty it was to have improved the Talents I received from Nature.*

Could any Man but he have staid after hearing so just and so publick a Reproach!— Could any Man but he have faced the indignant Censures of a thousand Tongues exclaiming in Chorus on his Barbarity! Yet did he keep his Seat, 'till he receiv'd the farther Mortification of the general Applause bestowed on his Nephew, after he had related the Circumstances of that unhappy Accident which brought him there, with all the Simplicity of Truth, but join'd with a certain Sweetness more engaging to the Heart than all the Ornaments of Rhetoric could have been. M 3 Mad

Mad with Rage at this unlook'd-for Difappointment, and impatient to vent the Ma-
lignity of his Soul, the wicked Count now
started haftily up, and rufhing thro' the Croud
with as much Precipitation as the thicknefs of
it would admit, flung himfelf into his Chariot,
muttering the moft unheard-of Curfes as he
paft. — One united Hifs purfued him till he
was out of Sight, and fome there were who
even followed to his Gates, exclaiming and
reviling; while the Chevalier was acquitted
without the leaft Hefitation, and the loud
Huzzas of all prefent teftify'd the high Satif-
faction they took in the equitable Judgment
of the Court.

To defcribe the fincere Joy of his Friends,
or the Tranfports of his amiable Wife, when
congratulating him on this happy Event,
would be altogether needlefs, fince there is
fcarce any Imagination fo cold, who having
read their Characters, but muft be capable of
conceiving what Words would but poorly exprefs. The Chevalier himfelf was the Perfon
who felt leaft Pleafure at his own Acquit-
ment, for though he rejoic'd his Innocence had
been fo fully cleared, yet to reflect that thro'
his Means a poor Man had been deprived of
Life, made a certain Heavinefs hang on his
Spirits, which all the Endeavours of his
Friends could not for a long time remove.

Yet could his cruel Uncle, guilty of the
moft premeditated Barbarities, while Villany
fucceeded, riot in Luxury; wholly incapable
of Remorfe, he felt no Anguifh but in the
Difappointment of his wicked Plots: To have

feen

feen one of his own Blood fall the innocent
Victim of his Fraud and Pride, would have
filled him with as exceffive a Pleafure as the
contrary Event now did with Defpair.

His frantick Rage was fuch at the Treatment he had received from the Populace, that
thofe whofe Place it was to be about him, felt
that Revenge he rather ought to have taken
on himfelf for his own Pride, Cruelty, and
Folly. But thofe were Vices too much a Part
of his Nature to be fhook off, and muft be ex-
ercifed on his poor Domefticks, having no
other Objects—he threw a Chair at one—
a Table at another—ftamp'd on a third—
kick'd a fourth down Stairs—wifh'd the
whole World in Flames—call'd for everlafting
Perdition on himfelf and all Mankind; and
fome aver, even curfed Heaven itfelf. His
Agents and Dependents endeavour'd to bring
him into better Temper for a long Time in
vain—they footh'd——they flatter'd every
Paffion——they fwore to retrieve all yet, and
either die or find fome means to revenge him
not only on the Pretender, as they call'd the
Chevalier, but alfo on all that had efpoufed
his Caufe——Join'd with him in the moft
horrid Imprecations againft *Amico* and *Macario* in particular.——*Rather than fee your
Lordfhip thus difquieted,* faid one of thefe
abandon'd Wretches, *I'll undertake to fend all
their Souls to Hell before another Night.*

To talk to him in this Manner was the
only way they had to continue their Impofi-
tions on him, and tho' no Man had more De-
ceit and Cunning than himfelf, yet was he fo
M 4 much

much blinded by his Vanity, that the very
Artifices he practised on others, could at any
time be made ufe of with Succefs upon himfelf. They were no Strangers to this Weak-
fide, and on any Event which they knew
would be perplexing to him, were always provided with fome Story to raife his Expectations of an adequate Satisfaction.———One
now told him of a Perfon he had heard of,
that had a large Sum of Money which he
wanted to put out, and that he believed with a
little Management it might be at his Lordfhip's
Service — Another offer'd to introduce him to a
beautiful young Girl juft come from theCountry,
yet had already attracted the Eyes of half the
Nobility in Town, and added, that he had
fuch an Afcendant over her, that he could almoft promife his Lordfhip he fhould have
the firft of her——But a third took a Letter
out of his Pocket, which he pretended to have
received that Day from the Confident of a Widow of Condition, who, he faid, was worth an
immenfe Sum of Money befides a great Join-
ture, and no Incumbrance of Children; and
finding his Patron inclinable enough to hear
it, read to him thefe Lines:

The Letter.

To Monfieur RELAYE,

SIR,

WHAT I told my Lady concerning the
Count *de Anglia*, made fo great an Im-
preffion on her, that fhe has talk'd of nothing
else

else since———She thinks him one of the most
agreeable Men in the World, and wants only
to be convinc'd of the Sincerity of his Passion
to make him a suitable Return———If he is
as much charm'd with her as you say he is,
let him make an immediate Declaration of his
Passion either by Letter or in Person, tho' I
believe, the former will shew most the Humility of a Lover who is not happy enough to
be acquainted with the Object of his Affection
———If the Affair succeeds, as I doubt not
but it will by my Assistance, I depend on you
for the Security of that Gratification which
my Endeavours will very well deserve——— I
shall be glad to see you at your Leisure, and
am,

Yours,

EMILIA.

All these Baits did the gull'd Count swallow
with the utmost Greediness; but the last most
engrossed his Attention. ——— A Lady with
that Fortune would be a sure Resource in case
of Accidents, and if the Right of the Chevalier
James took place against him, as he now began to fear, he should not at least be totally
undone. But then *Anadea* was a dreadful
Obstacle to his Designs on the Score of Marriage———He knew not but the first Ship
that arrived might bring that injur'd Fair,
whose Presence and Complaint would infallibly frustrate all Attempts of this Nature on any
other Woman.

M 5 On

On his suggesting his Apprehensions on this Score, another of his Instruments replied, that he had an Expedient which he would undertake should prevent her from giving his Lordship any Disturbance. —— It was this, —— He proposed to go and meet her on her landing, as from his Lordship, and then instead of suffering her to come to the Metropolis, conduct her to some House of his own providing, and keep her confined till she not only resign'd all Pretensions to him in Form, but also gave up whatever Credentials she might bring with her for the Probation of her Marriage.

The Count was so transported with this Thought, that he even envied his Agent the Glory of contriving it.—— *'Twill do,* cry'd he, *'Twill do, when once we have her to ourselves from all her Advisers, we will make her sign what we please, or it shall be worse for her--Shall a Man of my Quality be under any Apprehensions from such a Creature as she!*

In these few Words was his whole Soul delineated—his Cruelty, his Fraud, his Pride set forth to the Life ; as was his Vanity and Folly, in so easily giving Credit to any the most improbable Stories that sooth'd his Self-Conceit. He now forgot all that had so lately enraged him, and fired with new Desires and new Hopes, was for immediately putting in practice the Means of attaining them. In Compliance with the supposed Advice given by the Confident of the fair Widow, he wrote a Letter to her as follows:

The

The Count DE ANGLIA.

TO THE

Beautiful Relict of the Chevalier DU BRIS.

MADAM,

TO say I have had the Honour of seeing you, is sufficient to convince both yourself and the whole World, that I adore you; since with a much less Penetration than the World is pleased to allow me, I could not but discover Perfections in you worthy of the Coronet I beg leave to lay at your Feet, accompanied with a Heart which will ever be devoted to you.——If the Title of Countess *de Anglia* has any thing in it that may render the Visits of a Person who alone has the Power of conferring it on you, not altogether disagreeable, I intreat Permission to wait on you, in order to give you all imaginable Proofs of the Passion I am inspired with, and with how much Ardor and Sincerity I am,

Madam,

Yours Eternally,

RICHARD DE ANGLIA.

This

This being highly approved on by his little Council, the Person who had the Honour to be the Projector of this fine Scheme, was thought most proper to be the Bearer, while the others were employ'd on those Designs they had proposed to him.

The first acquitted himself in a short time of his Engagement, a Sum of Money was rais'd, tho' at an excessive Interest; for Count *Richard* never scrupled, for the sake of *a present* Expedient, to promise any thing, bind himself to any thing *in futuro*; was always extremely generous till the Day of Payment came, and then was seldom without an Evasion to avoid the Penalty.

The other, who had invented the Story of a young Beauty, merely to bring him into good Humour, and continue himself in Favour by being necessary to his Pleasure, was oblig'd to have Recourse to another Fiction to excuse the Disappointment, and to attone for it as well as he could, brought him in reality acquainted with a Girl, who had the Address to pass herself upon him for one that had never before made the least Step.

As for the Marriage-Jobber, he went boldly to the Lady he had mention'd, and without having received the least Encouragement, as he had pretended, or being even acquainted with any Person belonging to her, delivered the Count's Letter to her. As she was in effect a Woman of Fortune and Character, she was a little surprized at this Declaration of Love from a Person she knew only by Report, and could not remember she had ever seen, as

indeed

Indeed she had not. She however answer'd with Civility enough; but said, she thought it inconsistent with her former manner of Behaviour to receive the Honour of his Lordship's Visit, unless introduced by some Person of her Acquaintance, especially on the Affair he mentioned in his Letter; so having inclosed it under a blank Cover, she desired the Messenger would return it to him, with the Answer she gave by Word of Mouth.

The Fellow, however, knew his own Interest better than to obey her Orders, and only told the Count that she could not be spoke with, but that he had seen *Æmilia*, who had inform'd him, that a Relation was now in the House with her, who having strenuously recommended a Person to her, it would be better if his Lordship deferred his Visit till the Departure of this Friend, who else might put a thousand Things in her Head to his Disadvantage.

This Pretence was succeeded by others, which, together with the Hurry of Spirits the Count was now perpetually in, on the account of procuring fictitious Proofs against the real ones of the Chevalier, prevented that Deceiver of others from discovering he was deceived himself by the Wretches whom he fed.

In the mean time the Chevalier continued his Process, which was carried on with as much Success as the tedious Forms o a civil Court of Judicature would admit of. The Persons he was so fortunate to employ as Councel, Solicitors, &c.———happen'd to be Men of such unbiass'd Honour, Zeal and Integrity,

tegrity, that they always made their Client's Cause their own; and the uncommon Circum- stances of this agitating them with a more than ordinary Desire of bringing so iniquitous a Scene to Light, they were indefatigable in their Labours; and having good reason, by the whole of Count *Richard's* Behaviour, to be assured he would raise all the Money he could from the Tenants on the Estate, repre- sented the Affair in such proper Colours to the supreme Judge, that he granted them Writs of Ejectment, in order to prevent any Part of the Rents being paid till the grand Decision should be made.

This was gaining a great deal, and indeed all that the *just Claimant* could at present de- sire; but it made the *unwarrantable Possessor* almost beside himself with Rage and Appre- hension; especially when he heard Chevalier *James* was preparing to go himself in Person with those who were appointed to execute this Point of Law.

That injur'd Nobleman had an extreme Desire to see once more that Kingdom which gave him Birth, and his Friends highly ap- proving this Inclination in him; his Lady, whom it was judg'd improper should go with him, would not suffer her Tenderness so far to get the better of her Prudence, as to offer any thing in Opposition to it.

It was highly necessary *Amico* should stay to animate the Process, and keep the Wit- nesses together; various Stratagems being con- tinually put in practice by Count *Richard's* Tools, both to corrupt and terrify them. But *Macario*

Macario would not be separated from his dear Chevalier, and besides was a Person, who on account of his perfect Knowledge of the World, fine Address, and manner of Behaviour, might be of infinite Service to him on various Occasions. Two other Gentlemen also, to whom the Chevalier's Virtues and Misfortunes had made him equally beloved, would needs accompany him in this little Voyage; and the Progress he intended to make through all those Parts, where from a long uninterrupted lineal Descent, he was hereditary Lord, Baron, and Viscount.

It was not in the Power of all Count *Ricobard's* Invention, nor that of his Instruments, to put any Stop to this Expedition, the Event of which he had so much Cause to dread; but to render the Reception of the Chevalier and his Friends as disagreeable to them as possible, he sent three of his Emissaries with Letters and Instructions to some in that Kingdom; who by having been Partners with him in his Debaucheries, he imagin'd would assist his Schemes. The Substance of what he wrote to them, was, that a Bastard Son of his late Brother, had taken upon him to call his Title in question, and was coming over to forbid the Tenants from paying him any more Rent—and desired that they would prepossess the People with this Idea of him, and add also that he had been a Vagrant about the Streets of the Capital—had afterwards transported himself to *America*—return'd a common Sailor—had never been but a most abject Profligate, and was now only spirited up by three

or

or four ill-minded Perfons to diftrefs him in his Affairs.

Unexampled Barbarity! Hardnefs of Heart! not to be match'd but among thofe lying and implacable Beings that infpir'd it ! This was acting over again all his former Crimes, mifreprefenting every Fact, and pleading thofe very Miferies he had been the fole Author of, as Reafons for ill treating the illuftrious Sufferer.

The indefatigable Inftruments of their wicked Patron's Will, fet out with all poffible Speed on this Enterprize, after having flatter'd him with the Hopes that they would order Matters fo, as that his Competitor fhould be driven back with Shame and Confufion. But how far they were able to execute this execrable Commiffion, we fhall fee anon.

After the cruel Count had, as he thought, prepared an unkind Reception for his Nephew in the Land which gave him Being, he thought he ought not to be idle himfelf, and began to confider how he fhould diftrefs him in that he was about to quit ; therefore affoon as he heard the Chevalier, little fufpicious of thefe new Plots forming againft him, and having got every thing ready for his Departure, had taken Leave of *Amico,* and was fet out on his Journey, he caufed a Letter to be wrote to that worthy Friend of the Diftreft in an unknown Hand, the Subftance of which was as follows :

To Monfieur A m i e o.

SIR,

HAVING been a Witnefs of the Friendfhip fo long fubfifting between you and
the Count *de Anglia*, I cannot look on your
prefent Enmity without a great deal of Concern, as equally prejudicial to you both———
of all who efpoufe the Caufe of his Competitor and muft inevitably fall with him, there
is none for whom he is fo much troubled as
yourfelf———Believe me, Sir, that my Lord
has fuch unconteftable Evidences, that it is neither in your Power, nor that of all the World,
to fhake his Title———Be therefore no longer
deceived with the fpecious Pretences of an
Impofture, but return to your former Engage-
ments with a Nobleman, who, in fpite of all
you have done, has ftill a tender Regard for
you, and who, I can affure you, for I have
heard him fwear it, will not only forgive
every thing that is paft, but alfo make over
to you and your Heirs for ever, that part of
the Eftate mortgaged to you by the late Baron
de Altamont ———I imagine he will fend
Perfons to treat with you concerning this
means of renewing your former Amity; and I
wifh you fo well as to hope you will not
refufe the Offers he intends to make you, nor
any longer lend your Endeavours to prop a
falling Houfe which can only involve you in
its Ruins. I choofe to conceal my felf at prefent, but according as you purfue the friendly
Advice

Advice I give, shall at a more proper time
declare the Name of him who is,

Very much Yours.

Some Days after this, two Persons whom
Amico had often seen at the Count's, came to
him, as from him, and confirmed the Offer
made in the Letter—They even brought an
Instrument ready sign'd in order to convince
him there was no Deception in the Affair,
and also a full Receipt for that pretended Debt
for which he had been arrested before his
Voyage to *Altamont.*

Amico listned to what they said with a Patience and Attention which made them imagine
they had gain'd their Point; but when he found
they had fully executed their Commission —
*The Count, said he, is wondrous kind, but it
is not my way to abuse the Generosity of my
Friends; — Tell him therefore, continued he,
that I cannot accept the Gift he offers, because
I am very well convinc'd it is not his own
he would bestow—but in return for his Favours give him this Letter, that he may
know how to thank the Person that wrote it.*

With these Words he took the above Letter
out of his Pocket, and put it into the Hand of
one of them, who was indeed suspected by
Amico to be the same that wrote it. They
both looked very much confused at an Answer,
which by the beginning of his Treatment of
them they had not expected, and were preparing to add something to enforce what
they

they had already said on the Part of the
Count, but he prevented them by telling them
that he was surprized the Chevalier *Richard*,
after knowing him so long, shou'd know him
so little as to believe he wou'd undertake any
Cause without being well convinc'd of the
Justice, or that when he once was so, he
wou'd desert it for any Consideration whatever.

After this he wou'd enter into no farther
Conversation on this Head, but asked if they
wou'd dine with him; and behaved to them
with an ironical Complaisance that stung them
to the quick, and they were glad to get out of
a House where they found nothing but a just
Derision of themselves, and the Offers they
brought was to be expected.

The Count had not greatly flatter'd himself with Success in this Attempt, tho' he
made it, knowing very well if it succeeded
he should deprive the Chevalier of his greatest
Support; and if he fail'd, the Essay cou'd be
no Prejudice to him, being well assured his
Character cou'd not suffer more by it in the
Opinion of *Amico*, than it had already done
on other Accounts — he therefore bore the
Disappointment with more Patience than he
was accustomed, trusting entirely to the Success of those Agents he had employed abroad
against the Chevalier.

That much wrong'd Nobleman was now
pursuing his Journey with his three Friends,
one Valet-de-Chambre, and two Lackies, and
meeting with no Impediment either by Land
or Sea, arrived safely at that Capital from
whence

whence he had been so cruelly trepan'd,——
His Enemies had been there some time before
him, and were not idle in their Endeavours.
The first publick Place he went to, a Mob
was hired to insult and hiss him, and many
Affronts thrown on him as he passed the
Streets; but all this only shewed the mean
Malice of his Uncle, and was presently
quashed by the Respect which the Populace
soon found he was treated with by their Supe-
riors.

That good Woman who had reliev'd the
Distresses of his Childhood, when he was
indeed in that vagrant Condition with which
the Instruments of his cruel Uncle now up-
braided him, was still living, and conceal'd
nothing of the Chevalier *Richard*'s Behaviour
to him while at her House, and the Pretence
he made to take him thence.——Several
other reputable Persons also who had seen
him in his Infancy happening to be then in
Town, assured as many as spoke of the Affair, that the Baron *de Altamont* had really a
Son by his Lady, and that they saw not the
least room to doubt but that this Gentleman
was that Son. In fine, a very little time join'd
to his manner of Behaviour, which was far different from that of an Imposture, convinc'd
those least inclin'd to be so, that he was in
effect the Person he said he was.

Few Persons of Rank or Condition enough
to entitle them to such a Favour, but invited
him to their Houses, and intreated to be informed from his own Mouth the Particulars
of

of his Misfortunes——the moſt elegant Entertainments were made for him and his Friends ——the greateſt Marks of Diſtinction were beſtowed on him wherever he went; and inſtead of being treated beneath his Dignity, whoever had ſeen him either at Church, at the Play-houſes, Aſſemblies, Walks, Coffeehouſes, or any other publick Place, would have taken him for ſomething yet greater than he was, by the reſpectful and pleas'd Attention with which all Eyes were fix'd upon him.

But as to create Love and Eſteem were not the chief Motives which brought him to that Kingdom, he quitted the Capital, and went to the Province where he was born, and where lay a conſiderable Part of the Eſtate of his Anceſtors. The Wretches employ'd by Count *Richard*, had notice of his Intention, and finding their Schemes here render'd abortive by the Prevalence of Truth, and the good Senſe of the Perſons they had in vain attempted to impoſe upon, they hurry'd down to *Altamont*, hoping to meet with better Succeſs among the innocent Country People, on whom the firſt Impreſſion is generally the ſtrongeſt.

They got there five Days before the Chevalier and his Company, and having with a great deal of difficulty raiſed a *Poſſe* of about fourteen or fifteen, they took up all the Inns in that Town where the Chevalier was born, in order to diſappoint him and his Friends of any Lodgings at their Arrival.

Thi

This petty Mischief, as they thought, compleated, they dispersed themselves through the whole Neighbourhood, venting the most preposterous Falshoods of their own inventing, as Additions to those the Count had forged, in order to spirit up the Rusticks to drive him out of the Province as an Imposture come to betray and cheat them; but they little suspected the Shrewdness of these Country People; they knew, without these Creatures Information, that the Chevalier *James de Altamont* was on his Journey towards them, also on what score he came, and were full of Impatience to behold a Nobleman who was born among them, had so long been lost, and so miraculously recovered— They had always pitied the late Baron, had looked with a tender Eye upon his Faults, as believing him instigated to commit them by the wicked Insinuations of his Brother, whose very Name they hated, and whose Behaviour since he assumed the Title and Estate, made every Day more odious to them. All this joined to the History of the Chevalier's unexempled Injuries and Sufferings, as it was spread through the whole Country by those to whom *Amico* had related it, excited in every body a tender Prepossession in his Favour; which it was far from being in the Power of what these wicked Emissaries, of a more wicked Patron, could say against him to remove.

They concealed their real Sentiments however, seemed not to doubt the Truth of what was told them —— Drank the real Count *de*
Anglia's

Anglia's Health, and Confusion to the Pretender; which, being taken just the Reverse of what these honest People meant, gave an infinite Satisfaction to those employed to seduce them, and they expected no less than that the Chevalier and his Friends would be mobbed and almost torn to pieces the Moment they approached: Little did they think what sort of Preparations were then making to receive him, and that the seeming Credit given to their Suggestions, was done with no other Intent than to heighten his Triumph by so unexpected a Mortification to his Enemies.

It was only their Ignorance of the exact Day in which they might expect him, that prevented him from being met at a great distance from the Town; but when the People were informed that he was near, by one of the Servants who rode before in order to provide Lodgings for that worthy Company, they ran out one and all, Shops, Streets and Houses were left to the care of little Children, or such Women who only wanted Strength, to gratify their impatient Curiosity; none but whom old Age or Infirmities kept Prisoners remained behind—happy were the foremost of this joyful Crowd——some press'd to kiss his Hands — Others clung about his Legs—— Some took the Bridle of his Horse, leading him as it were in Triumph, while those at greater Distance threw up their Caps, and join'd in the general Cry, *Long live the* Heir of Altamont—*our own true Lord.*

In this manner, amidst a shouting Multi-
tude, was he conducted to the best House the
Town afforded, and there left, after a thousand Benedictions, to receive the Congratulations of the Chief of the Province, who hearing of his Approach, had made all the haste
they could to meet him. Many of these remember'd his Birth, had often paid their Compliments to him in his infant Years, and in
spite of Hardships, Griefs and Troubles, sufficient to have fixed the most heavy Gloom
on any Face, could still trace great part of
the Baroness *de Altamont*'s Sweetness in a Son
who was once thought very like her.

While these were entertaining him with
some Discourse of his Family, and listening
with Horror and Amazement to the brief Recital he made them of his Uncle's Barbarity
towards him, the Populace were busy in making Bonfires, ringing the Bells, and other Demonstrations of a publick and sincere Joy.

Never had Count *Richard* been received in
this manner; for though the blackest of his
Crimes had 'till now been wrapt in Darkness
yet there were others too notorious to suffer
that the Person guilty of them should be
treated with any Marks of Love or Esteem.

But these Testimonies of Duty and Affection to their new-found Lord ended not with
the Night. Early in the Morning a Troop
of young Men and Maidens neatly drest, with
Garlands on their Heads and preceded by several Musicians, came before his Lodgings,
and presented him with a rural Entertainment
which in that Country they call the Long
Dance.

Dance. Never had the Chevalier and his Friends beheld a Scene more perfectly delightful -- the clear and ruddy Complexions join'd with the Youth and Innocence of these Performers gave a Grace to every Motion, and it was pleafant to obferve how, it being then the Seafon of the Year which afforded little Variety of Flowers wherewith to ornament their Chaplets, the Girls had cut Pieces of Ribband, to reprefent Rofes, Pinks, Lilies, *&c.* in fo lively a Manner, that they feemed fo many *Flora*'s celebrating the coming in of the Spring.

In fine, as his Reftoration to *Altamont* was like a new Birth, his Entrance into it was welcomed in the fame Manner his Entrance into the World had been, and the whole Time he ftay'd gave one continued Proof of the Sincerity of the People's Hearts towards him, and that they were not only convinc'd of the Juftice of his Pretenfions, but alfo that they thought him worthy of the Dignities he claimed.

How fevere a Shock was this to his Enemies, who from the Moment they found how he was received, durft not fhew their Heads for fear of meeting that Treatment themfelves which they intended for him and his Friends; but fculked in Corners 'till Night favoured their Efcape, and then went Poft to the Capital; from whence they wrote an Account of their Difappointment to Count *Richard*, and defired frefh Inftructions in what Manner to proceed.

The

The Chevalier and his Company having now ferv'd their Ejectments, were obliged to quit *Altamont* in order to go to thofe other Provinces where likewife he had Eftates, and where it was neceffary the fame Writs fhould be delivered to prevent his unjuft Uncle from receiving any farther Profits from a Patrimony to which he had fo little Right, and which he had but too long enjoyed.

The Reception they met with through their whole Progrefs, convinced the Chevalier's Friends that the extraordinary Rejoicings made for him at *Altamont*, were not altogether owing to a partial Indulgence to him as having been born among them, but to the Certainty every body had of his being the lawful Heir; fince not only at his own Eftates, but in almoft all the great Towns he had occafion to pafs through, he was complimented with Bonfires and ringing of the Bells.

The News of his Succefs in the Country having reached the Capital, the Careffes he before received there were redoubled at his Return by all the People of Diftinction; and it was highly fatisfactory both to himfelf and Friends to obferve, that thofe who moft publickly efpoufed his Caufe, were thofe who were themfelves the moft eminent both for their Rank and Virtue.

It was not indeed in Nature to be otherwife, we are all apt to commiferate thofe moft who we find have the neareft Affinity with ourfelves — How then could the *Highborn* but look with the greateft Tendernefs and Compaffion on the Orphan of fo illuftri-

ous

ous a Houſe, expoſed in infant Innocence to all the Miſeries Language can give Name to?—How could the *Worthy* and the *Good* but love and reverence thoſe noble Principles, which without the Advantages either of Precept or Example he had ſo ſteadily adhered to during the whole Courſe of his Misfortunes?—How could the *Learned* but reflect with Admiration on the Ardency of his Deſires for acquiring Knowledge, and with what Care and Aſſiduity he had improved every little Hint that Providence threw in his way for the Improvement of his Mind? And what Matter of Regret was it for all who truly lov'd their Country, to find a Genius capable of being ſo great an Ornament to it, had been by the moſt unheard of Barbarity deprived of all the means of exerting itſelf.

The Ladies too, I mean that part of them who gave themſelves the trouble of looking no farther than thoſe exterior Accompliſhments which compoſe what is commonly called a pretty Gentleman, could not forgive Count *Richard* for having denied him the Advantages of Dancing and Muſick: Charmed as they were with his natural Politeneſs and Complaiſance, they could not find Words to expreſs ſufficiently how great a Mortification it was to them that he could not make one with them at a Ball, or give them his Judgment on a Concert.

In a word, being ſo generally liked as he was, every one lamented moſt his Want of that Branch of Education which was moſt agreeable to their own particular Taſte; but

all

all agreed in this, that no Punishment ever yet invented could be equal to the Crimes of such an Uncle as Count *Richard*.

But while the Chevalier was receiving all the Demonstrations of Good-will and Respect he could defire, and infinitely more than he expected, a Plot was forming against him, fit only for the execrable Brain of him who had no other Ideas but what turn'd on Mifchief; but which, like those that went before, ferved only to bring Confusion on the Author.

That inexorable and remorfelefs Uncle being informed by his Emiffaries of his Nephew's Succefs, and the Treatment he had received, was ready to burft with Rage and Malice; and perceiving his *All* was going ---- that Juftice was ready to burft upon him like a Deluge, and fweep every thing away his Avarice and Ambition had ufurped, leaving him naked to Punifhment and Shame, he refolved on an Expedient no lefs bold than wicked, which was to caufe the Chevalier *James* to be arrefted in an Action of one hundred and twenty thoufand Crowns, flattering himfelf that it would be impoffible to procure Bail for fo large a Sum; that he would be thrown into Prifon, and by being prevented from returning, he would be rendered incapable of profecuting the Suit, and all his Friends difcouraged from affifting him. To the Orders he gave his Agents for this, he alfo added that they fhould fend Expreffes to all the Tenants, pretending that

that the Chevalier had been detected in his Forgery, had given up his Claim: and then to demand what Rents were owing, in the Name of *Richard* Count *de Anglia* and Baron *de Altamont*, the real and true Owner of the Estates appertaining to thofe Titles.

The Wretches to whom thefe Inftructions were directed, fail'd not to obey them punctually to the utmoft of their wicked Power: They got a Writ immediately made out and prevail'd on an Attorney to back it; but when they came to the Office, met with a Difappointment they had not forefeen: All they could fay being ineffectual to get it feal'd: The Perfon appointed for that Purpofe had heard the whole of the Story, and faid he would not venture on fuch a Thing, unlefs he had the Sanction of one of the Judges to indemnify him. This Sanction the Count's Engines labour'd to obtain, but without Succefs'; thofe wife Difpenfers of the Law immediately faw into the Villany of the Defign, and thofe that requefted it had a fevere Reprimand inftead of a Grant.

Nor was it probable the Tenants, fo afcertain'd as they were of the Juftice of the Chevalier's Claim, and fo true an Affection as they had for him, would have been deceived by any idle Story to his Prejudice, much lefs have been prevail'd upon to pay any Money which muft infallibly have been to their own Lofs: The Chevalier, however, having been inform'd by fome of his Friends of this Defign upon them, caufed printed Advertife-

N 3   ments

ments to be fent down into all Parts of the Country, fetting forth the true State of the Cafe, and thefe laft Stratagems attempted to be put in practice againft him.

This made a very great Noife all over the Kingdom, and fet the real Character of Count *Richard* in fo ftrong a Light, that thofe who before had fome Doubts concerning the Chevalier *James*, were now entirely on his fide, judging with Reafon, that Truth and Juftice have no Occafion to purfue fuch clandeftine Meafures, and that thofe taken by the Count was a plain Proof that neither his *Claim* nor *Actions* would bear the Teft of Examination, but that to *fecure* the *one* and *fcreen* the *other*, he was under a Neceffity of going on in a continued Succeffion of Crimes.

This was indeed fo natural an Obfervation, that it could not efcape the moft narrow Capacity; the loweft and moft abject Delinquents are fenfible of it, and generally make it Part of their Confeffion in their lateft Moments.————The fmalleft Vice indulg'd, leads on to greater, till the whole Soul becomes one general Blot.

All thefe things were new Misfortunes to the difconfolate *Anadea*: She was preparing to appeal to the Legiflature, to give Proofs of her Marriage, and endeavour to force her wicked Hufband to allow her a Dowry befitting a Wife of Quality; but the general Opinion now giving her Reafon to believe it would foon be out of his Power, as before it was out of his Inclination, to do any Juftice to her,

put

put a Stop to all her Proceedings againſt him, and obliged her to wait till the Affair between him and the Chevalier *James* ſhould be determined. The Villanies practiſed on herſelf gave her but too much Cauſe to fear he was not, in relation to his Nephew, leſs guilty than he was repreſented: She reflected, as ſome Author has it, that;

" Juſtice is Juſtice, even to the Meaneſt,
" And thoſe who ſcruple not at petty Crimes
" To purchaſe petty Pleaſures, will, when
                                    [greater
" Excites the Appetite, act greater ſtill.

She therefore gave herſelf and Children over as deſtin'd to be unhappy Sufferers for another's Faults, nor could the moſt ſanguine of her Friends now flatter her with any Proſpect of Redreſs.

The cruel Count in the mean time receiving every Poſt Intelligence of ſome freſh Diſappointment, was full of Horror and Confuſion —a Viciſſitude of the moſt dreadful Ideas roſe in his diſtracted Brain---he felt by Turns every Pang that Guilt and enervate Rage can poſſibly inflict---he found the Hand of Heaven was againſt him---that all the Arrows ſhot againſt his innocent Nephew recoil'd upon his own Breaſt---that the more he endeavoured to defame him the more Shame he brought upon himſelf; and that all he did, inſtead of creating him Enemies, ſerved only to raiſe him up new Friends. Yet did not all this

this excite in him any true Repentance—tho'
he saw unavoidable Ruin stare him in the
Face, still he perfisted obstinate in Iniquity—
he had now recourse to the most paltry ill
concerted Falshood that ever was invented,
which was, to spread a Report that the Person
who call'd himself the Chevalier *James*, was
of himself a poor ignorant silly Fellow, and
only made by *Amico* and *Macario*, whose
Tool he was, to assume the Name of *Altamont*, and put in a pretended Claim to Estates,
which if obtain'd, they were to have the best
Share of.

One would think by broaching such an ab-
surd Story he must have been really as weak
as he took others to be, otherwise he might
have form'd something which would have had
a little more the Appearance of Truth, or at
least one that might not be so easily detected;
since even a Child might have refuted this, by
asking, Where was *Amico* and *Macario*, when
the Chevalier *James* deliver'd his Memorial to
the Admiral?—Had he then ever been in the
Kingdom where they were? or had they ever
taken a Voyage to *America* on purpose to find
a Person to raise up as a Pretender to the Titles
and Estates of the Count *de Anglis*?—Had
he at that time, or long after, ever seen these
Gentlemen, or even heard of their Names?
—If they then concerted with him this Plot,
it must certainly have been by Intuition, and
the whole Scheme carried on by intellectual
Conversations—gross Flesh and Blood could
never have passed such Lands and Seas invisi-
ble

ble to human Eyes. Nor, tho' both *Amico* and *Macario* were Men of excellent Sense, it was never suspected that they, any more than the Chevalier *James*, had studied Necromancy —were Doctor *Faustus's* in Disguise, and could with a Wish transport themselves wherever they pleased.

Nothing the Count had ever done render'd him more ridiculous than this Suggestion, his very Agents were asham'd of it, yet would he relate it boldly, and swear to the Truth of it, tho' he saw a Sneer in the Face of every one that heard it.——Doubtless he would have denied the Chevalier had ever presented any Memorial to the Admiral, would not the Letters wrote by that Great Man have been undeniable Evidences against him, and had he not been expected soon in Person to have given the Lye to so notorious a Falshood.

Every thing, in short, and himself most of all, seem'd to conspire to render this bad Man as contemptible for his Folly as detestable for his Wickedness, and 'tis possible the Consequences of his Crimes might now begin to make him feel some little Remorse, at least for those Parts of them which he found such ill Effects of, when all on a sudden he was presented with an occasion of Triumph he had little expected, and which, tho' short-lived, gave some Relaxation to his Vexation.

Intelligence had been sent him by his Emissaries, that the Chevalier and his Friends were preparing to embark in a small Vessel, the Name of which they sent him, belonging to a

Mer-

Merchant of that Kingdom ; and when every Day he was dreading his Return, the publick Papers gave an Account of that very Ship being wreck'd, and all on board her loft.

The Extafy he was in at reading a Piece of News fo flattering to his Wifhes, made him forget that in teftifying it as he did wherever he went, he difcovered the Apprehenfions he had been in for the Arrival of a Competitor, the Juftice of whofe Claim had been fo fully allow'd in one Kingdom, and in all Probability would have been fo in another, had not this unfortunate Accident put a Period, as 'twas thought, both to his Life and Expectations.

'Tis certain indeed, that the Chevalier and his Friends had intended to embark in that Veffel, but were ftill detained by the Perfuafions of feveral People of Diftinction, who found too much Satisfaction in their Society to be willing to part with them till the Neceffity of the Chevalier's Friends required it; and befide, it was thought derogatory to his real Dignity to go in that Manner: So that when they found him refolute to depart, and were convinced a longer Stay might be a Prejudice to him, the Government was applied to, and a Warrant for the Royal Yatch immediately granted—fure Mark of their being afcertain'd of his Birth! that being a Favour never allow'd but to Perfons of the firft Quality, or fuch, who by their high Offices in the State are put upon the fame Foot.

Every

Every thing now being ready — Bufinefs calling — Winds favouring — calm Seas inviting — no Pretext for detaining him remaining, the Chevalier with his Companions and Retinue, came on board, welcom'd by the Difcharge of the Cannon, and follow'd by the Prayers and good Wifhes of a Number of Spectators, who quitted not the Coaft till the Yatch was entirely out of Sight. The little Voyage was as profperous as could be hoped, and eight and forty Hours brought them to their intended Port, where being fafely landed, they made all imaginable Hafte to the Capital, their Friends having impatiently expected them for fome Days.

What a terrible Reverfe did this now give to the Expectations of Count *Richard!* —— to be told his Nephew was arrived when he thought him and his Pretenfions buried in the Sea, and that he arrived in the Manner he did, put an end at once to all his Hopes; nor was it in the Power of all thofe People, who earn'd their Bread by lulling him with falfe Imaginations, to footh his Mind or mitigate his Defpair, tho' they exerted all their Force of Diffimulation for that Purpofe. —— He found himfelf now without Money — without Credit — without Friends — without even Invention —— no Expedient offer'd to ward off the Blow, which muft inevitably fall and crufh him with its Weight, beyond all Poffibility of ever rifing more. —— He doubted not but the Chevalier would now bring things to an immediate Iffue, of which he knew the Confequence.

quence. Sometimes he was for flying the Kingdom, and thereby avoid the Punishment he
had Reason to expect for such a Series of
Crimes : But whither could he go ? where hope
to be received or protected? — What to do he
knew not, or how to behave in this Exigence
— Dependants importuning — Creditors per-
fecuting —— Wants within, and Dangers
without. Doors inceffantly perplexing him --
prefent Contempt and Fears of future Shame,
joining with fruitlefs Rage and difappointed
Revenge, drove him even to the Verge of
Madnefs.— At length, partly for the Relief of
his prefent Neceffities, and partly thro' Malice
to the real Owner, he made all the rich Furniture, Pictures, Bufto's, and other Curiofities
which the late Count *de Anglia* his Predeceffor
had collected, to be torn down and expofed to
publick Sale.   This was all that now remained in the Compafs of his Power, and was
indeed fome Occafion of Vexation to the Chevalier when he was inform'd of it ; not fo
much for the intrinfic Value of his Lofs, as
becaufe he regretted fuch curious Pieces of
Antiquity, as he had been told were treafured
there, fhould go out of the Family, and perhaps fall to the Lot of fome who knew not
how to make a proper Ufe of them.

   The whole Body of Nobility were no fooner
inform'd of this equally mean and unjuft Action, by the printed Catalogues every where
difperfed about Town, than they cried out
againft the Chevalier *Richard* ; and fome there
were, who in a publick Affembly were fo generous

nerous as to propofe raifing a Bank among them, in order to purchafe the chief of thofe Curiofities, and make a Prefent of them to the real Heir of that illuftrious Perfon to whom they had belong'd.

But here I muft give a Truce to my Pen, and for a while defer the Profecution of Adventures, which I doubt not but the Reader finds fufficiently interefting to create an Impatience for the Cataftrophe.——

O Time! in whofe tremendous Womb the Seeds of all things lie concealed, and who, fooner or later, ripens them to full Perfection, now fly fwiftly, as when happy Lovers meet, and bring me Opportunity and Means of gratifying the Curiofity I have excited, fo as the Event may give Honour to Juftice; and to Oppreffion, Fraud, Violence and Cruelty, the Shame and Punifhment they merit.

F I N I S.

ANti-Pamela, or Feign'd Innocence detected, in a Series of Syrena's Adventures.
A Narative which has really its Foundation in
Truth and Nature; and at the fame Time
that it agreeably entertains, with a vaft Variety of furprifing Incidents, arms againft the
fecret Mifchiefs arifing from a too fudden
Admiration. Publifh'd as a neceffary Caution to all young Gentlemen.

A Companion to the Theatre, or a Key to
the Play; containing the Stories of thefe ce-
lebrated Dramatick Pieces, viz. Abra-mule,
All for Love, Albion Queens, Amphitrion,
Beaux Stratagem, Bufy-body, Cato, Carelefs
Hufband, Conftant Couple, Committee, Con-
fcious Lovers, Country Wife, Diftreffed Mo-
ther, Don Sebaftian, Æfop, Fair Penitent,
Fatal Marriage, Hamlet, Hen. IV. Hen. VIII.
Julius Cæfar, King Lear, Love for Love,
Macbeth, Man of Mode, Meafure for Meafure,
Merry Wives of Windfor, Mourning Bride,
Mithridates, Oedipus, Orphan, Oroonoko, O-
thello, Provok'd Hufband, Provok'd Wife,
Rival Queens, Silent Woman, Spanifh Frier,
Phedra and Hippolitus, Timon of Athens.

N. B. The Story of each Play is here trac'd
to its Origin, brought down to the Opening of
the Drama, and carried into the Cataftrophe.
Each Character is drawn in its proper Colour,
no material Incident omitted; but the whole
appears one regular and continued Relation;
fo that a few Minutes employed in perufing
each Account, gives the Reader a juft Idea of
what is not otherwife known till the Conclufion of the Play. Price 3s.

An

An Apology for the Life of Mrs. Shamela Andrews, in which the many notorious Falf-hoods and Mifreprefentations of a Book call'd Pamela are all expofed and refuted; and the matchlefs Arts of that young Politician, fet in a true and juft Light. Together with a full Account of all that paffed between her and Parfon Arthur Williams, whofe Character is reprefented in a Manner fomething different from what he bears in Pamela; the Whole being exact Copies of authentic Papers deli-vered to the Editor. Neceffary to be had in all Families; with a modern Dedication after the Manner of the Ancients, efpecially Cicero. By Mr. Conny Keyber. Price 1 s. 6 d.

The Court Secret, a Melancholy Truth; (being the real Account of the late Earl of Scarb---h's Death) Tranflated from the Ori-ginal-Arabick. By an Adept in the Oriental Tongues.
Remember that a Prince's Secrets are Balm conceal'd,
But Poyfon if difcovered. MASSINGER.
Price 1 s.

A faithful Narrative of the Unfortunate Ad-ventures of Charles Cartwright, M. D. who, in his Voyage to Jamaica, was taken by a Spa-nifh Privateer, and carried into St. Sebaftians. His hard Ufage there, and wonderful Efcape from thence. Price 1 s.

The Death of Middleton in the Life of Ci-cero, being a proper Criticifm on that mar-vellous Performance. By an Oxford Scholar.
Monftrum horrendum, informe, ingens, cui lumen ademtum. VIRG. Price 1 s.

Are Thefe Things So? The previous Que-ftion, from an Englifhman in his Grotto, to a Great Man at Court.

Lufifti:

Lusisti satis, Edisti satis, atque Bibisti (alias
   BRIBISTI,
TEMPUS ABIRE TIBI——   HOR.
   'There being little Reason left to hope
'that either the Great Man, or his Tools,
'would put in a satisfactory Reply to that
'shrew'd Question, ARE THESE THINGS
'so? The Englishman himself has most
'obligingly sav'd them the Labour: Having
'just given us the Pleasure of an imaginary
'Tête-à-Tête Conversation Piece between
'his Honour and himself; in which he has so
'happily interwowen the Substance in a Thou-
'sand Gazetteers, that (were it not for the
'Vein of Irony which runs thro' it, and the
'Wit and Humour it every where abounds
'with) one would be apt to think it was really
'taken from the Life.'   See the Champion, N° 173.   Price 1 s.

The Great Man's Answer to Are These
Things So? In a Dialogue between his Ho-
nour, and the Englishman in his Grotto.
         Qui capit——
By the Author of Are These Things So?
Price 1 s.

The Skimmer: Or the History of Tanzai
and Neadarne.   In two Vols. Price 2 s. 6 d.

The Plain Truth, a Dialogue between Sir
Courtly Jobber, Candidate for the Borough
of Guzzledown, and Tom Telltruth, School-
master and Freeman of the said Borough. By
the Author of the remarkable Queries in the
Champion, October 7. Price 6 d.

The Trial between J. G. B——r, Plaintiff,
and M. M——y, Doctor of Physick, Defendant,
for Criminal Conversation with the Plaintiff's
Wife, on Tuesday the 30th of June, at Guild-
hall, London. Price 6 d.   The

The Genuine Speech of the Truly Honour-
able Adm— V——n, to the Sea-Officers, and
Council of War, juſt before the Attack of
C——a. As communicated by a Perſon of
Honour then preſent, in a Letter to his Friend.
Price 6 d.

A Second Genuine Speech deliver'd by
Adm—l V——n, after the Salley from Fort
St. Lazara. Price 6 d.

A Court Intrigue ; or the Stateſman detected. A Genuine Story, deliver'd by the Ora-
culous Ship. Addreſs'd to his Honour and
the Counteſs of Y—r—h. Price 1 s.

The Expediency of One Man's Dying, to
ſave a Nation from periſhing. A Diſcourſe
deliver'd before the Ancient Society of True
Britons, at their Annual Meeting, January 1,
1741-2.

*Hi medentur Reipublicæ, qui exſecant Peſtem
aliquam tanquam* Strumam *Civitatis.* Cicero.
By C. Thurloe, A. M. Chaplain to the ſaid
Society. Price 6 d.

A KEY to the Buſineſs of the PRESENT
S——N, viz. 1. His H——r's Speech to his
Life-Guard of Switzers, at their general Ren-
dezvouz in D—g S—. 2. Certain Important
Hints deliver'd to an Aſſembly of Independents
at the Fountain Tavern in the Strand.
There is a Tide in the Affairs of Men,
Which, taken at the Flood. leads on to Fortune ;
Omitted, all the Voyage of their Life
Is bound in Shallows and in Miſeries.
On ſuch a full Sea are we now afloat,
And we muſt take the Current while it ſerves,
Or loſe our Ventures.
                                    SHAKESPEAR.

The

—————————— The Gods
Grow angry with your Patience: 'Tis their Care
And must be Yours that guilty Men escape not.

JOHNSON.

Justice hath laid her Sword within your Reach.

DAVENANT.

N. B. *This is the Pamphlet which has already had the Honour of being* Six Times BEGAZETTEER'D.
And greatly conduc'd to the Removal of Sir R. Walpole from the Ministry.   Price 1s.

The Champion: Containing a Series of Papers, Humorous, Moral, Political and Critical. To each of which is added, a proper Index to the Times.   In Two Volumes.   By Henry Fielding, Esq; and others.

Quem legis, ut nôris, accipe.   OVID.

The other Side of the Question: Or, An Attempt to rescue the Characters of the two Royal Sisters, Queen Mary and Queen Anne, out of the Hands of the Duchess of Marlborough: In which, not only the most notable Strokes in her Grace's late unparallel'd Piece are fully stated, and as fully answer'd, but many important Particulars are remark'd on, and several are explain'd and set in a true Light. Among others,

1. Her Grace's Treatment of the Birth of a certain Person. 2. The true Reason of carrying on a Land War against France, and neglecting our Marine, in the Reign of Queen Anne. 3. Tory Lords (bred and born) became Whigs in 1701. 4. Why Tories Whigs (turn about) were for inviting over the Electoral Prince. 5. The Transactions of Parliament. 6. The Advances made by France towards Peace. 7. Why Peace was not made
by

by France at Gertruydenburg. 8. The Renegade Ministry in that Year fcreen'd by the Miftake of their Ay and No Men in the Houfe of C——, then humbled upon new Lights from their Leaders ; and then fcreened again ; all in a Week. A third Part of the Army in Spain allow'd for Officers Servants, fwallow'd at the Word of Command. 9. The fecret Hiftory of Mr. Harley and Mrs. Mafham. 10. The Hiftory of the good-for-nothing tall ragged Boy and his Sifter, her Grace's Coufins. 11. The Broils among the Whigs. 12. The total Change of the Adminiftration. By a Woman of Quality. *He that appeareth firft in his own Caufe feemeth juft, but his Neighbour cometh after him and fearches him.* Solomon. *N. B.* The Earl of Iflay faid ; This was the beft wrote Book he ever read, and the neareft High Treafon. Price 5 s.

The affecting Cafe of the Queen of Hungary ; in Relation both to Friends and Foes : Being a fair Specimen of Modern Hiftory. By the Author of the Court Seeret. *Behold and fee if there be any Sorrow like unto my Sorrow.* Lament. *The World had never taken fo full Note of what thou art, had'ft thou not been undone.* S. Daniel. Price 1 s.

A fhort Treatife on the Game of Whift ; As play'd at Court, White's and George's Chocolate-houfes ; at Slaughter's, and the Crown Coffee-houfes, &c. &c. Containing the Laws of the Game, and alfo fome Rules, whereby a Beginner may, with due Attention to them, attain to the Playing it well. Calculations for thofe who will Bet the Odds on any Point of the Score of the Game then playing and depending. Cafes ftated, to fhew
what

what may be effected by a very good Player in critical Parts of the Game. References to Cases, viz. at the End of the Rule you are directed how to find them. Calculations, directing with moral Certainty how to play well any Hand or Game, by shewing the Chances of your Partner's having 1, 2, or 3 certain Cards. With Variety of Cases added in the Appendix. By Edmund Hoyle, Gent. The fourth Edition. Price 2 s. *N. B.* At the particular Desire of several Persons of Quality, the Laws of the Game are printed on a fine Imperial Paper, proper to be fram'd, or made Screens of, that the Players may have them before them, to refer to if any Dispute should arise. Price 2 s. 6d.

A short Treatise on the Game of Back-Gammon : Containing, A Table of the 36 Chances, with Directions how to find out the Odds of being hit upon single or double Dice Rules whereby a Beginner may, with due Attention to them, attain to the playing it well. The several Stages for carrying your Men Home in order to loose no Point. How to find out who is forwardest to win a Hit. Cases stated for Back-games, with Directions how to play for one. Cases stated, how to know when you may have the better of saving a Gammon by Running. Variety of Cases of Curiosity and Instruction. The Laws of the Game. By Edmund Hoyle, Gent.

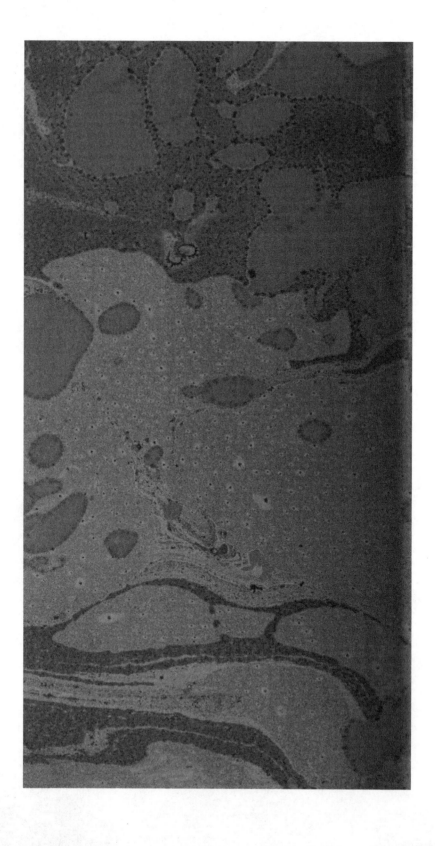

CPSIA information can be obtained
at www.ICGtesting.com
Printed in the USA
BVHW041051190720
584083BV00006B/212

9 781376 131673